An Introduction to
Political Thought

An Introduction to Political Thought

A Conceptual Toolkit

Peri Roberts and Peter Sutch

Edinburgh University Press

ATLANTIC®
PUBLISHERS & DISTRIBUTORS

ATLANTIC®

PUBLISHERS & DISTRIBUTORS
7/22, Ansari Road, Darya Ganj
New Delhi – 110 002
Tel: 2327 3880, 2327 5880, 2328 0451
Fax: 91-11-2328 5873
E-mail: info@atlanticbooks.com
Website: www.atlanticbooks.com

Published in India by
Atlantic Publishers and Distributors, New Delhi
in association with
Edinburgh University Press Ltd
22 George Square, Edinburgh, U.K.

First published 2004 by Edinburgh University Press Ltd
First Indian Reprint 2005

ISBN 81-269-0553-0

Typeset in Sabon and Gill Sans by
Pioneer Associates, Perthshire, and
printed in India by
Pushp Print Services, Delhi

Contents

Section III: Contemporary Understandings of Political Thought

Section IV: Challenges to Universalism and Foundationalism

Acknowledgements

Peri Roberts: This has been a difficult and interesting project. My thanks go to Kai, Rowan and Beck and to Mum and Dad.

Peter Sutch: Once again, this book could not have been written without the patience and encouragement of Nicola, Victoria and Matthew.

Our approach to political thought has been shaped over many years by engagements with Bruce Haddock, David Boucher and Rex Martin. Thanks are due to them and to the students that we have both taught and learned from over the years. Also, we owe thanks to the editors and readers at Edinburgh University Press.

Swansea and Cardiff

INTRODUCTION

HISTORICAL

The Nature of Political Thought

CONCEPTUAL

Conceptual Tools for Everyday Living

As we write this introductory chapter the news is on in the background giving the world a briefing on those things that are of real importance to us. The news is of war in the Middle East, of the Presidential elections in the USA, of the UK government appearing before a public inquiry, of tax laws and public-sector wages, of education reform, international business, of refugee crises, asylum seekers and immigration and of continuing starvation in the developing world. As we think about these issues over our morning coffee we are already engaged in political thought. We are being asked to reflect on some very difficult and profound issues. Was it right for the USA/UK alliance to go to war with Saddam Hussein's regime in Iraq or should the United Nations have made the decision? Is war ever right and, if so, under what conditions should we interfere in the affairs of other countries? Who should rule and how should they be accountable to the people? How much tax should we pay and why? Do we have a duty to those suffering outside our immediate society? If so, what should we do about it? How, if at all, should we adapt to a multicultural world? These are not abstract questions. The fact that they arise in the normal run of things and require an urgent answer impacts heavily upon our lives and the lives of others.

Thinking about politics is unavoidable and not just for those of you beginning university courses. Everybody has to do it. More importantly, we believe that everyone has a right to do it. This last sentence is worth thinking about a little more. First and foremost note that it is a **normative**, or moral, claim. We think that everyone has a *right* to an equal stake in politics. This kind of statement is characteristic of **political thought**. Answering any of the questions mentioned above requires us to make **normative judgements**. The role of political thought is to explore the nature and character of such judgements with a view to helping us understand the reasons for past judgements and to help us make better ones. Why do we think that everyone has a right to an equal stake in politics? On what grounds can we discriminate between this claim and counter-claims that assert that the poor, or women, or immigrants should not be allowed a voice? Exploring the normative claims that permeate our social world is a fascinating and demanding experience.

The task of courses in political thought (sometimes called political theory or political philosophy) is to help you explore these issues. The study of political thought will not give *the right answer* to moral and social questions. It is not that sort of discipline and they are not those sorts of questions. We will explore this a little further later in this chapter. It can, however, introduce you to the complexities of the questions themselves and to the conceptual tools you can use to address them. When we do grapple with the big questions of political life we are dealing with some profound issues. What is justice? What does it mean to say we know what is morally right or wrong? These are, for most people coming to the subject for the first time, new and unfamiliar sorts of questions. But they are questions that have been a constant feature of human society for millennia. It is certainly the case that the ways in which they have been posed and answered over the years vary across time and place. But in one form or another all human civilisation, from the ancient Greek *poleis* (city-states) through the modern nation-state to the contemporary globalised world, asks challenging normative, moral and political questions.

This is an introduction to political thought. Our goal is to make the unfamiliar familiar and to give you a conceptual toolkit that will help you understand and engage with political ideas. One of the principal driving forces of this book is the belief that there are two sets of tools that students of political thought need in order gain critical purchase on the subject. The first is a basic sense of the history and development of political thought; the second is a critical grasp of the theoretical or philosophical issues at the heart of politics. A sense of the historical context of political debates gives us a clearer grasp of the issues that confront us. For example, our contemporary understanding of the importance of human rights to justice has its own specific history. It is a product of the post-World War Two environment. It was not until we realised the danger that some sections of a society could face from their own government that we really pressed ahead with the idea of a universal set of individual rights that were to be policed across sovereign borders. In the face of Hitler's genocide we decided that the suffering of citizens of other countries really was our business. A grasp of how the emphasis on human rights arose allows us to appreciate the role such rights have in our political context and thus to refine the instruments of their development and execution. An understanding of how other, earlier, attempts to claim universal rights for man (*sic*) arose, the issues they were addressing, their successes and failures, gives us further conceptual leverage when we are thinking about the issues at stake. Similarly a grasp of the historical development of concepts such as 'the state', 'sovereignty', 'citizenship' or 'justice' offers huge insights into the basic building blocks of politics. We still need, however, to supplement this historical understanding with a critical perception of the core theoretical issues at stake. Human rights are not just defended as measures designed to cope with a specific historical threat. They are also defended as morally correct. They are viewed as the most ethically important rights, which may not be violated for any other political, religious or cultural reason. How do we evaluate this sort of claim? Over the centuries there have been many arguments about who, or what, should be accorded moral standing. It has been variously claimed that only fellow citizens count (and that foreigners can be killed or enslaved), that the interests of the state are more vital than those of its individual citizens (and thus people can be sacrificed to the greater good), that only white men count (and that women or coloured people are simply not worth the same and should be treated differently), that only law-abiding citizens count (and that criminals lose even the right to life) or that only adults count (and that children have no rights in their own person). On what grounds might we discriminate between these claims and the current thought that all persons, simply by virtue of their being human, have a certain moral standing that endows them with inalienable rights? In order to face this normative challenge we need to learn the language of moral and political argument.

In order to develop this conceptual toolbox we have split our table of contents into two parts. One table of contents is organised according to a chronological history of political thought, arranging chapters around particular thinkers and the development of political theory. The second table of contents is organised conceptually and highlights the theoretical questions and issues that each theorist is used to illustrate. Each chapter explicitly draws out important elements of both the historical and conceptual vocabularies. In doing so the reader is guided through the construction of their own critical glossary of important terms in political theory, thus furnishing them with a basic political vocabulary. This is intended to leave the reader with an historical and conceptual map to aid them in further study and a clear grasp of the basic vocabulary in which such study is undertaken. Most importantly it should give them the ability to add their voice to the debates. Beginning with the idea that laws and constitutions (the instruments of politics) are only good laws and constitutions in so far as they give effective expression to our considered moral and political beliefs, we invite the reader to explore the suggestion that moral and political ideas are the **foundations** of politics. Our aim is not only to highlight *what*, in the history of political thought, has counted as an adequate foundation, but to show the reader *how* (at an introductory level) such arguments work. In exploring these issues we guide the readers through a critical engagement with key arguments in the history of political thought and contemporary political theory. Just as importantly, we guide the readership through a critical engagement with their own moral and political beliefs.

The structure of the book is guided by these twin aims. The story of the development of political theory is told only in so far as it highlights key theoretical ideas and so this book does not aim to be comprehensive as a history. This is true in two ways. Firstly, while our book stretches from the work of Plato to contemporary antifoundationalism we do not cover the Roman philosophers or the medieval thinkers such as St Augustine or St Thomas Aquinas. Doubtless there is much to be gained from such a study but in the first instance the key conceptual ideas can be expressed more clearly in the works of Plato and Aristotle than in Christian neo-Platonism or neo-Aristotelianism. For similar reasons we do not examine the works of Machiavelli, Kant and Hegel. The omissions are to be regretted but in striking a balance between a conceptual and an historical introduction some tough decisions needed to be made. In any case we do not view this work as anything more than a comprehensive introduction to the discipline and console ourselves with the thought that this book may (we hope will) encourage you to delve deeper into the history of political thought. Secondly, we do not aim to do full justice to any particular thinker. Individual theorists are included to highlight key ideas. For example, in dealing with Plato we examine his contention (in *The Republic*) that political rule is a technical skill and the foundation to this argument that one can, given the right intellect and education, come to *know* what justice is. It is beyond doubt that this does not explore all there is to know about Plato. Nevertheless it is also beyond doubt that the reader will have learned something vital about Plato and about the nature of justice and politics and the type of arguments that support claims about justice and political institutions.

Making normative judgements: the nature of political theory

In approaching the subject this way we intend to give the reader a conceptual vocabulary that is indispensable to a critical and knowledgeable discussion of political issues. This is all the study of political thought can offer. It cannot offer you an easy route to *the right answer* or *the truth* about politics. Moral and political positions are not measured on a single scale with 'truth' at one end and 'falsity' on the other. In fact there is even considerable disagreement about what standard they are to be measured on at all. Indeed giving reasons why one set of moral and political claims has firmer foundations than others and should be thus given priority over them forms a large part of the debates in political theory. We can approach this issue by contrasting political thought with another aspect of political studies, **political science**. Most people coming to the study of politics for the first time will take a variety of courses. Almost everyone will take political science, which is the study of political institutions, constitutions and policy processes. Political science aims at an accurate description and explanation of these features of politics. It is an **empirical** (or positive) science in that it seeks to collect data and analyse it much as a natural scientist would collect a sample and put it under the microscope. The accuracy of an empirical claim can be tested against what is out there in the world. Either the civil service plays a positive role in policy-making or it does not. Either the Supreme Court has the power to veto unconstitutional legislation or it does not (of course political science can be much more complex than this). The empirical study of institutions and laws is a vital part of any study of politics. Political thought (or political theory/philosophy) is a very different discipline. Rather than being empirical it is normative. A normative project seeks standards that enable us to judge human action or to prescribe the best course of action. If political science asks '*what* are the key building blocks of politics?' political theory may ask '*why* are these the key building blocks of politics?'. If political science identifies human-rights legislation as a key feature of contemporary politics, political theory might ask 'is this just?'. Political science is the study of facts and political thought the study of values.

The advantage that political science has over political thought is that the standards by which the claims of political science are to be judged are generally accepted. Scientific objectivity is a standard we are all familiar with (at least in principle). The idea is that we can establish, through the application of scientific methods of data collection and analysis, the verifiable truth. This is certainly an important standard and the world has benefited hugely from its refinement and application. However, there is no reason to believe that it is the only standard by which knowledge is to be judged or that it is appropriate to normative reflection. The very first step a student of political thought has to take is to recognise this. It is a difficult step to take partly because non-scientific standards of judgement receive so little attention in our education systems and partly because science and the belief in scientific progress is the ideology of the contemporary period. Between the 1920s and the 1970s the scientific paradigm, the belief that all that counted as knowledge had to be scientific, came to be imposed upon the social sciences and humanities. The claims popular around this time were that we had left our religious and metaphysical infancy and developed science. Thus 2,000 years of philosophical and normative thought were dismissed. This quirk of intellectual history went beyond empirical study to make claims about the very nature and possibility of knowledge. These debates, called **epistemological debates** (from the Greek *epistēmē*, meaning knowledge), are key to political theory and we will explore them over the course of this book. Our first step along this route has to be a brief examination of the claim that all knowledge must be scientific. Here we are not concerned to deny the role or importance of science but simply to establish the place of normative political thought within the social sciences and humanities.

Between the 1920s and the 1970s the belief that scientific knowledge was the only true form of knowledge gained huge support. Empiricism became the mainstay of logical positivism through the work of the Vienna Circle in the 1920s and 1930s. Positivism became further refined in the behaviourist movements of the 1950s. These hyper-empirical schools of thought argued that scientific verifiability was the sole criterion of knowledge. In very broad terms they argued that there were only three types of statement. The first were statements of empirical fact such as 'the cat is on the mat'. This is acceptable as we can verify the statement by simply looking at the mat. The second were analytic statements of logical necessity such as 'all bachelors are unmarried males'. This is acceptable as its truth is given logically. Finally there were normative utterances. These were dismissed as 'ejaculations' (A. J. Ayer) or as 'nonsense'. They were treated derisively as they could not be subjected to empirical verification or falsification (for a very good discussion of these debates see Ball 1995).

The obvious starting point for a case against the claims of the hyper-empiricists is simply that their position is counter-intuitive. It goes against our general thinking on the matter. Nearly everything we do or say that is of any interest to us is normative and to dismiss all this as nonsense is a little startling. Take the statement 'it is wrong to eat babies'. This is not merely a frivolous example. In 1729 Jonathan Swift published a pamphlet proposing that the starving Irish should sell their children as food, thus solving the associated problems of poverty and high birth rates amongst Irish Catholic families. The proposal was made to shock and highlight the issues but its shock value relies upon the moral idea that it is wrong to eat babies. This is not an empirically verifiable idea but it does say something very important. To deny this statement the status of 'knowledge' and to dismiss it as 'nonsense' is to say that we cannot make such a judgement. But society is structured by such judgements. 'The government should be responsible to the people', 'theft is wrong', 'all human beings are equal in dignity and rights': these statements are the core of politics. Laws, governments and institutions are structured and restructured to reflect our considered moral and political judgements. Our lives make no sense without this 'nonsense'.

Political thought is not primarily concerned with the facts of political life. It is normative in that it is concerned with values, moral codes, social standards and ideals. Normative standards often conflict. Disputes over social welfare, capital punishment, abortion, gender equality, political accountability, warfare etc. are commonplace. The standards by which people live their lives cannot be measured scientifically. So how do we begin to think about the issues? The first step is to abandon the thought that all 'knowledge' can be judged on a single scale. Normative concepts are most often value judgements. People come to their values, beliefs and opinions in a whole variety of ways and because of this we have come to think of normative concepts as 'essentially contested concepts' (for a very useful discussion of this idea see Gallie 1956). This means that we recognise that there is a whole variety of perspectives that we can take on most issues, even the most fundamental ones. We generally accept that there is no single right answer to profound normative questions such as 'what is right and wrong?' or 'what is justice'. Nevertheless there is a huge difference between accepting this basic idea and accepting the further idea that all opinions are equally worthy. This last idea is termed **relativism** and it gives us no critical purchase on the debates. Relativists claim that because there is no one standard by which we can judge normative claims we have to accept that each claim is as valid as the next. Thus if one section of society wishes to prevent its children from receiving certain types of health care or education, or if it wishes to enforce certain gender roles within the family, or wishes to use capital punishment, or is pro-abortion, then there is nothing that another section of society that may view these practices as unjust can say, let alone do, about it. We do not want to encourage you to make a judgement about these specific issues here. What we do want you to do is to consider the twin facts that (1) normative clashes are an everyday occurrence and (2) unless we can generate standards that help us to solve or at least mitigate these clashes then the prospects for peace and prosperity are negligible. Normative thinking is essential to political stability.

There is no one correct set of answers to the issue of what is to count as an appropriate normative standard. So how do we go about discriminating between them? Political thought is concerned with exploring this very issue. Its role is the criticism of bad standards and the search for good, beneficial or defensible ones. Its goal is to discriminate between the good and bad opinions, practices and ideals that structure human society. It does this by subjecting the core principles of political and social life to critical scrutiny. Behind every moral and political principle is a justifying argument, what we term the theoretical foundations of a principle. More often than not the foundations of a principle are hidden away in the background. Foundational claims are the reasons people have for holding certain opinions. When people say they support human rights or despise racism they are expressing an ethical principle. The foundations of their argument may well be a belief in the moral equality of all human beings. Exploring this foundational claim, its relative validity in the face of claims to the contrary, is a core part of political thought. There are many different moral and political opinions in the world and throughout the course of this book we will be exploring the foundations of many different positions.

Foundational arguments take many forms. A cursory glance would reveal moral, religious, rationalist, epistemological, historical and sociological arguments. We will also explore anti-foundationalist arguments that criticise this way of thinking about ethics and politics. We need to learn to identify these arguments and to develop the critical and technical skills that help us assess them. This is where the real battles of politics are fought. We build democracies because we believe that each person should have an equal stake in politics. We build complex legal systems to give institutional expression to our understanding of justice. We build armies and fight wars, under the auspices of the United Nations, because we believe that genocide is wrong. The foundational arguments here are the specific conceptions of equality, justice and human rights that support the political, legal and military processes. Democracies, legal systems and armies are merely the instruments of our considered moral and political judgements. But they are immensely powerful instruments. They have a dramatic effect on our lives and those of others and so it is important that we keep a critical eye on the validity and coherence of the foundational arguments that drive them.

Here we shall not say any more about the role of political theory in general. Each theory that we will meet in the coming chapters has its own view of what (if anything) makes a solid foundation for political ideals. Each theory will enhance or deny all that we have said in this introductory survey. Each stage of this book will introduce you to a clear moral and political argument and will begin to show you how each position is defended. Engaging with these positions and exploring the claims they make is a fascinating experience. Typically people coming to the subject for the first time are so taken by each encounter that it is not unusual for them to agree wholeheartedly with each argument they come across (even when it contradicts the position they embraced the week before!). There are at least two good reasons why this is the case. First, each argument is so powerful that it has carved a place in history. The arguments we examine here have had a profound influence on their time and ours. Some have played vital roles in revolutions and others have had a more subtle influence but all are classic examples of political thought. Second, it is often the case that readers have not encountered the foundational arguments in support of each position before. The sheer power, or explanatory force, of these arguments can be amazingly compelling. It is quite easy to get overwhelmed by the depth and detail of these arguments but remember this is only an introduction. You are not expected to come to a complete understanding or any easy moral and political decisions straight away. Our immediate goal is to help you get a sense for the 'shape' of normative political thought. Our secondary goals are to enable you to make critical judgements about the arguments and to help you enjoy what is necessarily a life-long engagement with the world around us.

An introduction to the book

By way of further introduction to the discipline and to the book we shall take a brief overview of its content. This will introduce you to the variety of ideas we shall confront and to the structure of the book. The book is organised into four major parts, each of which is given structure by the dual table of contents discussed above. These four parts are: I Classical Origins of Political Thought; II Modern Developments in Political Thought; III Contemporary Understandings of Political Thought; and IV Challenges to Universalism and Foundationalism. We have chosen to begin with Classical Greek thought partly because Plato and Aristotle have had such a huge influence on political theory as a discipline and partly because their work illustrates some key ideas. The question that dominates Plato's *Republic* is 'what is justice?'. For Plato, and arguably for us too, this is the key question of political thought. Plato's answer to this question (which he gives to us through his portrayal of the character of Socrates) begins to show us what an answer that aspired to objectivity might look like. One of the key issues that we are looking at here is the question of how a normative argument might be objectively true, rather than subjective – just what we do around here. In examining this we come to Plato's account of metaphysics and his claim that it is possible to come to *know* for certain what justice is. For many of you this is the first time you will have come across metaphysics and it is important that you do not get overwhelmed or intimidated by the term or its meaning. It really only means that which is beyond the empirical or physical world and as we have already seen that is the area that normative thinking must engage with. Having gained some idea of what a metaphysical argument looks like we then turn to Aristotle's famous claim that 'man is by nature a political animal'. Aristotle also offers a metaphysical argument but it is very different from Plato's. Here we have our first example of how metaphysical arguments differ from one another and we can begin to try and discriminate between them. Both Plato and Aristotle argue that politics is natural to humans. As we come to understand human nature and the idea of 'the good' or 'justice' we can see how to make political judgements. But Aristotle's conception of human nature and his understanding of how we come to know what morality is are very different from those of Plato. In reading Aristotle and Plato we begin to think about the relationship between ethics and politics and to critically engage with differing positions within normative argument.

The next section of the book leaps straight to modernity. We have chosen to do this because it gets us into arguments that are vitally important to our own reflections about the political world. There is much we could take from a study of the Roman and medieval political philosophers such as Cicero, St Augustine or St Thomas Aquinas or from key Renaissance figures such as Niccolò Machiavelli. But this is not intended to be a comprehensive retelling of the history of political thought. The next challenge we want you to face is the very modern idea that politics is in fact artificial, rather than natural as both Plato and Aristotle believed. By the middle of the seventeenth century the political world (in western Europe at least) was changing. One of the driving forces of that change was the idea that we are naturally free. This radically changes the way we look at politics and our relation to its institutions and rules. It opens up the issue of why we have politics at all and how, if it is an artificial creation, we should structure it so it reflects, enables or mitigates our natural freedom. The assumption that we are morally free agents is the foundation for much modern and contemporary thinking. In this second section of the book we confront three attempts to show why we should begin our explorations of politics here and what natural freedom means to us. In Chapters 3 and 4 we take three of the greatest thinkers on the social contract, Thomas Hobbes, Jean-Jacques Rousseau, and John Locke, and invite you to compare and contrast their conceptions of natural liberty. What does it mean to say we are naturally free? What follows from it and how does this feed in to our political needs and aspirations? Once again we will encourage you to begin to seek out the differences in the arguments to see what makes each account of freedom differ and to think about which you find more compelling. It is truly stunning just how much any one view of human freedom affects one's political viewpoint. Here again our focus is on equipping you with the vocabulary to draw insight from and to judge between these extraordinarily influential arguments.

The final chapter of the 'Modern Developments' section (Chapter 5) looks at another hugely influential tradition that plays a large and critical role in our political and intellectual history. Here we invite you to discover the force of the arguments of Karl Marx and the socialist writer Robert Owen. The challenge laid down by this tradition is to the assumption that there is a fixed human nature (whether naturally social or naturally free) that forms the necessary true foundation for politics. For Marxists and socialists human nature was itself an artificial creation. What we view as natural about ourselves, and the political institutions that we view as flowing naturally from it, are themselves the creation of a particular time and place. Just as we underwent political revolution to get rid of the idea that the natural political order was hierarchical along monarchical or aristocratic lines, so, argue the socialists, we need a revolution (violent or moral) to rid ourselves of the view that free human relations are naturally competitive, productive and based on a capitalist hierarchy. Having rid ourselves of aristocratic privilege and established the basic premise that all men (*sic*) are equal we felt that free competition was the fairest way to distribute goods. Those that lost in the marketplace of life were lazy, unlucky or simply not good enough but they were not treated unfairly and they had the same chance as everyone else. It is this myth that the socialists challenge. They show that this conception of freedom (which had been wrapped up in a picture of human nature) is itself a product of a specific time and place and point to its weaknesses. This challenge to capitalism found massive expression in socialist and communist movements and also features heavily in left-wing liberalism. The 'left wing' appears to have fallen out of fashion but in these traditions we can find the supports for claims about 'fair trade' goods and services, criticisms of the World Trade Organisation and the desire to reduce or drop the debt the developing world owe to the rich Western states, which do form a vital part of our political agenda today.

Armed with this broad understanding of the debates that inform the history and development of our normative political sensibilities we then turn, in the final two sections of the book, to contemporary political thought. The first of these sections, 'Contemporary Understandings of Political Thought', introduces the reader to three mainstream debates. The first examines the question of whether 'it is the greatest happiness of the greatest number that is the measure of right and wrong' (FOG Preface: 2; see Chapter 6) or whether we should think of each individual as having rights that are inviolable. The issue is a fairly clear one: if sacrificing one person is to benefit society overall should we do it? On the 'yes' side of this debate we have utilitarianism and in particular the work of one of its founders, Jeremy Bentham. Bentham believed that talk of rights was 'nonsense upon stilts' (AF: 405). In its place he proposed to put a consequentialist calculus. This sounds complicated until we realise that he was proposing to judge all things by the overall level of happiness (or utility – hence utilitarianism) they produced. In defending this idea, the foundation of utilitarianism, Bentham showed that everything was good in so far as it tended to produce a higher rather than lower level of happiness in society. This was true of political institutions such as laws and prisons (indeed he argued that it would be possible to work out how much disutility a criminal caused and thereby work out the tariff to be paid) and people.

The utilitarian argument defines what is right in terms of what is good. For society to sacrifice one life for the greater good (providing you can demonstrate the good to be gained) is therefore right. On the other side of this argument are those who believe that there are uninfringeable rights and that therefore the right is different from (and morally superior to) the good. This is a familiar position and one we will have had some experience of in our reading of modern thought. In this instance the argument is developed for the contemporary reader by Robert Nozick, Ronald Dworkin and John Rawls. Here, even if the sacrifice of one was to the benefit of the many, we are obliged to respect the rights of the one. They are morally unchallengeable. The sorts of arguments and foundations that underpin these two traditions of thought are discussed in Chapter 6. Learning the vocabulary of both allows us to judge between them and this is important because we do need to judge the actions of ourselves, of others and of our societies. Some societies claim that they are founded on the rights of man (*sic*). Yet we are used to our politicians relying upon internment (or imprisonment without trial), or conscription, in times of crisis. If we have a right to due process, or to life, then it seems incongruous at best to argue that these rights can be removed for the greater good in times of conflict. Indeed it seems that our governments were backsliding from a moral commitment to rights to a consequentialist conception of the good when they interred Japanese immigrants during the Second World War, Irish men and women during the 'Troubles', or Al-Qaeda suspects during the second Gulf war. Judging our rulers requires that we have the conceptual and historical tools provided by our exploration here.

Building on these key traditions in contemporary thought we then move on to an exploration of two further debates. The first (Chapter 7) focuses on the issue of distributive justice or how we allocate benefits and burdens in a society. These are the principles that inform our taxation and social-welfare systems, and public education and health care provision. The second (Chapter 8) examines multiculturalism. These debates are distinct but share a common concern. How do we work out what we owe to each other? When doing so should we take account of different tastes or preferences? If so, which preferences are more significant or morally relevant? The multiculturalist debates take culture, ethnicity and religion as the morally relevant sources of preference. The claim is that our very identity is given through our cultural affiliations and heritage and that to ignore it is to make the idea of social goods irrelevant to us. For example, a decision to distribute a pork surplus equally throughout a society that contained among its citizens Jewish and Muslim people would not only fail to realise its goal of equity; it would be hugely insulting. Of course justice is about more than merely avoiding insulting our fellow citizens. The question is wider and concerns how far we ought to go to accommodate ethno-cultural difference. It may be, so the multiculturalists argue, necessary to treat people differently in order to treat them equally. This position is also present in the wider debates concerning distributive justice and Chapter 7 divorces the issue from the specific subject of culture and searches for the wider principles of justice. This asks us to dig deep into the foundations of our moral and political lives. The answers you will meet range from the claim that justice demands that we treat every individual equally and thus in the same way to the claim that we need to take account of certain morally relevant differences. This latter position is itself divisible into a wide range of positions. Here the real foundation lies in discovering what morally relevant differences are and in working out how a society might go about taking account of them. Some argue that it is necessary to arrange the distributive mechanisms of society to take account of undeserved constraints on freedom such as educational ability or physical prowess, gender or race or class. A society that limited freedom (consciously or unconsciously) based on these characteristics might be considered flawed. Some positions go further and argue that we have to take account of different tastes and preferences. Michael Walzer claims that we need a grasp of 'complex equality' that can take into account the social meaning of certain goods. Some communities value health care more highly than education and thus social equality requires us to take account of this when distributing goods across communities. In these chapters we ask you to explore the complexities of the notion of justice. In equipping you with the vocabulary to critically evaluate different claims and in giving you prominent examples of how some people have proposed to resolve the debates we intend to introduce you to a deeper understanding of the nature of politics. The understanding of how distributive mechanisms (such as public health or education services) work that you might gain from the news or, in rather more detail, from political science classes is supplemented with a grasp of why things are arranged as they are. The knowledge that some sections of society believe that it is wrong to require them to obey laws that reflect the social norms of the dominant culture in society rather than their own customs and moral traditions is supplemented with the critical vocabulary to engage in this real-life debate and to begin to think about the justice or otherwise of culturally differentiated rights as opposed to a unified conception of citizenship.

The second section concerned with contemporary political thought focuses on challenges to universalism and foundationalism. These are challenges to the whole idea of normative political theory as we have presented it in this book. In ending our introduction with these challenges we do not want to suggest that the normative project of political theory is finished. Rather, we hope to lay down a series of real challenges to normative political theory in the hope that, by this stage in your reading, you will be equipped to engage critically with them and to draw some important insights from them. The challenges we explore in this final chapter are very serious ones. Such challenges are not entirely novel. In one sense political theory is all about normative challenges and some of the responses to multiculturalism that we examined in Chapter 8 can also be viewed as challenges to universalism and foundationalism. Nor are such challenges the sole product of contemporary debates. Conservatism (Chapter 9) and feminism (Chapter 10) both have long histories that run alongside Enlightenment universalism. The conservatives in Chapter 9 challenge the positions that we engage with in the rest of the book. They do so by attacking the commitment of these other positions to abstract philosophical projects that underpin normative interventions in politics. They accuse political philosophers of simply failing to come to terms with the complexity of the social world, with dangerous consequences. Humanity's capacity for reason is not sufficient to meet the demands of practical politics and so we should rely on tradition rather than reason to guide our actions.

In the first part of Chapter 10 we explore the contribution of feminist political theory to the canon. It is overwhelmingly obvious that the vast majority of voices in political theory have been male. What does this say about the history of politics and the discipline of political thought? The history of politics is a history of gender discrimination. Some feminists have sought to deal with this fact by exploring the place of the rights of women within the discourses that have traditionally been about the rights of man (and here finally we can drop the rather apologetic '*sic*' that usually follows such statements). These thinkers, from Mary Wollstonecraft in the late eighteenth century to thinkers such as Susan Moller Okin and Carole Pateman in the contemporary period, are usually thought of as liberal feminists. These thinkers seek to reform and extend liberalism from within its basic theoretical boundaries. For other feminist thinkers, however, the very basis of liberal thought is suspect. Its claims to universality are challenged because they are the product of a male-dominated development that seeks universal human reason but finds only universal male reason. For some theorists the claim that women have different conceptions of morality and thus different political needs and aspirations is a product of a sexually particular way of being in the world. This claim is (to put it rather simplistically) based on the view that such differences are biologically hardwired into women and have been repressed by centuries of patriarchy. An importantly different claim is that women have a different conception of morality and thus different political needs and aspirations because of their gender or their experience of being treated as 'women' and given certain social, most often reproductive, roles (Gilligan 1982). Here gender is a social rather than biological fact. In exploring these challenges we explore the thought that all that has gone before has been hideously one-sided and does not speak for (or to) more than half of the world's population.

In the second half of this chapter we begin to explore antifoundationalism. In this present chapter we have begun to think about the foundations of politics (moral arguments, conceptions of human nature, of the good and of the right) as central to the understanding of politics. Antifoundationalism views this as utterly wrong. Indeed our principal proponent of this view, Richard Rorty, believes that this way of thinking about politics is wrong, outmoded and part of the problem rather than part of the solution (Rorty 1993). In addressing this challenge we are asked to consider, at a more general level, a concern (shared with some feminist thinking) that the way we are inviting you to do political theory will cause you to discriminate, against people. Political theory has been used to justify war, slavery, genocide, gender and sexual discrimination to name just a few of its achievements. After 2,000 years it may be time to try something else. This last thought asks you to think about what that 'something else' might be, or even to consider the prospect of a future that cannot rely upon modes of moral or social justification. We end with these challenges because they confront us here and now and require us to think deeply and critically about our normative projects. It is a lot to ask you to face up to in an introductory book but if you accept the challenge the rewards can be immense.

Conclusions

As an introduction to political thought this book is both wide-ranging and intellectually demanding. It has to be because the issues we have to deal with as scholars, students, citizens and as human beings are wide-ranging and demanding. As you begin to immerse yourself in 2,000 years of political and moral argument remember that your task is not to learn by rote the answers given to difficult political questions by those figures we explore here. Rather you are encouraged to get a sense for the broad sweep of the history of political thought and for the ways in which moral and social positions are justified and defended. It is, in our experience, much easier to engage with the detail of these vital arguments armed with a broad grasp of what political theory is all about. In one sense there is far more detail in the rest of the book than you will need in your first engagement with the subject. This detail is there to help frame the general debates and to offer you something to encourage you to revisit them. You are not required to have mastered each chapter before you go on to the next. Nor are you required to agree with everything you read. Every engagement with the issues turns out to be a new experience and every new voice in the discourses of politics brings new inspiration. We hope that this book encourages you to add your voice to them.

Topics for discussion

1. What is normative thought?
2. What is the relation between ethics and politics?
3. Why do political theorists think that scientific standards of judgement are not the only standards we need to think about? Are they right?

Critical glossary

This book has two main aims. Firstly we intend to introduce you to a broad range of some of the most important issues in political thought. This survey covers a wide variety of philosophical and historical traditions, drawing, for example, on ideas developed in Ancient Greece, Enlightenment Europe and in the present-day USA and UK. In doing so it examines questions such as 'why should we obey the rules of politics?', 'what is freedom?' and 'are contemporary political institutions justifiable?'. The second aim of this book is to give you a firm grounding in the complex philosophical and technical concepts that surround the analysis of politics. When individuals or governments give their support to (for example) human rights or democracy they often do so by referring to an enormous range of moral and practical reasons. Our aim is to introduce you to the necessary skills that will allow you to critically engage with such claims. You need to able to understand the way arguments work, the consequences of holding any particular moral or political position and the origin and content of these arguments if you are going to be able to make an informed judgement about the validity or otherwise of various political issues.

While a large part of this knowledge can be acquired by learning about the development of political thought this book makes the expansion of your awareness of the issues and your analytic skills a priority. A recurring theme is the construction and organisation of what we have called a critical glossary. As we go through the course we will add words and concepts to our glossary, drawing out the key themes and ideas that will play a part in your study of politics. Someone defending liberal democracy will often do so for 'individualist', 'universalist' and 'deontological' reasons. In order to critically assess the argument for liberal democracy you must be aware of what these arguments are, their strengths and weaknesses and any plausible alternatives. At the end of this book you will.

The ideas covered by this glossary are not presented as dictionary definitions. Instead we focus on the use of each concept in the context in which you come across it and aim to show you how it informs the argument or expresses a core principle. Each term may have alternative or broader meanings in other contexts and, because of the nature of political studies, many terms have contested meanings. Each term is intended to start a discussion about its meaning, not to end it.

Important terms that you have dealt with in this chapter include:

Normative Normative refers to the complex (and hotly contested) web of standards, concepts and ideals through which we make value judgements.

Political Thought Political thought is synonymous with political theory and political philosophy. It refers to that part of the discipline of political studies that concerns itself with the values, ideas, norms, and concepts (theories) that inform politics taken generally. The place of theory in the study and practice of politics is itself contested because there are contested understandings of the role and content of theories. In this book political thought refers to the normative aspect of political and social life and is contrasted with political science.

Foundations The foundations of politics are the moral, social and cultural ideas and customs that justify political institutions. One important role of political thought is to elaborate and scrutinise these (often unspoken) foundations.

Political Science Political science is used in two ways. First, it is often used as a generic term for the study of politics and suggests a unidisciplinary approach to the subject. Second, there is a more technical usage and this is the one we will adopt in this book. Here political science is taken to be the empirical (scientific) branch of political studies. An essential aspect of political studies, it concerns itself with the recording and analysis of observable data such as policy processes, institutional structures and government.

Empirical Empirical refers to that which is based on experience. This is often contrasted with normative (as normative standards are not necessarily based on empirical experience).

Epistemological From 'epistemology', meaning theory of knowledge. How do we *know* what is good, bad, just or unjust? A surprising amount of moral and political theory is tied up with epistemology. It focuses both on the status and authority of knowledge (for example as truth or as consensus) and on the justification of claims to knowledge.

Relativism	The idea that there is no absolute or universal criterion sufficient to generate cross-cultural comparisons or value judgements. The idea is simply that such standards are relative to specific times and specific places.

List of references / Further reading

AF Bentham, J. [1843](2001), 'Anarchical Fallacies', in *Selected Writings on Utilitarianism*, Ware: Wordsworth Editions. References are to chapter and paragraph.

Ayer, A. J. (2001), *Language, Truth and Logic*, London: Penguin.

Ball, T. (1995), *Reappraising Political Theory*, Oxford: Oxford University Press.

FOG Bentham, J. [1776] (2001), 'A Fragment of Government', in *Selected Writings on Utilarianism*, Ware: Wordsworth Editions.

Gallie, W. B. (1956), 'Essentially Contested Concepts', *Proceedings of the Aristotelian Society*, 56, 167–98.

Gilligan, C. (1982), *In a Different Voice: Psychological Theory and Women's Development*, Cambridge, MA & London: Harvard University Press.

Rorty, R. (1993), 'Human Rights, Rationality and Sentimentality', in S. Shute & S. Hurley (eds), *On Human Rights: The Oxford Amnesty Lectures*, New York: Basic Books.

SECTION I

CLASSICAL ORIGINS OF POLITICAL THOUGHT

CHAPTER ONE

HISTORICAL

Plato

CONCEPTUAL

Is There a Universal Moral Order?

The first person we will encounter on our journey through the history and concepts of philosophy is a Greek philosopher called Plato. Plato was born in 427 BC and died in 347 BC, living most of his life in Athens. Whilst he was by no means the first philosopher he was one of the earliest to leave us a significant body of work, as well as being one of the most influential of all philosophers. Most importantly for us Plato has been so influential because he spends time asking and providing answers to questions that have always troubled people. Even today, nearly 2,500 years after Plato's death, if we think about politics and the problems of living together the issues that confront us again and again very often involve the sorts of questions that Plato's *Republic* can help us think about in a more focused and sophisticated way. Questions we ask regarding the best form of state, about whether democracy is a good idea, about why politicians make mistakes and especially about whether there is anything absolutely morally right or wrong in politics are among those that Plato can help us to think about.

We can best understand the issues that concerned Plato by taking a look at the circumstances of his life in classical Greece. Although the Greeks thought of themselves as a single people, distinct from, say, the Persians, Macedonians or Egyptians, Greece was not a single country. Instead it was divided up into a number of small self-governing city-states or *poleis* (singular *polis*) that formed shifting patterns of enmities and alliances. Politically, each *polis* was often very different from the next. Whilst one *polis* might be ruled tyrannically by a single man and others by benevolent monarchs, still others were oligarchies, ruled by a small but wealthy group of aristocrats, and others again were democracies, where all adult male citizens were involved in ruling. At the same time the Greeks were becoming more aware of other cultures. The Greek historian Herodotus recounts the story of the ruler of Persia considering the practices of the Greeks and certain Indians concerning the disposal of their dead. Whilst the Greeks thought it proper to burn their dead, amongst the Indians it was proper to eat them. Each group was horrified by the 'unnatural' practice of the other, regarding it as a desecration of the dead. The Persian concluded that 'custom was king', that there may not be a right way of doing things but that different people regard different things as right and wrong and that this might be all we can say on the matter. Political variation within Greece and cultural confrontation beyond it made this question of **relativism** an issue that seems to have concerned Plato. Is there a single and definitive right way of doing things or do right and wrong vary relative to (or depend upon) cultural context? Are morality and politics simply matters of 'what we do round here', custom or convention in the same way as is which side of the road we drive on? You will have recognised that relativism is also an issue that anyone thinking about politics today must confront. When we consider the 'clash of civilisations' in world affairs or the problems of multicultural politics we must ask ourselves if there is only one right and justified way of acting and organising ourselves politically and whether that just happens to be the way that we currently do things.

Plato was also concerned with the related problem of **subjectivism**. This is again an issue concerned with standards of morality, of right and wrong. However, whilst the relativist regards these standards as given by communities, the subjectivist believes that each man sets his own standards. Just as one person may prefer vanilla ice cream and another strawberry depending on their differing sensations of taste so what is right for one person may differ from what is right for another because they are in different circumstances or have different desires or interests. We have all encountered subjectivists in conversations whether we were aware of them or not. When asked to defend their actions or words we are familiar with responses like 'well, it is true *for me*' and 'I was right to do it because it felt right *to me*'. In these answers the standards appealed to are subjective; they are dependent upon the person making the judgement. Another Greek, Protagoras, summed this up in the claim that 'a man is the measure of all things' and we shall encounter the same attitude later in this chapter from the sophists (teachers of philosophy and rhetoric in classical Greece). What relativism and subjectivism have in common is their mutual claim that there are no absolute standards of right or wrong in morality or politics. Both positions deny the **objectivity** of values or standards. As we shall see, Plato, like most of us most of the time, wants the values he relies upon and defends to be objective values, to be the right values and to be true values.

The political pluralism of Plato's world posed to him other important political questions. Recall that the *polis* or city-state took on a number of political forms. Whilst Plato was growing up democratic Athens and her allies had been at war with the oligarchy of Sparta and her allies. During this conflict there had been struggles within Athens for political control between democratic and aristocratic political factions. Plato, born into a distinguished aristocratic family and living in a democratic Athens ultimately defeated by the oligarchy of Sparta, must have been affected by these events. Indeed, much of *The Republic* details Plato's thoughts on the best form of political organisation. He addresses issues such as 'who should rule?', 'how should they rule?' and 'why should they rule?'. Plato's answers to these important questions force us to consider, as they did Plato himself, whether democratic government is a good idea. He rattles our complacent assumption that **democracy** is the best form of political system, considering it fickle and arbitrary and instead supporting a form of **elitism**.

The final piece of Plato's context that we need to be aware of is his relationship to Socrates, another Athenian philosopher and Plato's friend and teacher. As a philosopher Socrates was constantly cross-examining people about their beliefs and convictions. He would question them about what they believed justice or courage were, for example, and then demonstrate that their beliefs were muddled or confused. As you can well imagine this questioning of their traditional beliefs upset many people and, coupled with the fact that he associated with aristocrats naturally sympathetic to Sparta (such as Plato), led democratic Athens to execute Socrates on charges of impiety and corrupting the young. Plato regarded this as a huge mistake and, together with the mistakes made in the conduct of the unsuccessful war, it encouraged his concern with the question of why politics goes wrong. Why do politicians and governments consistently appear to make poor decisions, do the wrong thing or exhibit gross errors of judgement? Again, these are questions we hear voiced just as loudly today.

These then are Plato's concerns: the issues of relativism and subjectivism, of the best form of political organisation, and of why politics goes wrong? These are big questions. They are also among our questions whenever we try to think hard about politics. They can also be united in a single question, 'what is **justice**?'. If Plato could provide us with an objective account of the nature of justice then we could counter the relativist and subjectivist, would know how best to organise ourselves politically, and would be best equipped to avoid political disaster. It is this question, 'what is justice?', that occupies Plato in *The Republic* and to which we look in it for an answer. We must be aware that Plato's answer may not be ours, or even be anything resembling what we might expect an answer to look like. Indeed, Plato's study of politics led him to the conclusion that

> all existing states were badly governed . . . I was forced in fact, to the belief that the only hope of finding justice for society or for the individual lay in true philosophy, and that mankind will have no respite from trouble until either real philosophers gain political power or politicians become by some miracle true philosophers. (This is from Plato's *Seventh Letter*. Taken from the translator's introduction to *The Republic*, p.16; see also 499b)

The conclusion that philosophers should be rulers might surprise the modern reader, and it surprised many of the Greeks too, but we would ask you to reserve judgement until you have had a chance to consider Plato's arguments. It may also be that even if we disagree with Plato we will learn much from understanding both with what, and why, we disagree. We should be able to helpfully separate Plato's specific answers to his questions from, firstly, the importance of the questions he asks and, secondly, from the way he goes about answering them, from the method he adopts. Even if we do not turn out to be sympathetic to Plato's answers we might still acknowledge the centrality of the issues he addresses and learn a lot about the sorts of arguments we might have to make if we are to answer them differently. If we are concerned about cultural relativism and subjectivism, about justifying moral and political standards, about justifying human rights, or about judging or criticising the actions of governments or individuals then we might have to make the same sorts of arguments as Plato.

Setting up the question

The Republic is not what we would expect a book on politics to be, or even one such as Aristotle wrote. We do not find in it an account of prominent political figures and there are no histories of political factions, regimes or constitutions. Neither is there an account of meticulous data collection about political attitudes nor the statistical analysis that accompanies it. Indeed, there is nothing we would recognise as political science with its reliance on empirical (value-free) method. Nor do we find a legal analysis of rights, or of the manner in which law manages conflict between individuals and classes. Instead what we get from Plato is a normative (value-laden) attempt to address the questions about justice that we have highlighted. However, these questions are not addressed as we would normally expect a book to address them. Plato wrote his books as *dialogues*, conversations between two or more people on the topics that concerned him. The conversations he recounts are not real conversations, but the people in them are usually real people associated with he views he places in their mouths. The central character of these dialogues is Socrates and it is through him that we are told what Plato thinks on the matter in hand. Whenever we read what Socrates thinks about something we can assume that this is what Plato thinks.

At the start of *The Republic* Socrates and several others are gathered in the house of the wealthy and elderly Cephalus when the conversation turns to justice. Cephalus ventures the opinion that justice is 'truthfulness and returning anything we have borrowed' (331c). In reply Socrates argues that doing right must be more than fulfilling our obligations. If we had borrowed an axe from a friend who later went mad, returning his weapon to him would not be the right thing to do, nor should we answer truthfully if he asked us where it is. This sort of argument can be found for any answer similar to the one Cephalus gives. If we try to answer the question 'what is justice?' simply by listing examples of just actions then counter-examples can always be found where acting in that way seems wrong. Trying to catalogue examples of justice doesn't look to be the right way of finding out what justice actually is. Polemarchus takes up the argument that 'it is right to give every man his due' and appeals to the poet Simonides to support his claim (331e). He refines his views so that he argues that 'justice is to benefit one's friends and harm one's enemies', again defended by appeal to the poets (332d). Appealing to poets as authorities might seem strange to us but to the Greeks the works of the poets were the closest thing to a Bible they possessed. Polemarchus is doing just what many people today do when they look to the Bible or some other holy book for an authoritative answer to difficult moral questions. In the course of conversation it becomes apparent that Polemarchus has thought little about the question of justice himself, simply accepting the authority he cites, and so he is in no position to defend his claims when questioned. Indeed, he ends his active part in the conversation agreeing with Socrates that rather than harm one's enemies the just man should harm nobody, the opposite of the position he set out defending.

Cephalus and Polemarchus highlight two possible ways of answering our questions about justice: we can try to list right actions or we can unreflectively appeal to certain moral authorities for an answer. Neither avenue leads to an understanding of justice, listing actions is vulnerable to counter-examples and unreflective acceptance of authority leads to confusion when unfamiliar situations or questions call on us to think about how to apply these poorly understood traditional ideas. Nor can appeal to authority be a satisfactory justification for anyone who doesn't share our opinion about what is authoritative. Appealing to the revealed word of God as contained in the New Testament will fail to move an atheist or a Muslim. If we find these traditional answers to our question unsatisfactory, and reject them, the alternative might be a scepticism about justice. In *The Republic* we find this sceptical attitude in the mouth of Thrasymachus. Thrasymachus storms aggressively into the argument, claiming that justice is none of the things they have discussed so far. Instead 'justice or right is simply what is in the interest of the stronger party' (338c). He continues, claiming that 'each type of government enacts laws that are in its own interest . . . what is "right" for their subjects is what is in the interest of themselves, the rulers . . . right is . . . the interest of the established government' (338e–339a). Socrates argues that ruling is a craft or skill like that of the doctor or ship's captain, and like the doctor with his patients or the captain with his crew the ruler exercises his skill not in his own interest but in the interest of his subjects. This 'craft analogy', where ruling is regarded as a sort of skill, becomes very important later on. Here, however, Thrasymachus responds that the ruler is instead like the shepherd who might look after his flock and appear to be considerate of their interest but only so as to fatten them for his profit. Justice and morality are simply the rules of behaviour imposed by the strong upon the weak in order to make the weak, or just, work in 'someone else's interest', that of the strong or unjust. Thrasymachus thinks that the pursuit of self-interest rather than what is usually called justice brings rewards of wealth and power. Not only that, he seems to regard the pursuit of self-interest as a prime human motive and therefore as natural and right.

These themes are picked up by Glaucon and Adiemantus. Glaucon argues that men are hopeful of being free to do wrong and benefit from it whilst, at the same time, suffering no wrong done to themselves. This, however, is not generally possible and so people will agree to

> make laws and mutual agreements, and that what the law lays down they call lawful and right. This is the origin and nature of justice. It lies between what is most desirable, to do wrong and avoid punishment, and what is most undesirable, to suffer wrong without being able to get redress; justice lies between these two and is accepted not as being good in itself, but as having a relative value (358e–359a).

Justice is merely the result of compromise between human beings, each of whom agrees to the laws because he can't do wrong and get away scot free (359d). Even the just man is being motivated by self-interest; acting justly is the best he can get away with in the circumstances. To add weight to his claim Glaucon tells a story about a shepherd who found a ring that can make its wearer invisible, the Ring of Gyges (359c–360d). When he realised what the ring did the shepherd used it to seduce the queen, kill the king and steal the throne. Glaucon's point here is that the just and unjust man would behave in the same way if they possessed the ring. If he could steal what he liked, seduce who he liked and kill who he liked without fear of capture the temptation would be too much for any man. If he can get away with it the just man will behave in the same way as the unjust man because they are both self-interested: 'no man is just of his own free will, but only under compulsion . . . he will always do wrong when he gets the chance' (360c). You might want to think about what you would do if you found such a ring, and whether the temptation to do wrong might be too much to withstand. Would you too be governed by 'self-interest, the motive which all men naturally follow if they are not forcibly restrained by the law' (359c)? Is the law that restrains you simply a set of conventions forced on you as a compromise between your injustice and that of others? Do you only act morally out of fear?

Do people act justly only because they are afraid of the consequences of not doing so? Do they act justly only because society rewards what it regards as good acts and punishes those it regards as bad? If so then it is not justice that is good but only those things that go along with justice, the rewards of acting justly such as a good reputation and the wealth and power that reputation brings. Adiemantus points out that in fact it is best to be unjust but to mask this with a reputation for justice. If the unjust man can appear just he will 'have a marvellous time' and do what he likes (365b–366d). This lays the ground for the specific task Socrates sets out to complete in *The Republic*, to prove that justice is good in itself and not for its consequences. Socrates is asked to show that we should act rightly whatever the benefits or punishments we might receive for doing so.

The challenge laid down by Thrasymachus, Glaucon and Adiemantus is a challenge to us as well as to Socrates and Plato. Each of these characters argues that instead of being good, full stop, justice is good only relative to something else. Justice is in fact made relative to the interests of particular people. What is just depends on the interests of the stronger or the ruler (Thrasymachus) or on the interests of a group of people who get together to agree on rules of justice because they cannot consistently get away with advancing their interests in any other way (Glaucon and Adiemantus). A change of ruler, of interest or circumstance, since justice is relative to these, may lead to a change in the content of justice.

The Greeks distinguished between *physis* and *nomos*. *Physis* referred to things that existed by nature, *nomos* to things that existed as a result of human organisation. In many ways this is similar to the modern distinction between natural and artificial. Thrasymachus and Glaucon argue that what we call justice is a product of *nomos*, human custom and convention. Justice is artificial rather than natural. In this way they are similar to the social-contract theorists such as Hobbes who appear in later chapters. If justice is artificial instead of natural it might not be the same everywhere. What is called just will vary in relation to the interests of rulers or to the customs agreed upon. Custom, it seems, *is* king and justice is just 'the way we do things round here'. Man *is* the measure of all things as he weighs everything against his interest. This is the challenge of relativism and subjectivism restated. Are justice and morality everywhere the same or do they legitimately vary from place to place? If what is right is relative to interest or circumstance, should justice and morality be abandoned or discarded if our interests or circumstances change? This is our central concern in this chapter and one of our central concerns whenever we think hard about politics.

What is justice?

The first important aspect of Plato's answer to this question is that politics is natural, not artificial. By this we mean that Plato thought that a specific form of political organisation is especially justified in that it is most in accordance with our nature. Human beings have a definite nature that mandates a particular sort of political organisation, and the politics that best suits our nature is just. An important implication is that if justice fits with human nature then justice will be the same for all people since all share the same human nature. It will be helpful if we briefly look at Plato's specific account of justice and the important manner in which he argues that it is the correct account. Through Socrates Plato says that the nature of justice is a very obscure subject but we can cast light on it by looking at it on a large scale, in the city, before moving on to examine the nature of the just individual (368e–369a). The claim that political justice (the just city) and personal justice (the just soul or psyche) will be sufficiently similar for this method to be helpful may strike us as unusual. It is a claim we can revisit, but for now it is enough that we let Plato point out that we call both men and institutions just and this must reflect something they have in common.

We have already come across Plato's claim that political justice will be found only when philosophers become rulers or politicians become philosophers. It is now time to examine the arguments that he marshals in favour of philosopher-kings. It is suggested that 'no two of us are born exactly alike. We have different natural aptitudes, which fit us for different jobs' (370a–b). We are each born with differing capacities, talents and abilities, a different natural endowment of skills. Plato argues that there is a natural division of labour that should reflect these differences of ability, and so each of us is suited for a different sort of work. Some of us will be good farmers, others good builders and yet others good smiths. Plato contends that it is best 'when a man specializes appropriately on a single job for which he is naturally fitted' (370c). Each person should specialise in the job that they are best suited to perform. Plato's vision of the just city reflects this ideal division of labour by institutionalising two broad classes of people, the artisans or businessmen and the guardians. The guardian class is further subdivided into the auxiliaries (soldiers) and the guardians proper (philosopher-kings). These classes are then hierarchically ordered: the guardians are the rulers and, supported by the arms of the auxiliaries, they rule over the artisans, who constitute the overwhelming majority of workers in the *polis*.

The life of the artisans was to be the ordinary and everyday life of the marketplace. Plato envisaged their lives carrying on much as they did in the Greek *poleis* of his day. However, the lives of the auxiliaries and the guardians were to be very different indeed. These classes of citizens would be permitted to own no property. They were to be allowed no money, no gold or silver (416e–417a), nor were they allowed property in housing or provisions. Instead, 'they shall eat together in messes and live together like soldiers in camp' (416e). Private property was not to be the only institution abolished amongst the ruling classes; the family was to receive similar treatment. Rather than develop special attachments to any other guardians in particular, 'all the women should be common to all the men; similarly, children should be held in common, and no parent should know its child, or child its parent' (457d). Instead special 'marriage' festivals were to be organised where lots would be drawn in a 'fixed' lottery to ensure that the best guardians of both sexes mated together to produce superior offspring, in much the same way that horses and dogs have been bred by stock breeders (458e–460b). The children that resulted were to be brought up in communal nurseries (460c). These measures embody Plato's attempts to prevent corruption of the rulers. If the guardians cannot own property then they cannot be tempted by riches into tyranny; if they have no family then they cannot be tempted into nepotism (417a–b, 464e).

Plato has presented us with a city divided into three very different classes. The artisans or workers would be a mixture of all sorts of people following various trades and living relatively normal lives with their families. The auxiliaries are a kind of army and police force for the defence of the *polis* against its enemies. The rulers are philosopher-kings, the best of the auxiliaries and thus best suited to leadership. These classes were organised hierarchically and rigidly. If you were best suited to be a member of one then that was where you were to belong. Plato's belief that we have different abilities, that we each do one thing better than we do anything else, and that we ought to do that at which we are best ensures this outcome. Despite having made the life of the guardians seem unappealing Plato is aware that there may be a popular reaction against this hierarchy. He counters this possibility in two ways. Firstly, and infamously, he proposes to tell the people a 'magnificent myth', often referred to as a 'noble lie' (414b–415d). Plato envisages convincing his community that this hierarchy is justified since God, when drawing men from the earth, added different metals to the souls of different men and that these metals correspond to social functions and classes. To some he added gold and these become rulers, whilst those with silver become auxiliaries and those with iron and bronze, workers. Secondly, in addition to giving this hierarchy mythical significance Plato would make it clear that all people were of the same stock. For this reason a child born of the working class could have gold or silver in his make-up and would then be taken for training as a guardian. Likewise the child of a guardian might exhibit traces of iron or bronze and the guardians would then 'assign it its proper value' and place the child with the workers. Once your place in life was identified the hierarchy was rigid and your place fixed, but there was room for movement between classes (promotion and demotion) across generations. The hierarchy was not hereditary and so the ruling class did not constitute a permanent aristocracy. Rather, membership of a class was purely a matter of your abilities and suitability for a role (415b–c).

Plato now feels ready to tell us what justice is. He does so by identifying the four cardinal virtues of the classical world, wisdom, courage, self-discipline (or moderation) and justice. When we have seen how the perfect state embodies the first three of these virtues what is left over will be justice (427d–434d). The state is wise because of the wisdom of its rulers, gained during an extensive period of training and education. It is courageous because of the courage and judgement of its defensive class, the auxiliaries. That the state has self-discipline is a result of the mastery of those best suited to be masters over those worst suited, and the acceptance by all of that hierarchy. Finally, the justice of the state is that which makes it possible for the state to exhibit these other virtues and which guarantees their preservation. What allows the rulers to be wise, the auxiliaries to be courageous and for all to accept discipline is that each is doing the job that they are best suited for and no one is doing anyone else's job. For Plato justice is just this, 'minding your own business' (433b, 434c). The state is just when each person and class sticks to its own task and does that for which it is naturally best suited. When this is the case the state or *polis* functions like a living being as an organic whole, with each person and class of persons being like the different parts of a body. No one of the limbs or organs can function alone or do the job of another body part, nor can they function properly unless all the other parts of the body are doing their jobs properly. However, when each part does its job, minds its own business, the body is at its most healthy and becomes more than the sum of its parts. Likewise, when each part of the state minds its own business and works in harmony with the other parts then the state will exhibit a unity that makes it as healthy as it can be.

Having provided an account of the just state Plato moves on to check that this pattern of justice makes sense when applied to individuals. Is justice in the individual also somehow a matter of everything minding its own business? Plato answers that it is, with the three hierarchically organised parts of the city being mirrored in the proper ordering of the three elements of the just soul or personality. Just as the state is made up of rulers, auxiliaries and workers so the soul consists of reason, spirit and desire or appetite. Reflection on our own experience may make this a plausible account of our personality. We each are aware of appetites, of drives such as hunger and thirst or for such things as riches or sexual satisfaction. Plato concludes that these drives are all types of desire, and that desire is a part of the personality of each of us (437d). We are all equally aware that we do not think it proper for us to succumb to our desires every time we experience them. If we do so we might, for example, descend into gluttony, lose our friends if we fail to temper our desire for riches in our dealings with them, or lose our jobs if we succumb every time we want to laze around in bed watching television all day. Nor are we capable of satisfying all our desires at once. Plato identifies the faculty that takes a broader look at our interests, balancing and judging between our desires and at times suppressing them, as reason. Reason is the reflective element in our personality that is often capable of mastering our irrational appetites (439c–d). Plato's third element of the soul is usually translated as spirit although this is an approximate term and may include qualities such as indignation, ambition and determination (see the translator's notes at 434d). For Plato, spirit is roused by a person's reason when righteous indignation is appropriate and motivates us to fight for what is right (440c). Although directed by reason, spirit forms a separate element since children can be full of spirit at birth and then only later (sometimes never) acquire a degree of reason.

These three elements of the soul are the same as those of the city, in so far as they have equivalent roles to play and are arranged hierarchically in the same way (441c–442d). Reason should rule the soul as the philosopher rules the city since it is the seat of wisdom. Spirit, like the auxiliary class, exhibits the virtue of courage and should support the rule of reason as the auxiliaries support the guardians. Together reason and spirit should discipline appetite and give it direction. A soul organised in this way also exhibits the virtue of self-discipline. Finally, 'the individual man is just in the same way that the state is just . . . when the three elements within it each [mind] their own business' (441d). In the truly just man each of the three parts of the soul is in its proper place, fulfilling their roles in harmony, and so exhibiting a unity. This three-way division of the soul enables Plato to explain the existence of three classes of men. In each of the classes a different part of the soul is predominant. In the artisans desire predominates, suiting them for business and wealth accumulation. In the auxiliaries spirit is dominant so they are naturally the best soldiers. In the souls of the guardians reason predominates and so they are best fitted for ruling. These links that Plato draws between the parts of the soul and parts of the city lend credence to the 'myth of the metals'. This is not so much a 'noble lie' in fact; Plato regards it as a way of conveying to the masses the truth about the suitability of people to jobs. This city, it seems, matches human nature. The correspondence between the city and the soul demonstrates that this city is organised in accordance with human nature. Political organisation, what kind of state we ought to have, is not arbitrary and contingent. Man has a nature and our nature mandates this particular form of hierarchical political organisation as natural and justified.

Plato's conclusion that justice involves component parts of a whole 'minding their own business', properly fulfilling their function or acting in accordance with their nature underpins the rule of philosopher-kings. However, his conclusion that the philosophers should rule depends on there being a special skill of ruling that only the philosophers are capable of possessing. If we recall the 'craft analogy' used when arguing with Thrasymachus, Plato contends that just as there is skill in medicine exhibited by doctors and in navigation exhibited by ship's captains, the philosophers exhibit skill in ruling. In order for Plato to justify the rule of philosophers he needs to provide an account of what it is that this skill of ruling involves. What is it that suits the philosophers for leadership? Since the philosopher's soul is governed by reason they have the virtue of wisdom and to be wise is to be a lover of knowledge. The key question that Plato must answer to clinch his argument is 'what can the philosopher have knowledge of that is necessary to ruling and that is not available to any other group of people?'

Philosophers and the Forms

The knowledge that Plato claims philosophers have is knowledge of **'the Forms'**. To understand what the Forms are we have to follow some unusual arguments, starting with the claim that most of us never experience or gain knowledge of the real world. Plato distinguishes between the experienced world that most of us think of as reality, and 'the real world' of the Forms accessible only to philosophers. The world we ordinarily experience with our senses is just a superficial reflection of, or shadow of, the more real world of the Forms that remains invisible to all but the greatest of philosophers. To understand why Plato might make such a claim we can consider a list of things that people commonly regard as beautiful (476b–d). We speak of beautiful people, beautiful landscapes, beautiful buildings, beautiful ideas, beautiful butterflies and even beautiful goals on the football pitch. It is obvious that these beautiful things have little in common except that they are all related to something called 'beauty'. Plato asks us to consider 'beauty itself' and argues that it must be something else quite apart from the range of beautiful things, something which makes each of them beautiful but is not one of them. Beauty itself must be something apart from any particular beautiful thing since any beautiful person or landscape may be at the same time both beautiful and not beautiful (479a–d). One person may think someone beautiful whilst to another they are ugly, just as at one time of day a landscape may be beautiful whilst at another time, in a different light or from a different angle, it may be daunting, frightening or merely nondescript. If any particular thing can be both beautiful and not beautiful it cannot be beauty itself. This idea of beauty itself, which all beautiful things reflect in some way, is the Form of beauty. Similarly, although we are aware of many things we call large they may also be called small in other contexts. A large building looks small next to a mountain just as a large jockey is small in comparison to a basketball player. Again there must be a Form of largeness itself that explains our understanding of the largeness of all these objects. Plato also argues that there are Forms of objects as well as concepts. He argues that there are Forms that correspond to beds and tables. The Form of the table is reflected in all the examples of tables of all shapes and sizes and enables us to recognise them all as tables (596b). In fact, everything we experience in the world is a reflection of one or more Form. It is knowledge and awareness of this 'world of Forms', which underpins the world we experience that marks out the true philosopher.

It is not just the existence of Forms that is important to us, it is their features also. By understanding Plato's conception of Forms we will be able to understand how he aims to address the questions posed by relativism and subjectivism that we took to be important. Plato believes that each Form is unique. There is only one Form of the table just as beauty itself is the single Form that all beautiful things reflect. It doesn't matter what beautiful thing is being contemplated, who is contemplating it, or whether they are doing so in Greece or in Australia; its beauty is always a reflection of the same Form. It doesn't matter when they contemplate it either since each unique Form is also eternal and unchanging. The Forms have always existed and will go on existing forever unchanged, always and in all places the same. A Form also perfectly embodies that which it is the Form of. The Form of Beauty is then perfectly beautiful just as the Form of the table is the perfect embodiment of 'tableness'. Because the Forms are perfect, eternal and unchanging Plato considers the world of Forms to be more real than the everyday world that reflects them, where objects and people are created, age and are destroyed or die. The world of things we ordinarily experience is transient and the things in it are shadows of the 'real' world and the Forms it contains.

Plato feels he cannot stop his account here. Whilst knowledge of the Forms is a higher kind of knowledge there is also a highest form of knowledge, knowledge of the 'Form of the Good' (505a). If each of the Forms is perfect then they each share the quality of being good. Their value as perfect examples of beauty or of a table is therefore dependent on how they reflect the Form of goodness. Just as the objects we experience depend for their existence on the Forms they are shadows of, so the Forms themselves depend for their existence on the Form of the Good. Plato feels unable to explain directly what 'the Good' is; such knowledge depends upon fifty years of the proper education (540a). Instead he describes something that seems to be 'a child of the good and to resemble it very closely', the sun (506e). The Simile of the Sun shows how the Good is like the sun. Just as the light of the sun makes objects visible to our sight, the 'light' of the Good makes objects intelligible to our faculty of knowledge. Further, just as the sun is the source of the energy necessary for the existence of everything on earth, so the Form of the Good is the source of the reality and truth that underpins the existence of the Forms in general (507b–509e).

We can now see clearly the hierarchical organisation of both objects and knowledge. The reality of objects can be represented on a vertical line (509d–511e). At the bottom are the least real, shadows or images or paintings of physical things, above them the physical objects themselves and above them the Forms. Standing above even the Forms is the Form of the Good, the most real of all. Gaining knowledge of each of these types of object in turn marks a progress from mere opinion towards true knowledge. Progress towards knowledge will not be made through our senses, for things can appear to our senses as both large and small or beautiful and ugly at the same time. Instead true knowledge can be achieved only through the exercise of reason, a position that has come to be known as rationalism. Since the souls of philosophers are the only ones dominated by reason only philosophers are capable of true knowledge, knowledge of the Forms and the Form of the Good, and so of ultimate reality.

To help understand the relationship between knowledge and opinion and between philosophers and others, Plato provides the Simile of the Cave (514a–521b). He pictures a group of people who have been chained in a cave since they were children so that they can look only straight at the wall in front of them. Behind them in the cave burns a fire, in front of which pass puppet-like figures of men and animals which cast shadows on the wall so that the prisoners can see them alongside their own shadows. Plato claims that these people would believe that the shadow world they see is the real and only world. If one prisoner were released he would, after initially being blinded by the fire, see the way the puppets caused the shadows and come to a deeper understanding of the way his world worked. If he were then dragged upwards out of the cave to the outside world lit by the sun he would again be blinded. However, he would gradually come to see the real things outside the cave of which the puppet figures are copies and again recognise them as more real or genuine than anything he had seen before. Finally the freed prisoner can look at the sun itself and see that it produces the seasons, makes the plants grow that feed the animals and people and makes it possible for him to see these other objects. Plato claims that most people are like the prisoners chained in the cave, seeing only a shadow of reality. Only the philosopher is capable of breaking out of the prison of our senses and, after the initial disorientation (blinding) caused by casting aside comfortable presuppositions, through education in the exercise of reason see 'outside' to the real world of the Forms and the Form of the Good that illuminates it. Plato likens the difference in understanding between the ordinary person and the philosopher to the difference between dreaming and full consciousness (476c–d).

We started this section with the question of what sort of knowledge it is that philosophers alone possess which suits them for ruling. We are now able to answer that they are capable of knowledge of the Form of the Good and of the Form of Justice. Where most men such as Cephalus and Polemarchus can give only partial accounts of justice the philosopher can give a full account of what justice is in both the city and the soul. Indeed his knowledge of the Form of Justice allows him to recognise that justice is the same sort of thing in both the city and the soul in so far as all just things reflect the Form of Justice. The philosopher is able to look upon the perfect and unchanging Form of Justice and bring this knowledge to bear in his governing the state. The Form of Justice is an ideal pattern, a pattern 'laid up in heaven', which only the philosopher-king can be guided by (472c, 592b). As such only the philosopher-king 'should be in charge of a state' as only so will the state be 'properly regulated' (484b, 506a–b).

Conclusions

We can summarise Plato's specific answers to the political questions broached at the start of this chapter.

What is the best form of state? Plato claims that the best state is the just state, and this will be organised therefore as to match human nature and so be appropriate to the sort of creatures we are. Justice is attained in both the city and the soul when each of their respective constituent parts 'minds its own business'. When so ordered both the city and the soul exhibit a unity that is to be valued as it reflects the Form of Justice. As well as being good in itself in this way, being just is also good in its consequences for the individual. In 'minding their own business' each person does the job to which, by their nature, they are best suited. Each person fulfils their nature and becomes the best that they can be. In doing so they will be happy.

Why elitism rather than democracy? Much of this chapter has been concerned with Plato's argument that the just state is ruled by a relatively small number of guardians rather than by 'the people' as a whole. Key to the argument has been Plato's contention that there is a skill to ruling that is dependent upon knowledge of the Form of Justice and that this knowledge is available only to a few. Without the guidance provided by the 'pattern' of the Form of Justice the political decisions of the masses will be fickle and arbitrary. 'The people' have no objective reasons to make one decision rather than another and so will make one decision on one day and its opposite on another, just as their mood and appetites change (561c–d). Rather than abandon society to this fate Plato's *Republic* embodies a rationalist vision of certain human beings able to understand social and political processes and capable of rationally planning and organising so as to properly permit human flourishing.

Why do things go wrong in politics? Not only is government by those unskilled in the art of ruling inherently unstable, it is also likely to issue in poor decisions. If my car breaks down I don't gather passers-by in the street and ask them all to make a guess at what is wrong with it. They are more likely than not to make the wrong diagnosis so instead I find a mechanic. If I am ill I don't ask the people in the doctor's waiting room to vote on my cure, I consult the doctor. If we recognise the necessity of specialist knowledge in these cases how can we fail to do so in the most important case of the government of the state? It is because we are most often governed by the unskilled that the decisions of politicians so often seem to be bad decisions. It was a failure to recognise the truth-seeking nature of the philosophic enterprise and its relevance to the moral and political well-being of the *polis* that led to the Athenian execution of Socrates. Likewise, instead of blaming others for the problems in society, Plato believes that politicians should recognise that it is their shortcomings that are ultimately responsible. Politicians are like the sailors on a ship who think the art of navigation unnecessary and blithely sail the ship into danger. The philosopher is the true navigator, who can sail the ship of state safely (488a–489c). How convincing do you find this argument? Even if you find it difficult to agree with Plato about philosopher-rulers you should think hard about how and whether democracy is justified. Is there any reason to assume that democratic government is better than the alternatives?

We now find ourselves in a position to address the main concerns we brought to this chapter, relativism and subjectivism. We saw that these were Plato's concerns too and looked to Plato for help in countering the claim that right and wrong, justice and injustice might vary from place to place, time to time, with circumstances or with the interests, desires or concerns of different individuals. Plato's answer was to argue for the necessity of the Forms, specifically the Form of the Good and of Justice. If justice has a Form then true judgements of justice cannot be dependent on context or vary in response to local concerns. Since the Form of Justice, like all Forms, is perfect, eternal and unchanging it can be the basis of the objectivity needed to counter relativism and subjectivism. Justice is not the artificial creation of man, varying from place to place as a matter of custom. Instead, the Form underpins a certain political organisation as natural for man and perfectly just. The justice of Plato's *Republic* is absolute. Whenever and wherever we are posed questions of justice the Form of Justice will provide us with the same true answer. This is Plato's answer to the relativist: there is indeed a universal moral order.

It is important, now that we have seen Plato's specific answers to this range of questions, that we step back and ask ourselves what we can take from Plato to help us answer our own versions of these questions. Just like the Greeks we are confronted by alternative ways of life and by different forms of political organisation, each reflecting different moral judgements. As such we are similarly faced by problems of relativism and subjectivism and by concerns about the best form of government. Whilst we may feel uncomfortable with Plato's elitism and antidemocratic standpoint, and whilst we may find his arguments strange, we can importantly separate the content of his specific answers to these questions from more general features of the way that he reaches those answers. We have already noticed that Plato is important because he seems to take seriously many of the same questions that we think are serious political questions. This alone gives us reason to examine what he has to say closely. However, we are more interested here in Plato's method, that is, with the type of reasons and arguments he feels are necessary to give a proper answer to questions of this sort. By thinking about why Plato makes the arguments he does we might understand what sort of arguments we need when we attempt to answer the same questions.

Firstly, Plato is clear that we must find guidance in our judgements of value, our normative judgements, outside the world that we experience through our senses. Questions such as 'what is justice?' and 'why is it wrong to hurt people gratuitously?' cannot be answered empirically. If we are unsure of the answers we cannot make much progress by simply looking more closely at the world before our eyes. If we are faced with a challenge to our commitment to human rights, for example, we might answer that these are rights to certain forms of treatment that all people have in virtue of their being human. When pushed to justify this we can try in vain to find empirical evidence to support our claim. At a cursory glance we might see that usually people have two arms, two legs and a head in virtue of their being human but we wouldn't notice any rights. Perhaps we feel we should look closer so we start a more thorough empirical examination. Taking up our scalpel we find that people usually have two lungs, two kidneys and a heart in virtue of their being human but still no rights. No matter how exact we make our examination we will not find our human rights.

Instead Plato shows us that this whole approach is wrong, answers to these sorts of questions must be normative. Values must be looked for and defended in the intelligible world, the world of ideas, not in the physical world. We all value some things just as we all regard some actions and principles as right and others as wrong. Plato's point is that to defend and justify these judgements we must step out of the 'real' world and into a world of ideas. *The Republic* is an attempt to defend the objectivity of moral values by doing just that. We might disagree with Plato about what he found when he climbed out of the cave and into the light but it is a climb we may be committed to making too.

Secondly, moving from the 'world of facts' to the world of ideas when looking to justify our normative judgements may involve endangering those very judgements. In many situations of disagreement we turn to the facts in the world to help us resolve our differences. If Anne and Bob have different opinions about the exact size of their kitchen or the make of car that their neighbour drives then they can find out quite easily whose opinion is correct. They can do so by going and taking a look in next door's driveway or by measuring their kitchen with a tape. In both cases the way the world actually is functions as an objective standard for their judgements, it anchors some opinions or statements to the truth. If we must cast ourselves loose from the world that we can measure or observe in order to think hard about justice or morality we seem to be depriving ourselves of an anchor to truth. If we have nothing against which to check our opinions then opinion is all they may be. Once we turn to the world of ideas we face a problem separating the good judgements of value and right and wrong from the bad. Indeed, it may be that there are no good or bad judgements, just mine or yours. Plato, aware of this danger, attempts to provide an anchor for such judgements; he tries to provide an objective foundation for claims of justice and morality. Having already rejected in Book I of *The Republic* the common-sense approach of Cephalus and Polemarchus's appeal to authority, Plato's rebuttal of Thrasymachus and Glaucon involves what is called a foundationalist approach. A foundationalist account of morality identifies a set of ideas, principles or values that underpin all moral judgements and serve to justify them. This approach attempts to establish a bedrock upon which a theory can be built, a rock-solid foundation. Only then can it provide the unshakeable basis to which all other moral claims refer and upon which they rely for justification. The foundation is the standard against which all other moral principles are measured and from which their status as moral is derived. In Plato's case the foundations are the Forms and ultimately the Form of the Good. All normative judgements can be right or wrong, and their correctness is measured by how perfectly they reflect the Forms. By regarding the world of Forms as more real than the world we experience Plato is reinstituting the 'world out there', against which we can check our judgements.

The sort of foundationalist response with which Plato meets the relativist challenge has a notable historical and theoretical pedigree. Much of the history of philosophy concerns different attempts to provide foundations, and we will encounter alternative accounts of those foundations later in this book. Besides Plato's Forms, prominent suggestions for the foundation of morality include the revealed word of God, a variety of accounts of a fundamental human nature, and the human rights possessed by all individuals. On this understanding, for something to be an objective truth, or for a judgement or principle to be objectively right, it must either correspond to the foundation, whatever that happens to be, or be derived via an error-free chain of reasoning from that foundation. The foundationalist claim is that if no such bedrock can be identified then there is nothing which can anchor moral principles or judgements, nor any measure or standard of rightness that can apply to them. Without a foundation to underpin a universal moral order we will be left without any way to discriminate between right and wrong principles or good and bad moral judgements. If such a foundation cannot be found then the truth really may vary with speaker or circumstance and we may be stuck with relativism after all.

Plato is important because he, like most of us, wants to defend certain values and principles and wants to justify them as universal and objective. In trying to provide such a justification he felt pushed all the way to claiming the existence of a more real world of Forms. In examining and thinking about Plato's attempt to provide this foundation we have been encouraged to think about how we might justify our own principles. If we are attached to our universal normative claims, such as the claim that all human beings have the right to certain forms of treatment, then in order to avoid relativism we may have to follow Plato's path. We may not feel able to follow exactly in his metaphysical footsteps but we may very well be committed to a similar project. If we cannot provide a foundation for our normative claims they will appear to be no more than our opinions, and a lot of people may hold different opinions. Giving up on Plato's project or on anything that resembles it may exact a heavy price, submission to relativism.

Topics for discussion

1. Do you think that there are objective standards of right and wrong, or does justice vary with context or with people's interests?
2. What do you think of Plato's attack on democratic politics?
3. How convincing do you find Plato's justification of inequality?
4. Do you agree with Plato's claim that the Forms are necessary in order to make sense of the world and of normative judgement? If not, then are you giving up on moral objectivity?

Critical glossary

Relativism The idea that there is no absolute or universal criterion sufficient to generate cross-cultural comparisons or value judgements. The idea is simply that such standards are relative to specific times and specific places.

Subjectivism This is again an issue concerned with standards of morality, of right and wrong. However, whilst the relativist regards these standards as given by communities, the subjectivist believes that each man sets his own standards.

Objectivity In opposition to relativism and subjectivism, the search for objectivity assumes the existence of absolute and universal normative standards that apply in all contexts.

Democracy Government by the people. In ancient Greece this entailed direct participation in government of every adult male citizen. Plato's political thought led him to reject democracy in favour of elitism.

Elitism The idea that a minority of human beings are in some way superior, as a group, to the majority. When this elite minority rule this is often referred to as an oligarchy. Plato's view of the knowledge

	necessary to political rule led him to argue that only an elite (philosopher-kings) were able to rule justly.
Justice	Contesting the meaning of justice is central to the project of political thought. Questions of justice, in the broadest terms, concern what we owe to each other. Plato argues that justice is 'minding one's own business', in the activity of ruling or being ruled both in the city and in the soul.
The Forms	Plato distinguishes between the experienced world and the world of the Forms, which is the basis for objectivity and value. The Forms are knowable through the philosophical exercise of reason.

List of references/Further reading

Primary text

Plato (1955), *The Republic*, Harmondsworth: Penguin. All references to *The Republic* are made by paragraph number and letter. These can be found in the margin of most editions.

Secondary literature

Melchert, N. (1994), *Who's to Say? A Dialogue on Relativism*, Indianapolis: Hackett.

Nettleship, R. [1897] (1964), *Lectures on the Republic of Plato* (2nd edition), London: Macmillan.

Pappas, N. (1995), *Routledge Philosophy Guidebook to Plato and the Republic*, London & New York: Routledge.

Sayers, S. (1999), *Plato's Republic: An Introduction*, Edinburgh: Edinburgh University Press.

White, N. (1979), *A Companion to Plato's Republic*, Indianapolis: Hackett.

There are also good chapters on *The Republic* in:

Boucher, D. & Kelly, P. (eds) (2003), *Political Thinkers: From Socrates to the Present*, Oxford: Oxford University Press.

Forsyth, M. & Keens-Soper, M. (eds) (1988), *The Political Classics: Volume 1*, Oxford: Oxford University Press.

CHAPTER TWO

HISTORICAL	CONCEPTUAL
Aristotle	**Is Politics Natural?**

The idea that there is 'something out there' that gives justice its content or justification is one that has stayed with political theory, and with mankind more generally, for thousands of years. It makes sense of one of the foundational categories of our moral and political lives. Yet, as no doubt you found out in the last chapter, even with the help of Plato's analogies of the Sun or the Cave it is hard to see clearly what that 'something' might be. Perhaps when we all reach the age of intellectual maturity that Plato suggested we will grasp his point fully. More worryingly, we might just have to accept that we are Plato's men of silver or brass and that we are never destined to understand these higher things. It is this last suggestion, rather than any philosophical problem with the idea of the Forms, that irritates the modern reader most of all. Surely non-philosophers have a stake in politics. Surely politics is a human activity and not a philosophical one. In any case, many of you will have had the chance to meet philosophers for the first time in your university careers. Do you really think that they should rule the world?

We do not have to look far to find a political philosopher who also seems to have thought this way. Indeed it was one of Plato's students who supplied this human touch. Aristotle, like his master, argued that politics was natural to man and essential to a life of virtue. Nevertheless Aristotle's approach to politics and ethics seems to capture the humanity of political life while showing us what is so morally important about politics. It was not only political philosophy that made Aristotle an historical figure. His life, the sheer breadth of his work, the dominance his work has had on the world (right up to the present day) make him a compelling figure. Born in Stagira in northern Greece in 384 BC, Aristotle was a member of Plato's Academy from 367 BC until Plato's death in 347 BC, at which point he left Athens. During his twelve year absence Aristotle was, among other things, tutor to Alexander (later 'the Great'), son of Philip of Macedonia. Returning to Athens in 335 BC Aristotle founded his own school, the Lyceum, where he worked for twelve years, founding the first real research library. His work was innovative and in many cases seminal in the fields of biology, cosmology, mathematics, dynamics, aesthetics, metaphysics and logic as well as politics, a subject that was for Aristotle a continuation of ethics. When Alexander died anti-Macedonian tensions caused Aristotle to leave Athens. One story has it that charges of impiety were brought against him. You may recall that this was a charge levelled at Plato's mentor, Socrates. For this crime Socrates was executed by being forced to drink hemlock in 399 BC. Plato famously dramatised Socrates' refusing the offer to escape his sentence (a fairly routine offer in Athens at this time). Socrates preferred to live up to his obligations to his 'mother and father', the laws of his native Athens. Aristotle, of course, was not Athenian and he fled Athens for Calchis, 'in order that the Athenians might not commit a second crime against philosophy' (Aelian, *Varia Historia* III, 36 in Barnes 1995: 6), where one year later in 322 BC he died.

If Aristotle's life reads like an essential part of the history of Greek civilisation then his influence beyond his lifespan reads like an essential part of the history of almost all civilisation. Although Aristotle's work was lost to the west for a considerable period it was retained in Syrian and Arabic culture. Reintroduced to the west early in the thirteenth century Aristotle's philosophy was first banned by the Council of Paris as being subversive but then assimilated totally into Christian teaching by St Thomas Aquinas. This total assimilation meant that between the thirteenth and eighteenth centuries if you referred to 'the Philosopher' everyone knew you were talking about Aristotle. In the universities of Europe Aristotelian ethics were taught not as one ethical framework among others but simply as ethics. Even today Aristotle's work forms a touchstone for many of the world's most famous political theorists.

What is it that makes Aristotle so impressive and durable? Answering that question has taken thousands of scholars tens of thousand pages to answer. Fortunately our focus is more limited. Our goal is to begin to understand just two of Aristotle's most famous claims. In the *Politics* Aristotle claimed that politics is natural to man and that happiness and moral virtue are to be found in citizenship (*Politics*: 1, 2, 1253a). All over the world human beings form themselves into political societies. Most of us are born in to a state of some sort and so we take it for granted. But just look at those who are born, or who are made, stateless – their biggest wish and most insistent claim is for the protection and benefit only a state can provide. Admittedly Aristotle is arguing a more specific case. His full claim is that the *polis* (a relatively small city-state as opposed to the nation-states we know now) is the best form of society. Nevertheless there is much we can draw from Aristotle's work. There is something intuitively engaging about his argument about the relationship between man and politics (and for Aristotle 'man' means man and not human beings more generally, something we will look at later). Exploring the mechanics of this claim (and others like it) is a large part of what political theory is. As we examine Aristotle's argument there are many things we can learn about politics and about our own intuitions and beliefs. We will also go a long way to answering the question of Aristotle's importance.

For some, Aristotle's greatness lies in his reputation as the father of political science. Aristotle is famous for his empirical work and had made a study of 158 contemporary constitutions, a foothold on reality that distinguishes him from Plato (whom Aristotle criticises for excessive idealism). But this misses the most important aspect of Aristotle's greatness. Aristotle's political science is far removed from the political science of the behaviourists and positivists you encountered in the Introduction. For Aristotle politics is a practical science and to live well a man needs practical wisdom, not just philosophical wisdom (early on in the *Ethics* Aristotle argues that knowledge of 'the Form' or 'the Idea' is irrelevant to political theory as politics must concern itself with real human beings and their capacities and happiness). This idea distances him from Plato but does not abandon the philosophical side of political thought. Political science of this sort has two vital features. Firstly, and most importantly, it is necessarily entwined with ethics. Political science done properly aims to tell us not just how others have lived, but how we, and others, can live well. This relationship between ethics and politics in Aristotle's work is typically Greek but if we generalise the idea it is also fundamental to political theory. We do not merely ask 'what types of political system are out there?'. Instead we ask 'what is the best type of political system out there?' and 'what features make it better?'. Secondly, Aristotle claims in the *Ethics* that politics is the controlling or **master science** (*Ethics*: 1, 2, 1094a25). (It should be mentioned that *Ethics* refers to the *Nicomachean Ethics* rather than the *Eademian Ethics*; in any case the former is more famous and widely used than the latter.) The goal of political science is to help us understand how to live well, which for Aristotle means happily and virtuously. The range of 'sciences' we need to draw upon to make these claims is huge and they are all in this sense subordinate to, or a part of, political science. Aristotle's claim gives us an understanding of both the importance of our task and the terrifying depth of our study. Thinking about politics is difficult but it is also very important and can be very rewarding.

The claim that we need to focus on is that politics is natural to man and that man's happiness is dependent upon being a citizen of a well-run *polis* or city-state. It is for this argument, above all else, that Aristotle is famous. The argument here is opposed to the claim that politics is an artificial construct designed to curb the worst excesses of human nature. In Aristotle's time this position was held by some of the Sophists, who, you may recall, were also protagonists in the Platonic dialogues. But this debate is not merely some ancient Greek curiosity. In the modern period it formed the core of the arguments between Thomas Hobbes, John Locke and Jean-Jacques Rousseau (see Chapters 3 and 4). Even today this debate is still vital. It is certainly the case that this discussion is culturally informed and therefore differently nuanced in each incarnation. But the question of whether we have politics to constrain the actions of human beings or to enable human beings to flourish must still inform our view of what the best sort of political arrangement is. Understanding the arguments that provide the foundation for this claim will require that we explore questions concerning human nature, human happiness, the nature of ethics, the constitutional possibilities of politics and the idea of justice. It sounds difficult and we should not underestimate the intricacy of any representation of this argument. However, in Aristotle's thought, as with all classic arguments, it is possible to identify the ideas that do most of the work, the motor of the argument. In Aristotle (as in Plato and as in virtually all political thought to the present day) it is the foundation of a political theory that does all the work. If you can grasp Aristotle's **teleology** you will have the tools to help you unlock both the *Politics* and the text that serves as its prologue, the *Ethics*, and gain access to his version of the claim that politics enables humanity to be the best sort of human beings possible.

Often in the study of political theory it is best to begin with a brief look at the working parts of an argument rather than with a retelling of the story. The story about how we naturally come to live in a *polis* is well told in Aristotle but the real force of his case lies in the argument he makes to justify his conclusions. Throughout the history of political thought, and throughout this book, you will come across many extremely persuasive stories about politics and ethics and it is easy to get carried away with the basic intuitive sense in each one. But it is important to remember that each story is the product of an argument that you are being asked to judge. Every story retold here has been persuasive enough to convince history to remember it. Your task is to learn how to discriminate between convincing stories and the best way to begin to do that is to learn how to uncover what supports each of the most important steps in the story. The best place to begin a study of the *Ethics* and the *Politics* is with the teleological nature of Aristotle's thought, as it provides the context for the questions he asks. Teleology sounds like an intimidating concept but it is not. The word comes from the Greek '*telos*', meaning 'end' or 'goal'. For Aristotle the final goal or endpoint of a thing is also its formal cause, through which we can understand its purpose. Focusing on the goal of a thing offers us a way to understand its nature. For example, the purpose of an acorn is to become an oak tree. We know that not all acorns become oak trees but nevertheless we could not understand what an acorn is if we did not have a grasp of its *telos*. An acorn that falls on barren ground or that ends up as squirrel food is not uncommon but in one fundamental sense it is a failed acorn. In thinking about acorns this way we have a grasp of what an acorn should be and what conditions contribute to the realisation of its potential. This teleological way of thinking about things is characteristic of Aristotle's political theory. The only real difference is that human beings are more complicated than acorns. Both the *Politics* and the *Ethics* are teleological in that Aristotle argues that questions concerning the best life for man can be understood by looking at his natural 'endpoint'. At its simplest Aristotle's question is 'what conditions allow man to reach his full potential?'. The answer is equally simple 'being a **citizen** of a just *polis*'.

Before we explore the answer Aristotle gives us, let's explore the question a little further. The question is formulated in the *Ethics*, where Aristotle lays out the scope, the limits and the form of moral and political enquiry. Even if we simply accept the sense in looking for the natural goal of a thing we still need to know by what criteria we can assess the natural goal of a man. Aristotle's answer is '**happiness**'.

> An end pursued in itself, we say, is more complete than an end pursued because of something else . . . Now happiness more than

> anything else seems unconditionally complete, since we always [choose it, and also] choose it because of itself, never because of anything else. Honour, pleasure, understanding and every virtue we certainly choose because of themselves, since we would choose each of them even if it had no further result, but we also choose them for the sake of happiness, supposing that through them we shall be happy. (*Ethics*: 1, 7, 1097a30–1097b5)

We can understand human potential by looking at what makes people happy. The Greek word used by Aristotle here is *eudaimonia* and often you will find that it is reproduced in this form. The main reason for this is that *eudaimonia* is a far more sophisticated notion than basic happiness. Sometimes this notion is described as activity of the soul in accordance with **virtue** or **excellence** (***aretē***) (Robinson 1995: 69; Barnes 2000: 124). The essence of the notion is that true happiness stems from being the best human being we can be, making the most of all our capacities. A man who does nothing more than eat Mars bars, even if he really likes them and is therefore satisfying that desire totally, is not able to achieve real happiness. Genuine and complete happiness requires an all-round game. A fuller idea of why Aristotle starts here can be gleaned from a brief look at his understanding of virtue or excellence (***aretē***). The achievement of virtue is a key part of achieving genuine happiness and Aristotle explains this idea through his **doctrine of the mean**.

The mean or moderate state is, for Aristotle, the virtuous state. To take a very basic example first: how does our Mars bar eater become happy? Eating too many Mars bars will make that person sick, or give him bad teeth or a nutritional problem. Yet denying himself the pleasure of eating Mars bars seems too extreme and an unnecessary denial of his basic desire. The Aristotelian answer is simple – eat Mars bars, but not too many. Both excess and denial are vices; they do not lead to happiness. Virtue lies in deciding accurately how many Mars bars will make us happy and sticking to our plan. It is a practical decision and it is relative to us. That means that there is no 'right' number of Mars bars for all (an ethical flexibility that can take account of the variety of human experience) and that living virtuously is hard, personal work. How often have you eaten or drunk more than you know is good for you?

> It is hard work to be excellent, since in each case it is hard work to find what is intermediate; e.g. not everyone, but only one who

> knows, finds the midpoint in a circle. So also getting angry, or giving and spending money, is easy and everyone can do it; but doing it to the right person, in the right amount, at the right time, for the right end and in the right way is no longer easy, nor can everyone do it. Hence [doing these things] well is rare, praiseworthy and fine. (*Ethics*: 2, 9, 11093a25)

Obviously Aristotle's full conception of virtue is more detailed and complicated than this but it will serve to help us understand Aristotle's most vital claims in the *Politics*. Aristotle's political thought is ethical reflection on a practical issue. What, he asks, does it take to make men happy? Or, under what conditions can man live to his full potential? It is certainly the case that these are more difficult questions than working out how many Mars bars will make us happy but the mechanics are pretty much the same. Understanding the basics of Aristotle's teleology and his conception of happiness offers us a way in to his answer to these questions, and the bigger question and its answer are a lot more interesting.

Politics is the key to man's happiness. To be a virtuous citizen is to be the best sort of human being possible. Politics is natural. These are massive claims and, if proven, will confirm politics as the master science. Aristotle's fundamental claim, the foundation for all of his political thought, is laid out clearly in what must be one of the most famous quotations of all time.

> It is evident . . . that a city-state is among the things that exist by nature, that a human being is by nature a political animal, and that anyone who is without a city-state, not by luck but by nature, is either a poor specimen or a superhuman. (*Politics*: 1, 3, 1253a)

You already have the intellectual tools to understand this as the foundation of Aristotle's politics. The first idea, 'that a city-state [exists] by nature, that a human being is by nature a political animal', is an expression of man's *telos*. The second idea, 'that [whoever] is without a city-state . . . is either a poor specimen or a superhuman', has also been expressed as ' . . . is either inferior or superior to man' (*Treatise on Government*). A little later on Aristotle puts it another way: 'Anyone who cannot form a community with others, or who does not need it because he is self-sufficient, is no part of a city-state – he is either a beast or a god (*Politics*: 1, 2, 1253a25–1253a30).' This can best be understood if we think of it as a generalised version of the doctrine of the mean.

If we initially take the second of these ideas much of Aristotle's thinking will become clear. Beasts do not have the capacity to live politically (even if they do live socially). They lack the powers of speech and reason that enable humans to live this way. Gods, we can assume (or believe), do not need the benefits of political society as they are self-sufficient. We can all think of examples of humans who are bestial and humans who shun the benefits of society. Humans who are incapable of living in decent society, perhaps because they follow their base (sometimes called 'animal') desires in an unconstrained way, we do think of as somehow not being fully human. Sometimes we lock them up as criminals or treat them as sociopaths. At other times we censure them as 'vulgar' or 'immoral'. At the other end of the scale we can imagine hermits, examples of the ascetic saints who engage in a life of spiritual contemplation in the desert (like Antony of Egypt) or up a pole (like Simon Stylites). Be they saintly or otherwise, it does not take a comic genius to draw out the absurdity in this way of life. Similarly the idea that philosophy is the perfect way of life for man (as in Plato) does not seem to capture the full human experience. Pure reason is too high a life for man. We are capable of philosophical reasoning. It is an important part of what and who we are. But if a life of contemplation is perfection how do we ensure we have enough to eat or propagate the species? Human virtue lies in finding the mean, a balance between the animal part of our nature and the rational part of our nature.

Returning now to the first idea (Aristotle's claim that '**man is a political animal**') we begin to get an idea of how we find this balance between our animal and rational sides. Aristotle's claim is that the balance is struck in becoming a citizen of the *polis*. The idea of citizenship is vital here. It is not enough for man to simply live in a *polis*. He must be a citizen. This is not true of all men or any women and it is a theme to which we shall return. For now we must focus on the idea that our happiness (and remember the particular meaning of happiness/*eudaimonia* here) depends upon citizenship or full membership of political society. Our nature dictates this and this is what Aristotle means when he says that we are a type of animal that is suited by nature for life in a *polis*. In this way human beings make no sense without the *polis* just as acorns make no sense without oak trees.

It is here that the acorn/oak tree – human/*polis* analogy begins to break down. Acorns never existed without oak trees; the whole (the tree) is necessarily prior to the part (the acorn). However, it is clear from history that humans existed independently of political society generally and the *polis* more specifically. Aristotle does not deny this and it makes no difference to the power of what is a subtler version of the same argument. Indeed he still claims that the whole (the *polis*) is necessarily prior to the part (the happy or excellent man) (*Politics*: 1, 2, 1253a19). Note the way we put that. We did not say 'man' but rather 'the happy or excellent man'. Aristotle's claim is that the life of the citizen is, was, and always shall be the route to human fulfilment.

In fact, Aristotle's claim is even stronger than this. His claim is not that citizenship is the key to happiness but that citizenship in the *polis* (rather than the empire or the nation-state) is the key to happiness. Life before the ancient Greek city-state, or outside it in confederations or nations, or beyond it in the modern nation-state, is not conducive to happiness. This is quite a claim and one that often turns people off from Aristotle's work. However, like much in the *Politics*, this does not follow necessarily from his argument. Rather it is what you might call 'cultural baggage'. It is built partly upon a culturally informed view of the role of women and slaves in society and partly on the view that a *polis* was just about the perfect size, balancing economies of scale and the potential to defend yourself with the feeling of being fully connected to your community (*Politics*: 7, 4, 1362b2–1362b7). Aristotle's view of the severely restricted role of women in society, and his further claim that some people are naturally slaves, are anathema to the modern reader. First we should look at the story as told by Aristotle and then we will suggest a few ways around what is a sticking point for many. Similarly the view that the best state is one where there is a strong sense of community and personal obligation is very important to Aristotle. Even so this does not have to be a problem for the modern reader. Many contemporary political theorists (later on you will come to think of them as communitarians) believe that politics and human happiness would be better served if we could foster a sense of community. The problems faced by political units larger than the *polis* may be more significant in this regard but that is not necessarily the case and Aristotle is merely drawing on personal experience and expressing a preference. More importantly there is a more universal message in the *politics*. As one authoritative commentary on the text notes, 'it is not really the *polis* which occupies Aristotle's attention in the *Politics*, but rather the "form of organization of the *polis*", namely its constitution, or *politeia*' (Johnson 1990: 2). It is life in a properly organised (or just) state that humans require for fulfilment and this is an argument that transcends the historical context that can seem to shackle Aristotle's work to the *poleis* of ancient Greece.

As we go through the arguments in the *Politics* it is possible to begin to distinguish between the philosophically vital 'core' of Aristotle's case and the 'cultural baggage'. You already have the conceptual tools to do this. Arguments that draw on the idea of teleology, or relate directly to the achievement of *eudaimonia* (happiness) or *aretē* (virtue) are the ones that you need to pay most attention to. Doing this allows you to look beyond the basic story told by Aristotle and to focus on those arguments about the importance of citizenship and the nature of the just state that made his work so important.

What evidence does Aristotle use to fill in his claims about man's *telos*? He begins by arguing that there is a series of natural relationships between a man and a woman and a man and his slave. There is, Aristotle generously admits, a difference between a woman and a slave (at least in Greek society) but they are similar in that a man needs them for survival. Women are needed for the sake of procreation and slaves (whom Aristotle likens to 'oxen' and 'animate tools') are needed for manual work. Man, the natural ruler, can organise these resources in a way that is beneficial to all (*Politics*: 1, 2, 1252a24–1252b15). Clearly this is not the sort of beginning likely to endear Aristotle to the modern reader. In our view most of this comes under the 'cultural baggage' category. The important claim is that the family (or the household as Aristotle puts it) is a basic natural unit among humans. The fact that the ancient Greek household included slaves (the labour-saving devices of the day) and assumed that women should be subservient to men is as culturally relative as the nuclear family of modern western societies. Nevertheless, Aristotle expends considerable energy showing that neither women nor slaves can run their own lives and so they 'fit' in his scheme of things in a manner that supports the *eudaimonia* of the full citizen. On first sight then he excludes all non-Greeks (barbarians or natural slaves) and all women from having the potential to achieve human excellence. In mitigation, Aristotle was not the first (or the last) man and ancient Athens was not the first (or the last) society to think this way. Also, we know (from his will) that Aristotle did free some of his own slaves and so could not have really believed that they were incapable of ruling themselves and were therefore natural slaves. So what can we learn from these opening arguments? First, humans naturally work in groups. The basic unit of humanity is not the individual but the family. In fact the various social groupings that humans live through are always more important than the individual as the individual cannot live without these groups. This is an important claim and has significant political implications. The focus on individual autonomy that is the basic assumption of much modern western political thought is far more recent and changes how we think about politics (something we will examine closely in later chapters). From Aristotle's perspective engaging with the group's dynamics rather than protecting ourselves from the group is the key to happiness. This is something that seems to make sense of the basic human condition. Second, and because we naturally work in groups, ensuring the smooth running of the group is vital. Ruling and organising are key virtues. In the recognition that we are communal animals we find the origin of the claim that we are political animals.

The family, or household, is the most basic unit but it is not the culmination of our social instinct. As natural as the family, argues Aristotle, is the village. Here a 'natural' hierarchy of rule by the eldest leads a group of families that can enjoy modest economies of scale and the protection of 'safety in numbers'. This development is straightforward. Life in a village is more efficient. But it is not the most efficient.

> A complete community constituted out of several villages, once it reaches the level of total self-sufficiency, practically speaking, is a city-state. It comes to be for the sake of living, but remains in existence for the sake of living well. That is why every city-state exists by nature, since the first communities do. For the city-state is their end; for we say that each thing's nature – for example that of a human being, a horse, or a household – is the character it has when its coming-into-being has been completed. (*Politics*: 1, 2, 1252b26–1252b30)

Here there are three things you must note. First, this is a clear expression of Aristotle's teleological method. Second, self-sufficiency is the mark of a political community (something we will look at shortly). Third, the end of a city-state goes beyond living effectively to living well; that is, politics takes us way beyond mere economies of scale to justice, the very thing that has the power to perfect humans (*Politics*: 1, 2, 1253a32).

When Aristotle argues that the political life in a just *polis* is natural to man he is not claiming that we would naturally evolve into just citizens. Citizenship and justice need to be worked on and sometimes coercively enforced. Nevertheless the potential is always there. We can see this, Aristotle claims, in our powers of speech and reason.

> It is also clear why a human being is more of a political animal than a bee or other gregarious animal. Nature makes nothing pointlessly, as we say, and no animal has speech except a human being. A voice is a signifier of what is pleasant or painful, which is why it is also possessed by other animals (for their nature goes this far: they not only perceive what is pleasant or painful but signify it to each other). But speech is for making clear what is beneficial or harmful, and hence also what is just and unjust, and the rest. And it is community in these that makes a household and a city-state. (*Politics*: 1, 2, 1253a8–1253a18)

Note the final sentence here, 'it is community in these that makes . . . a city-state'. Aristotle's version of justice and politics here is very down to earth. Working together to make practical decisions about how to maximise benefit and avoid harm is justice. It seems simple, even commonsensical and perhaps not deserving of the 2,000 years of attentive study it has received. However, therein lies its appeal. All of the reasons that Aristotle has given in support of this conclusion provide the grounds we need to discriminate between good and bad types of polity and serve to outline the practical advice citizens need if they are to live well.

Thus far in our exploration of Aristotle's political theory we have only been looking at a very small part of his thought. Although we have been drawing on the *Ethics* in order to fill out some points we have really only been thinking about one chapter in the *Politics* (book one, chapter two). Before we go on let us just recap the ideas that have been doing the most work. In claiming that politics is the **master science** (or controlling science) Aristotle has made the case for political theory as a practical science. His **teleological method** leads him to argue that politics enables man to achieve **happiness** understood in a particular way as ***eudaimonia***. By this Aristotle means that the man of **virtue** or ***aretē*** (the excellent or most fulfilled man) is a just **citizen** of a well run state.

The rest of book one and book two of the *Politics* go a long way towards clarifying Aristotle's understanding of the life of a citizen (household management including slave ownership, wealth acquisition etc.) and provide an overview of the types of constitution, both real and theorised, that Aristotle drew upon. If you come to study Aristotle later in your university careers these books will offer you a way in to the specifics of his thought. As an introduction, however, we can move straight on to Aristotle's exploration of the nature of citizenship and the state. The questions left for us to explore are 'what is citizenship?', 'what is justice?' and 'what is a well-run state?'. The way Aristotle reaches these questions dictates the form in which they are answered. Clearly he is not asking purely empirical questions. Nevertheless Aristotle's initial definition of a citizen seems straightforwardly empirical – anyone who is eligible to participate in deliberative and judicial office (*Politics*: 3, 1, 1275b16–1275b20). This is a definition that gives us a small insight into life in the *poleis* of ancient Greece. We have already drawn your attention to the fact that Aristotle valued communal participation in society. This meant participation in military, judicial and political decision-making and action. Such a huge personal investment in one's society was fostered by the limited size of the *polis*; these aspects of your life really had an impact upon your well-being. It is for this reason that Aristotle favoured a small political unit limited by 'self-sufficiency'. Nevertheless this empirical definition begs all the really interesting questions that we want to ask about the nature of citizenship. Who should be allowed to participate? We already know that Aristotle excluded all minors, women and resident aliens (we might think in terms of immigrants although that wouldn't really capture Aristotle's meaning) from citizenship. Is there anything we can say about that? Also we are aware that throughout history there have been tyrannies or oligarchies where one person or a really exclusive group has had total power. What can we say about this? We have already learned that citizenship is more than mere participation in social events. It is the way we fulfil our human potential; it is the way we are in control of our own destinies (necessarily in conjunction with others); it is the way we achieve full happiness. How do we judge political participation?

In the *Politics* Aristotle does approach these questions. In order to understand what he is doing you have to be aware that at different points in the text Aristotle is doing different things. At one point he is trying to offer practical advice to the citizen. At others he is measuring politics against his absolute standard of justice. The two arguments seem to conflict but if you keep this distinction in mind the conflict is easily sorted out. Essentially Aristotle encourages a citizen to participate fully in his own community (for the reasons we noted above) and notes that how one achieves this depends on the sort of constitution that governs the *polis*. A good citizen respects the norms and customs of his community and takes his turn at ruling (where appropriate) and being ruled. The key to grasping this part of Aristotle's theory is to notice that good citizenship is relative to the constitution the citizen lives under. Here Aristotle lays out his famous classification of constitutions and begins to show us how we can judge political participation. But being a good citizen (in this part of Aristotle's theory) is not identical with being a good man (the human who has reached their *telos*).

> The virtue of a citizen must be suited to his constitution. Consequently, if indeed there are several kinds of constitution, it is clear that there cannot be a single virtue that is the virtue – the complete virtue – of a good citizen. But a good man, we say, does express a single virtue: the complete one. Evidently, then, it is possible for someone to be a good citizen without having acquired the virtue expressed by the good man. (*Politics*: 3, 4, 1276b29–1276b35)

Here, in his practical advice section, citizenship does not necessarily entail participation in ruling. Rather it is reduced to sharing in the benefits of membership of a state. To elaborate freely on Aristotle's theme: there are several types of state (some democratic, some not so democratic) and many cultures in the world. Different religious backgrounds, different ethno-cultural heritages, different socio-economic conditions, different human resources and different geographical situations all place their own demands on a community and have to be managed in different ways. Politics is a practical thing and we (humanity) have developed a number of different ways of managing our lives. We have to acknowledge the validity of these different structures for their own citizens. Being a good citizen means being a good citizen within these constraints. If one person rules, or if a few wealthy or well-born rule, it does not automatically mean that those states are immoral. Similarly just because the masses have a role in politics it does not necessarily make that state morally superior (something we should perhaps keep in mind more today). Politics/ethics is more subtle than this, it is not merely a question of numbers. Nevertheless it is important that we can still say of some states that they are bad. Also we can get somewhere near thinking about the best kind of state, which is the one in which being a good citizen does coincide with being a good man. Aristotle does not overstate his case and this is one of the great strengths of his argument. His theory is realistic and pluralistic without ever subordinating the critical power of ethics to the flaws of the real world.

There are lots of different types of state that are self-sufficient. Any community with an authority that establishes a constitution, makes and prosecutes laws, sets foreign and domestic policy and controls the armed forces can be said to be a state. What distinguishes states from each other, argues Aristotle, is whether or not they are free and the sort of constitution that they adopt. A constitution that is organised for the good of the community is just, regardless of its shape. For Aristotle a monarchy or kingship (rule by the one), or an aristocracy (rule by the few), or a polity (rule by the multitude) can all be just constitutions. But there are perverted constitutions, deviations from these models, where only the good of the rulers is furthered and these are bad or unjust. Here Aristotle lists tyranny, oligarchy and (more surprisingly for us) democracy (see *Politics*: 3, 6 & 7). What distinguishes a just from an unjust state is simply that a just state is ruled in the common interest of all whereas in an unjust state the ruling class rules in its own favour. 'For tyranny is rule by one person for the benefit of the monarch, oligarchy is for the benefit of the rich and democracy is for the benefit of the poor. But none is for their common profit' (*Politics*: 3, 7, 1279b5–1279b9).

The first thing we should note is that these six types of constitution are pure or ideal types. Aristotle, you will remember, had made a study of 158 different constitutions and was aware that there were many mixed constitutions, but all constitutions are a blend of these basic types. You are probably already familiar with the basic features of most of these ideal types. Aristotle has a specific view of each and some very interesting things to say abut them but this is something we can postpone until you study Aristotle in more detail. You are probably less familiar with 'polity' used, not in its generic sense as a word for a political society, but as a specific type of constitution: the good form of the necessarily corrupt 'democracy'. We want to focus our attention on these two, not because Aristotle was exclusively concerned with them (he wasn't), but because we can start using Aristotle's tools to think about the relative merits of democracy. Often we support democracy as the best form of politics without thinking about it. Exploring the relative merits of democracy through Aristotle's theory can be quite a useful exercise.

Let's start with what we think we are sure of. Democracy, for us, is rule by the people. This rather general starting point is as far as we go with the Athenian understanding of the term, which stems from the

Greek *demos*, meaning 'people'. When we say democracy we usually mean representative democracy (where we elect a representative) rather than direct democracy (where each citizen really gets involved in decision-making). That is the first difference. We also have a very different understanding of who 'the people' are. For those of us in the UK 'the people' in this context is everyone over the age of 18 (bar sitting peers in the House of Lords, convicted prisoners and those in mental hospitals with criminal convictions). For Aristotle this would be ridiculous. Children, he would agree, are too immature to vote. Women would be disqualified because they do not have the capacity to command; their *telos* is satisfied in the household. Metics or resident aliens (of which Aristotle was one) had no political rights and slaves were merely animate tools. Democracy, as we understand the term, was rule by everyone even if they had none of the necessary skills to rule. 'The people' were, for Aristotle, the freeborn men of a city-state. More strictly they were the common freeborn men of the city-state. If these people were well off enough to afford the armour and arms of a hoplite soldier (an infantryman) then rule by the people might just about have a chance as the multitude would at least be capable of military virtue. But this was not democracy. For Aristotle this basic property and character qualification paved the way for what he termed polity (or timocracy in the *Ethics*). Democracy was the form of constitution where the poor ruled in favour of the poor. The difficulty with rule by the multitude is that not everyone is going to be virtuous – especially if they are so poor that they have to worry about material survival and work hard, at the expense of education, to assure it. The tendency would be for the mob to seek freedom from all restraint rather than the virtuous freedom that would lead to *eudaimonia*. Even if some among the mob are virtuous their voice would be drowned out by the insistence upon equality of the multitude. In any case, does it not make more sense to have the virtuous, even if they are the minority, rule?

Aristotle's criticisms of democracy are sharp and sustained and add weight to his claim that citizenship (in the actual world rather than in ethical theory) should be understood as sharing in the benefits of virtuous rule rather than active participation in the ruling of a *polis*. If you have one outstandingly virtuous man then let him rule (monarchy). If the best are the most wealthy (oligarchy) or well-born and well-educated (aristocracy) then let them rule. Of course, Aristotle argues, there is a sense in which the more qualified citizens there are available to rule the better but it is unlikely that 'the people' could manage it. At the very best the middle classes or hoplite classes should rule.

Aristotle's argument is fascinating in itself but let's try a small experiment. Is it possible to make a case for democracy within the rough outline of his framework? In order to do this we need to question the exclusion of women and slaves and Aristotle's favouring of the middle and upper classes. We also need to revisit the key concept of Aristotle's thought.

First then let's think about who 'the people' are or should be. Aristotle's usage is, again, culturally and historically nuanced and refers to a particular class of people rather than a numerical concept such as the majority. Nevertheless the way this class is defined is, as we have seen, based on some central ideas. In a polity the phrase 'the people' refers to the hoplite class. This is because they have the potential to be virtuous; they are 'political animals' where the mob, the women and the slaves are not. Aristotle's argument here is based on those technical ideas that we explored earlier in this chapter. So what is it that grants them this feature? There are two basic layers of argument here. The first is that women and slaves are naturally subordinate. The claim is that women achieve their natural end in the household (in child-bearing) and that slaves are born 'animate tools'. Both require the rule of the male head of the household. Aristotle has to sustain this claim or the subordination of women and the practice of slavery would be seen as unethical. It cannot be seen to be merely conventional, it must be natural or nothing can justify their subordination. Few of Aristotle's arguments here are convincing. The second layer of argument goes some way towards explaining why he took this route. To be a political animal is to be a fully rounded human being. This involves being the head of a family and good enough at wealth acquisition both to satisfy our basic needs and to have the leisure time to develop the intellectual skills that serve a man well in political life. The political animal of Aristotle's work relies upon his wife and his slaves to give him the leisure time necessary. Neither argument is necessary to us. Even Plato had a vision of gender equality (albeit in a very strange set of communal relationships) and there is no reason why the biological function of child-bearing should limit a woman's role in political life. It certainly does not follow that because women have the children they are naturally subordinate. As for slavery, well, the basic tools of economic management have developed far beyond the need for slaves and history has shown that even non-Greeks are capable of citizenship! It is possible to flesh out his line of thought and to claim that 'humans are political animals' (but that is something we'll leave you to think through). Of course just because humans are political animals it does not mean that in actual fact all people will exhibit the virtue necessary for ruling, just as not all acorns become oak trees. Nevertheless if genuine human happiness requires the correct balance between the satisfaction of basic desires, the development of rationality and participation in political life then society should provide the opportunities for full participation – say a universal education system, the redistribution of wealth to ensure at least basic equality of opportunity and a revamped representative democratic system that really encourages people to engage with their society.

This of course is just the beginning of an argument. Nevertheless reflection on the basic elements of Aristotle's work offers a series of important insights into politics. You could develop this basic argument in any number of ways, drawing on Aristotle's theory in some parts and challenging him in others. Political theory does not really offer you a complete set of answers (and you should be very wary of a theory that claims to do so). Instead it offers an entry into some of the most complex and pressing problems we face. Aristotle's longevity stems from the way he helps us think about what he termed the master science. If we draw together some of the basic features that we have looked at it is clear that his legacy is a wealth of conceptual tools that offer us an introduction to ourselves.

One of the first key insights that Aristotle gives us concerns the nature of political theory itself. The claim that politics is the master science may be a trifle grand but politics is about living well or managing our lives to get the best out of them. Everything else is geared to this end. The big claim is that we are political animals. Aristotle's reflection on this leads him to suggest that citizenship is the key mode of human life and that the state (in one particular form) is the key context in which we can achieve our potential. Thinking about how a state should be organised and how we are to live as citizens is thus hugely important. More important still is the claim that follows from this argument. Without the state, without community in citizenship, we are nothing. Living justly with our fellow citizens is our goal and not (as many moderns have it) finding the space to pursue our private self-interest. Politics is a practical science and there are many ways to pursue happiness but the basic context is membership of a just state.

Topics for discussion

1. How does a grasp of Aristotle's teleology help us understand the essence of his claim that man is by nature a political animal?

2. How do you think Aristotle's conception of happiness as virtuous citizenship compares against your understanding of happiness?
3. What sense can you make of Aristotle's claim that a state is prior to its constituent parts? What impact does this notion have on your understanding of the relationship between you and your society?
4. Why does Aristotle think that democratic states are 'deviant'? What qualifies a person to participate in politics?

Critical glossary

The Master Science	Aristotle had a very specific view of what political thought is. It is a practical science and is necessarily entwined with ethics. It is also the study of the highest good as a state is prior to the happiness of its members. Ultimately politics scaffolds all virtuous human existence. Thus the study of politics is the master science.
Happiness/*Eudaimonia*	Aristotle's conception of happiness is closely linked to his conception of **Virtue/*Aretē***. It is sometimes translated as 'virtuous activity of the soul'. The key to happiness (which is the final end of all things) is living a fully rounded life where all our capacities are satisfied and balanced against each other.
Teleology	The defining concept of Aristotle's political thought. The essence of a thing, its final cause and end, can be grasped by understanding its most perfect or developed state. The word comes from the Greek *telos*, meaning 'goal' or 'end'. If you understand this then you have the key to understanding Aristotle's political thought.

Man is a Political Animal	A gendered concept in Aristotle's work but it does not necessarily have to be so. The idea is that our very nature means that we are happiest or most fulfilled in political society. Citizenship is the key to happiness, the state the only context in which human perfection is possible.
Citizen	A full member of a state. For Aristotle this excludes children, women, resident aliens and slaves. A citizen is someone with the right to participate in ruling and in enjoying the benefits of rule. But it goes beyond this. Citizenship is community in the constitution, a full engagement with one's society and a necessary part of human fulfilment.

List of references / Further reading

Primary texts

There are many editions and translations of the Politics and the Ethics. At this stage in your careers it does not really matter which editions you use as long as you are making some attempt at reading the primary sources. Translations differ as each scholar strives to present Aristotle's meaning and to present his style. In this chapter I have been quoting from:

Aristotle (1998), *Politics*, translated and with an introduction and notes by C. D. C. Reeve, Indianapolis & Cambridge: Hackett.

Aristotle (1985), *Nichomachean Ethics*, translated and with an introduction, glossary and notes by T. Irwin, Indianapolis & Cambridge: Hackett.

Aristotle (1912), *A Treatise on Government*, translated by W. Ellis, London: Dent.

The references to each quotation take the form of Book, Chapter, Line, rather than page references to these specific editions. Generally speaking the texts are reproduced in the same order and have the same line numbering (drawn from the Bekker page numbers).

Secondary literature

Over the last two millennia plenty has been written about Aristotle's work.

Aristotle

The following guide to further reading is not intended as a comprehensive bibliography but to suggest a few sources from the next 'step up' in the introductory literature.

Barker, E. (1959), *The Political Thought of Plato and Aristotle*, New York: Dover.

Barnes, J. (1995), *The Cambridge Companion to Aristotle*, Cambridge: Cambridge University Press.

Barnes, J. (2000), *Aristotle: A Very Short Introduction*, Oxford: Oxford University Press.

Hughes, G. (2001), *Routledge Philosophy Guidebook to Aristotle on Ethics*, London: Routledge.

Johnson, C. (1990), *Aristotle's Theory of the State*, Basingstoke: Macmillan.

Mulgan, R. (1977), *Aristotle's Political Theory: An Introduction for Students of Political Theory*, Oxford: Clarendon Press.

Robinson, T. (1995), *Aristotle in Outline*, Indianapolis & Cambridge: Hackett.

SECTION II

MODERN DEVELOPMENTS IN POLITICAL THOUGHT

CHAPTER THREE

HISTORICAL

Hobbes, Locke and Rousseau

CONCEPTUAL

Liberty and Human Nature: What is Freedom?

Jumping from ancient Greece to what political theorists call modernity misses out a wealth of Medieval and Renaissance thought. It is always a huge loss, in historical and intellectual terms, to skip over the works of great thinkers such as Cicero, St Augustine, St Thomas Aquinas or Niccolò Machiavelli. Nevertheless, for our purposes this dash to modernity allows us to begin thinking about our own political heritage. By this we do not mean to imply that we owe nothing to the Roman, medieval or Renaissance thinkers. Everyone can gain enormous insight into the nature of political obligation, natural law and, in the case of Machiavelli, the darker arts necessary to the political pursuit of freedom by reading into the history of political thought. However, by starting with something that you will be more familiar with we have an opportunity to confront the normative issues that we face here and now rather than those faced by our ancestors. This does not mean that we are consigning all that is 'past' to a study of history rather than political theory. In fact the opposite is true. One of the main reasons we have chosen to skip straight to 'modern' political thought is that it will allow us to begin to focus on the **historicity** of our own political ideas. Use of the technical term 'historicity' here is a deliberate attempt to make you focus on what is a key issue in political theory. Historicity refers to the historical context, or historical situation, of ideas, beliefs and cultures. It is absolutely vital that you begin to think historically as well as philosophically about concepts that most people take for granted. It is often easier to think historically about ideas that are clearly 'a part of history'. For example, we are able to think about Aquinas's understanding of the relationship between human law, natural law and divine law (in the classic *Summa Theologiae*) as the product of the thinking of a thirteenth-century monk. But what about the ideas that are at work in your conception of the political world? When we use 'modern' understandings of key issues such as freedom, legitimacy, justice, obligation etc. what do we mean? There is a rich history to the way we think about what it is to be free here and now, a rich history to our political aspirations and identities. By exploring one of the key intellectual traditions to come out of the European **Enlightenment**, a tradition that helped forge what we think of as **modernity**, we are able to gather the historical and conceptual tools necessary to an understanding of some of our most sincerely held (and seriously contested) beliefs. Coming to terms with the historical depth of modernity in order to appreciate the subtleties of politics is a difficult introductory exercise. However, the rewards outweigh the complexity of our task. As we begin to think about the nature of humanity, freedom and morality, or the reasons why we are obliged to obey governments and laws, or the limits of political authority, we enter fully into some of the most fundamental debates of our lives.

If we are to answer the question 'what is distinctively modern about our political ideas?' we need to have some conception of what **modernity** is. Many readers, coming to the issues for the first time, will often equate 'modern' with 'contemporary'. Yet we will begin to explore modern political thought in seventeenth-century Europe. Periodisation in history is itself an analytical structure imposed upon the past by historians, philosophers and students of politics in order to emphasise particularly important themes or ideas. For someone interested in (for example) international politics modernity is usually dated from 24 October 1648. It is of course absurd to date something as elusive as modernity so precisely but in on this day in 1648, after four years of negotiation, the Thirty Years War was brought to an end by treaty between the Holy Roman Emperor and the King of France and his allies. This historic treaty (the Treaty of Westphalia) represents the confirmation and legal recognition of a system of sovereign and territorial states, one of the key features of modern world politics. As political theorists interested in the key ideas that drive modern politics we can also find our historical roots deep in this period of history. The tensions surrounding the period from the English Civil War up to the Glorious Revolution (1642–88) and later the tumultuous events leading up to the French Revolution (latter half of the eighteenth century) were the anvil upon which modernity was forged. Central both to these revolutions and to our understanding of what it is to act and think politically are three very distinct thinkers and writers, linked by their use of an idea that has come to characterise modern political thought: **the social contract**.

It is almost impossible to overstate the impact that Thomas Hobbes, John Locke and Jean-Jacques Rousseau (and the social contract tradition of which they are the finest exemplar) had on their time and ours. They were not the first or the last to explain politics using the social contract. However, their most famous works in political theory, Hobbes's *Leviathan* (1651), Locke's *Two Treatises of Government* (1690) and Rousseau's *The Social Contract* (1762) redefined the key concepts of politics and laid the foundation for modern and contemporary debates. Before going any further it is important to be clear that Hobbes, Locke and Rousseau differ on almost every significant point in political thought. Nevertheless their use of the idea of a social contract gives us the opportunity to compare and contrast their key ideas.

One of the key differences in the way we moderns think about politics is that we do not think of it as 'natural' like the ancient Greeks did. In fact we are much more accustomed to thinking of politics as something artificial, even alien to us, as something imposed upon us. Whether or not this is a good thing is, of course, a matter for considerable debate. Nevertheless it is a feature of modern life that we often think of political institutions both as constraining our individual liberty and as requiring our consent to their authority. How did we come to see ourselves as individuals distinct from our community? How did we come to identify freedom with self-interest? Exploring these questions offers us critical insights into the foundations of modern politics. Exploring the writings of Hobbes, Locke and Rousseau brings us a double benefit. First, we get to examine three arguments that contributed hugely to this radical change in thinking. Second, we get the opportunity, by virtue of the fact that they use the same explanatory mechanism, to focus on those key ideas that shape the way we view our social world.

Hobbes, Locke and Rousseau present three very different conceptions of human nature, freedom, **morality** and politics. They do so by imagining what life would be like in '**the state of nature**'. The state of nature is a depiction of life before politics and society. As such it invites us to consider the bare essentials of human nature and what it means to be free from the laws, the moral norms and the coercive institutions that constitute political society. All three thinkers that we are going to look at offer very different, but hugely compelling, conceptions of life in this pre-political condition. This leads inevitably to a question that we rarely ask: why are we in political society at all? It is a question that offers a remarkable opportunity to consider the fundamentals of politics and for this reason even a basic tour of these classic 'state of nature' arguments is tremendously enlightening. As Hobbes, Locke and Rousseau lay out their answers to this question they invite us to imagine a social contract that outlines the obligations and rights of rulers and citizens alike; they ask us to imagine what people would agree to given the choice. What sorts of institutions and rules would free individuals sign up to? Obviously the rules and institutions that people would choose are informed by the sorts of problems that exist in the state of nature. The thought here is that if we were not faced with a series of what Locke charmingly calls 'inconveniences' in the state of nature we would not have bothered with politics at all. The telling of each of these stories carries with it a series of insights into the nature of humanity, freedom, morality, justice and society that have the power to help each of us understand the driving forces of politics. Take, for example, the following snapshot of the hugely influential arguments that the next two chapters will explore.

For Hobbes the main problem we face in the state of nature is a naturally selfish and unconstrained desire to satisfy our appetites. This feature of human nature, linked with the fact of scarce resources, led inevitably to what Hobbes most famously described as a 'warre of all against all' (Hobbes 1968: 186). Politics is thus founded on the need to constrain our natural freedom to satisfy our desires; because of this (and because we cannot be trusted to simply keep to our side of the social contract) politics must be grounded firmly on an absolute, all-powerful sovereign. For Rousseau, on the other hand, 'Hobbes's horrible system' rests on a fundamental mistake. Selfishness is born of corrupt politics, not of nature, and so a Hobbesian social contract compounds rather than solves our dilemma. For Rousseau the real problem we have to master is the transition from primitive life (marked by sparse population, abundant food and a marked absence of moral sense) to social life (where we are permanently confronted by other human beings competing for scarce resources). Politics is about helping us to swap primitive freedom for social freedom. For Locke neither of these stories makes sense of the human condition. In particular they do not take adequate account of man's moral condition. Here we are invited to consider another of the fundamental issues of human social life: what is morality and how does it relate to politics? For Locke, we are naturally moral beings (although we are not always clear about what morality requires) and it is our inability to fully comprehend and give expression to the natural law that obliges us to enter into a social contract and thereafter form a government. For Locke our natural freedom is constrained by a natural moral code (he uses the term 'law of nature'). Effectively giving expression to that moral law is the reason for political society.

Each of these stories offers us a series of piercing insights into the human condition – natural, moral and political. Despite the fact that taken as a whole they are mutually exclusive it is not unusual for people coming to these great texts for the first time to be so taken by the depth of their vision that upon first reading Hobbes they become committed Hobbesians then, in turn, committed Lockeans and Rousseauians. The task of these next two chapters is first to introduce you to those ideas that have made these texts classics, to allow you to experience (as generations of students have done) the force of the insights that they offer. But we also intend to help you get beyond that to equip you with the knowledge and conceptual tools necessary to make intelligent and discriminating judgments between them. The arguments of these three theorists are not just intuitively insightful. They are also philosophically rich in detail and a grasp of the core elements of their arguments will allow you to consider the key questions that underpin our political preferences. When we make these judgements we are going a long way to understanding the question that is the focus of this chapter. The question is put quite simply: what is **freedom**? This is one of the most fundamental questions of politics, as we need to understand the idea of freedom if we are to understand the reason for politics. How can political organisation and its guiding rules (law and justice) help us preserve or gain freedom? The question might be simply put but finding an answer to it has proved rather less simple. In turning immediately to three hugely influential, but ultimately incompatible or opposed, accounts of freedom we can begin to get a sense of the complex issues we need to broach.

Thomas Hobbes

Thomas Hobbes was the most self-conscious moderniser of any of the thinkers we will examine here. Coming to Hobbes's masterpiece, *Leviathan*, for the first time really allows us to begin to get a feel for the modern period. Hobbes was born in 1588. He was the son of a clergyman, he studied at Magdalen Hall, Oxford, and went on to work as a tutor to the son of the Earl of Devonshire. It seems hard to imagine a more orthodox context for this most radical of thinkers. Yet Hobbes's work had a huge impact on his time and ours. In his own time it angered both sides in the Civil War, clashed with the scientific and ecclesiastical establishment, was condemned by the authorities at Oxford, and was even cited in 1666, in the House of Commons, as one of the causes of the Great Fire of London. For our time it has had a more positive effect. As C. B. Macpherson puts it in the introduction to his edited version of *Leviathan* Hobbes 'dug the channel in which the mainstream subsequently flowed' (Hobbes 1968: 24). Hobbes's intellectual career was notable because he disagreed so roundly and radically with the prevailing orthodoxy of his time. He loathed the Aristotelian Schoolmen of Oxford where he studied; indeed his work is littered with sideswipes at these 'deceived or deceiving schoolemen' (Ibid. 99). Later, inspired by the new scientific method being applied in fields such as medicine and cosmology, Hobbes set out to rewrite political theory and to create a true science of man. It was an ambitious beginning, but it was an ambition that was to see him bring politics and ethics into the modern period. What can we know with scientific certainty, he asked, about the nature of man? This scientific approach was to dominate Hobbes's thought and it must be viewed as the foundation of his political theory.

There is more to it than this. There is Hobbes the actor on the political stage of the Civil War, Hobbes in social and historical context. There is also a series of complex debates about the nature of Hobbes's method. These are important issues but they can be usefully postponed until a later engagement with Hobbes, perhaps in a history of political thought class later in your university career. Our task here is simply to get a basic grasp of the 'shape' of Hobbes's famous argument. In order to do this you can usefully think of *Leviathan, or the Matter, Forme & Power of a Common-wealth ecclesiasticall and civill* (to give it its full title) as a story much like any other. Every compelling story has a narrative (or story line) and several key moments, or building blocks, that make that story interesting or moving. A critical understanding of the story grasps these moments fully so it can show us how the story works. The general pattern of *Leviathan*, understood in this way, then takes the following form:

The general pattern of the basic argument of Hobbes's *Leviathan*.

1. A scientific method that leads to an enquiry into the basic elements of society. *This in turn leads to*
2. A description of individual men *(and)*
3. A description of these agents in a pre-social condition – the 'state of nature'. *These three elements lead to*
4. A picture of the laws of nature (precepts of reason that lead us to recognise the origin of politics). *This in turn leads to*
5. An understanding of the nature of political legitimacy and obligation. *And*
6. A realisation that sovereign authority must be absolute.

With this outline as your touchstone we can explore the text.

Hobbes's new scientific and modern approach to philosophy was based on what is known as a 'resolutive-compositive' method. This means that everything is broken down into its basic parts and then reconstructed to see how it works. It was a method pioneered by leading scientists of the day such as Galileo (whom Hobbes travelled to meet) and, for Hobbes, it was part of an all-encompassing, modern approach to knowledge (for more on this see the discussion in Hampton 1986). As the subject matter he chose to examine was political society the basic parts were individual men. Thus by understanding the nature of man, taken independently of all those things that are not absolutely natural to human nature (such as politics, law, justice, morality), we can gain insights into the forces that drive humanity and thereby come to understand the real role of politics in our lives rather than the role prescribed by priests and schoolmen, who come to the debate prearmed with ideas about the highest good for man. This of course is an eminently sensible proposal, but there is one issue you might highlight for further exploration a little later: is it really self-evident that individuals are the base elements of human society?

Armed with this new scientific approach Hobbes sought the answer to the question 'what can we say with scientific certainty about the nature of man?' His answer brings us to the core of his political theory and the beginning of Chapter 13 of *Leviathan*, a wonderful passage and the one where you should begin your first close reading of the text itself. The chapter opens with the bold proclamation 'Nature hath made men so equal' (Hobbes 1968: 183). For Hobbes this is a brute, scientific fact and not a moral declaration. The simple fact is that, taken scientifically, we are all simply walking bundles of desire or appetite, all seeking ways (power) to satisfy those desires. We are, to use terms Hobbes would have used, all simply matter in motion and the only thing that can stop or hinder our motion (or prevent us from acting on our will) is another force (most importantly other humans with competing desires). Viewed scientifically all humans are pretty much equal. Some are stronger, some are smarter. But the smarter can be defeated by the stronger and the stronger outwitted by the smarter. In any case all have to sleep at some time and thus we are all equally vulnerable. Again there is nothing that seems particularly objectionable here. But this equality is the source of all our troubles. Equality, for Hobbes, means that everyone has equal hope of achieving what they desire and this leads to

> three principall causes of quarrell. First Competition; secondly Diffidence; Thirdly, Glory. The first maketh man invade for gain; the second for safety; and the third for reputation. The first use violence to make themselves master of other men's persons, wives, children and cattel; the second to defend them and the third for trifles, as a word, a smile, a different opinion, and any other signe of undervalue, either direct in their Persons or by reflection in their Kindred, their Friends, their Nation, their Profession, or their Name. (Ibid.: 185)

Do you recognise your species? Hobbes's description of human nature stripped of the constraints of society has been taken as the basis of a huge amount of political thinking that purports to take seriously the dynamics of power. Our goal is what Hobbes calls 'commodious living' and in the state of nature we are all equally free to decide what our 'good life' is and to pursue it through any means necessary. As a 'realistic' description of our basic condition this picture is very engaging but it is hardly surprising that Hobbes thought it would generate such conflict.

Hobbes's description is engaging on two levels. The first is simply intuitive. Human beings do act selfishly and, given the right circumstances, will do all they can to further their own ends. This factor seems to be exacerbated under those conditions in which the legal constraints and moral norms of society grow weak. Take, for example, the atrocities Hobbes's peers will have witnessed as civil war gripped England or the human catastrophe that we saw in Kosovo as law and order crumbled there. Without what Hobbes describes repeatedly as a 'power to keep them in awe' human beings act selfishly out of a combination of fear (of not being able to get what they want) and self-interest. The unconstrained pursuit of power as neighbour turned brutally on neighbour in the former Yugoslavia, or in mid-seventeenth century England, or in any number of examples of human selfishness that you can recall, seem to confirm Hobbes's thesis. We might view these political disasters as a return to the state of nature and the actions of the people involved as a simple reversion to type. But Hobbes was not merely offering anecdotal evidence or appealing to our ever-confirmed pessimism about human nature, although he does invoke some of this to back up his claim (Ibid.: 187). In fact he was making a scientific point. Hobbes's state of nature was not England in 1650, still less Kosovo in the 1990s. It was a hypothetical pre-political condition. It was a theoretical model that 'resolved' society down to its basic parts so that we can see what drives it just as, Hobbes tells us, we could take a watch apart to see how each component acted on the others to make the whole. It was to be 'Man' stripped to its essence and examined individually. Away from all the constraining and supporting mechanisms of society what is there except self-interest? Reason, Hobbes argues, is a vital part of human nature but it is harnessed to our desire for power and naturally outweighed by our passions. This last point is really important to Hobbes's case and there are two aspects to the claim that you should take a moment to consider. The first is that passions have greater motivational force than reason. For Hobbes it is 'Feare' that outweighs all. Fear of not being able to get what we want, fear of death. It is this fear that prevents us from moving out of the state of nature, something that becomes vital when we consider the 'laws of nature' and the 'modified state of nature' in a moment. On a slightly less dramatic level we also have plenty of examples of our passion getting the better of our reason. Was the famous sacrifice of Romeo and Juliet based on passion or reason? How many times, despite knowing that eating too much chocolate is bad for you, have you ended up feeling rather sick? The second is that if passion does outweigh reason, and the solution to our predicament is to be found in reason (as Hobbes maintains (Ibid.: 188)), then we have to find an artificial way, 'a common power', to bring the passions in line with reason. This is politics.

Hobbes sums up his description of the state of nature with one of the most famous passages in the history of political thought, indeed in the history of literature. He writes:

> Hereby it is manifest, that during the time that men live without common power to keep them in awe, they are in that condition which is called Warre; and such a warre, as is of every man, against every man. For WARRE, consisteth not in battell onely, or in the act of fighting; but in a tract of time, wherein the Will to contend by battell is sufficiently known. . . . In such a condition, there is no place for industry; because the fruits thereof is uncertain . . . and which is worst of all, continuall feare, and danger of violent death; And the life of man, solitary, poore, nasty, brutish and short. (Ibid.: 186)

This famously damning, but compelling account of human nature is not intended to make us out to be immoral. It is an amoral account of our natural condition. In a passage that foreshadows the rest of his work Hobbes is insistent that

> the Desires and other Passions of man, are in themselves no Sin. No more are the Actions, that proceed from those Passions, till they know a Law that forbids them: nor can any Law be made, till they have agreed upon the Person that shall make it. (Ibid.: 187)

From Hobbes's scientific perspective justice and injustice are qualities that relate only to social man and in the state of nature, far from being vices, force and fraud are 'cardinall virtues' (Ibid.: 188). But this is our natural liberty, our inherent freedom. Equality and competition are brute facts of free and unconstrained human nature and the pre-political state of nature is a very scary place indeed. In this amazing description we find that two vital concepts that we are accustomed to thinking of as noble are base facts of human existence. Equality and freedom are at the root of all our troubles.

Of course the story does not end here. But how are we to overcome this war of all against all? Where in this bleak account of our natural condition are the foundations for politics? It is here that we must return to the battle between reason and our natural passions. For subdued by our fear and self-interest, Hobbes argued, are the rational principles, the 'laws of nature', that can help us achieve peace and 'commodious living'. The 'laws of nature' seems to be a very imposing title, and not one you would normally associate with a scientific and amoral doctrine. However, the laws of nature are merely 'precepts of reason' that show us the route out of the state of nature.

> The Passions that encline men to Peace, are Feare of Death; Desire of such things as are necessary to commodious living; and a Hope by their Industry to obtain them. And Reason suggesteth convenient Articles of Peace, upon which men may be drawn to agreement. These Articles, are they, which otherwise are called the Lawes of Nature. (Ibid.: 188)

The laws of nature are just as scientific in their formulation as the state of nature. It is not an expression of natural law in the religious sense but a dictate of right reason. It is clear that living in the state of nature is not a good thing and so equally clear that we need to get out and the laws of nature tell how to approach this task. The laws of nature help us cope with freedom and equality.

All of Hobbes's laws of nature, which are discussed in Chapters 14 and 15 of *Leviathan*, are derived from the first or 'fundamentall law of nature', 'That every man, ought to endeavour Peace, as farre as he has hope of obtaining it; and when he cannot obtain it, that he may seek, and use, all helps and advantages of Warre' (Ibid.: 190). Hobbes goes on to point out that this is itself divided in two parts with the first clause (endeavouring peace) being the first law of nature and the second clause (war) being more properly called the fundamental right of nature. Let us focus briefly on each of these in turn beginning with the right of nature. Our natural liberty, our freedom, entails a very basic right to everything, even, Hobbes tells us, 'one another's body'. In one obvious sense this means nothing as no one has a corresponding obligation to supply us with anything. The fact that everyone is free to take whatever they want if they can get it does leave the idea of natural liberty particularly empty. But that is the stark message Hobbes gives us. If we cannot do any better then we are free to try and get what we want by force or fraud. There is something important about our natural right. Our right to preserve our life as we see fit is an inalienable right and the base line point of politics. If our lives are ever threatened (say we are found guilty of a capital crime or the army in which we serve as conscripts is routed) we revert to our natural liberty. Everything beyond this basic freedom is, as it were, an optional extra. To be sure, given that the state of nature is so awful, these optional extras are very appealing, but they are optional – we need good and stable incentives to move beyond our natural right to everything.

The first law of nature is simply that we should 'endeavour peace'. If we can do it then we *ought* to do it. It follows that if the state of war is the problem then instituting a state of peace is the solution. The real core of the argument lies not in this statement but in the detail of how we go about making this transformation. However, there is something very important to point out here. Note the way Hobbes puts his point: we *ought* to endeavour peace. For Hobbes the natural law and the moral law are the same thing. We have a moral duty to institute a state of peace. Here we can learn much about Hobbes's conception of morality and about the mechanics of moral theory more generally.

It probably seems strange, given Hobbes's mechanistic science of man, for him to make the claim that we have a moral duty to end the state of nature. This is because we are accustomed to thinking about moral duty or obligation as a duty or obligation that we must undertake regardless of its consequences. That is, we are used to thinking of morality in **deontological** terms. Deontological moral theories are usually contrasted to **consequentialist** or **instrumentalist** theories, which lay all their emphasis on the end that is to be achieved or the consequences of an action. Often deontological principles are considered to be higher principles, perhaps simply as moral principles in contrast to the pragmatism of instrumentalism. Those that make these claims often find justification for their stance in the claim that the deontological force of such principles stems from the fact that they are God-given or metaphysically necessary. Despite some famous arguments to the contrary (Taylor 1938; Warrender 1957) this is not what Hobbes is doing. His claim is that moral principles are instrumental. That is, those precepts of reason or rational principles that tell us successfully how to escape the war of all against all and are thus deemed laws of nature are moral principles. It is worth noting that not just any instrumentalist principle counted as moral but only those that performed this particular function. (For example, Hobbes was an instrumentalist through and through. John Aubrey, the celebrated biographer, tells a story of Hobbes in his *Brief Lives* that recounts the fact that Hobbes used to sing loudly, but only for the consequences it had for his lungs, and used to drink to excess, but only once a year, and then only 'to have the benefit of vomiting'. These may be the most instrumentalist reasons ever for singing and drinking but they are not moral.) Nevertheless for Hobbes there is no preconceived morality, no justice and injustice in the state of nature. All we have to work with are our natural appetites and aversions, our experience and our reason.

This is a rich area for reflection and debate and a very useful starting point is found in Hampton's *Hobbes and the Social Contract Tradition* (Hampton 1986: 27–57). However, here all you need to focus on is the idea that Hobbes's morality is secular, instrumentalist and very modern. This is not to suggest that Hobbes's argument set a secular seal on modern ethics. This would be very far from the truth and would ignore many of the key debates that were to come. But this approach to morality is one of the many reasons that Hobbes was so important to his time and to ours. In the Europe of Hobbes's day politics was gaining a new independence from religion and it is interesting that he endows ethics with this political character. Freedom, equality and morality are to be thought of as straightforward concepts. If you were to ask 'why is this a moral principle?' the answer would simply have to be that it is the only way to ensure we remain out of the state of nature, rather than 'because God said so' or 'because it corresponds to the Form of the Good'. The deontological account of ethics and the instrumentalist account of ethics are wholly opposed and this is something to bring to any other investigation of claims about the nature of morality. There are many types of deontological and instrumentalist accounts (for example, Plato and Aristotle have different deontological accounts) but an initial answer to the question 'what sort of moral theory is this?' can usefully begin with a deontological–instrumentalist divide.

The second law of nature follows as easily as the first. If our having an unconstrained right to everything is the cause of our problems then we must be prepared to relinquish it.

> That a man be willing, when others are so too, as farre-forth, as for Peace, and defence of himselfe he shall think it necessary, to lay down his right to all things; and be contented with so much liberty against other men, as he would allow other men against himselfe. (Hobbes 1968: 190)

This is, perhaps, the very core of Hobbes's work. It is not the most important insight or the most innovative but it does capture Hobbes's political theory. Given human nature the point of politics is to achieve a stable peace. This requires that we give up our natural liberty. There is still much to be said about how we go about doing this but this simple expression of the point of politics is the key.

There is one more step in Hobbes's description of the state of nature that tells us why we need a political or social contract to help us 'endeavour peace'. This step focuses on the question of how we might go about giving up right to everything. At the beginning of Chapter 15 Hobbes writes:

> From that law of Nature, by which we are obliged to transferre to another, such Rights, as being retained, hinder the peace of Mankind, there followeth a Third; which is this, *That men performe their covenants made*: without which, Covenants are in vain, and but Empty words; and the Right of all men to all things remaining, wee are still in the condition of Warre.
>
> And in this law of Nature, consisteth the Foundation and Originall of JUSTICE. (Ibid.: 201–2)

There is a lot in this quotation. It ties together much of what has gone before and lays the foundation for all that is to come. First, if a right to everything is natural then it follows that not having a right to everything must be artificial in some way. We can be robbed or even killed but we still have the rather empty 'right' to everything. The only way we can lose this right is to go beyond nature and covenant, or contract, it away. This is also a product of right reason. Our natural right to everything is the problem so the only obvious solution is for us to give it up. Once again this is an instrumental or prudential issue. But it is also on Hobbes's terms a moral issue (the foundation of justice) because making and keeping promises is the way to 'endeavour peace'.

You may recall, however, that principles of right reason are not strong enough to help us escape the state of nature on their own. Our passions, particularly fear, are stronger than reason. What guarantees do we have that those with whom we make such convenants will uphold their side of the bargain? Humans, we know, sometimes take the selfish, passion-driven, route when it seems in their immediate interest even when rationally they know that long-term interest is best served differently. The real problem is that while it is obvious that contract can establish peace and justice it cannot by itself establish the background conditions for acting justly. Social scientists have spent years trying to calculate the likelihood of social co-operation without politics (Hampton 1986: 58–79). This is something you might think about, because Hobbes's conviction that humans cannot be trusted to keep their covenants leads him to believe that, while the concept of justice is to be found in promise-making and -keeping, 'yet Injustice actually there can be none, till the cause of such feare be taken away; which while men are in the naturall condition of Warre, cannot be done'. (Hobbes 1968: 202).

Hobbes's conclusion here sets the scene for the next part of his theory, in which the *social* contract effectively brings the state of nature to an end. The difference between the social contract and any other contract is that it is to be overseen by a power of such awe and might that it can guarantee the keeping of covenants. This is the 'Leviathan' of the title and the subject of the next chapter. Hobbes continually refers to his solution to the problem of natural liberty and human nature as 'some coercive power', or 'a power to keep them in awe'. As Hobbes put it 'covenants, without the sword, are but words' and we will explore the political consequences of this state-of-nature argument a little later.

First let us pull some of the conceptual issues together. We have looked at steps 1–4 of our general outline of *Leviathan*. The story is hugely compelling. Natural liberty and equality are just not compatible with 'commodious' and peaceful living. Indeed they lead to competition and fear. This is the basic matter that politics has to deal with. The story is compelling intuitively but how does it stand up to more rigorous theoretical analysis? Obviously it has stood up well enough. If generations of scholars had thought it ridiculous we wouldn't be considering it now. But making your own judgements requires that you take (at the very least) a view on human nature, on Hobbes's scientific method and on the nature of morality and justice. If after all of this you still agree with Hobbes then, as we shall see in the next chapter, it will radically affect the way you think about politics. For now, however, let us turn immediately to a competing account of the nature of freedom.

John Locke

As we turn to the state-of-nature argument of John Locke we find a very different story indeed. Locke's conception of natural liberty is a moral conception of 'perfect freedom' and equality. His view of the law of nature is a normative rather than a descriptive one – a discussion of what people, living up to their duty to God, *ought to do*. For some students coming, as most do, to Locke after Hobbes, Locke's approach seems almost archaic. But Locke, as much as Hobbes, was a pioneer of modernity. Locke was at the cutting edge of the epistemological debates of the seventeenth century and embraced the new empiricism of his time. His rationalism offers genuine insights into a morally charged, deontological, law of nature. His liberalism, while radical for its time, is almost standard now (what higher praise could there be). Indeed it is mostly his utter rejection of the kind of absolutism that Hobbes's political theory calls for (see Chapter 4) that endears his legacy to us.

What appears to concern most contemporary students new to Locke's work and maybe even new to historical and philosophical study is his reliance upon God. For some it is a reaction to the retreat from the apparent secularism of Hobbes. This rests on an understandably biased reading of Hobbes. The heavy religious tones found in *Leviathan* are quite rightly overlooked by most lecturers teaching Hobbes's work as part of an introductory course. But a quick glance at the full table of contents of Leviathan shows that religion was an indispensable part of the debates of the day: chapters 32–47 are concerned with religious matters. Of course it is perfectly reasonable to suggest that Hobbes was masking a modern secularism. However, modernity is not characteristically secular. Indeed the influence of religion on the modern and contemporary world is massive and even if you cannot share a thinker's beliefs it is important that we can understand the cultural and historical development of contemporary ways of life (a point that goes well beyond a study of Locke). However, there are difficulties that arise within a reading of Locke that are caused by his merging of ultra-modern political and philosophical concepts and a very traditional faith in a Christian God. As W. M. Simon noted,

> although individualism could hardly be more plainly stated than in [Locke's thought], we are still plagued by Locke's concept of natural law, which limits not only empiricism as a political method, but also individualism as a political tenet, since men's natural rights, guaranteed by natural law and common to all, obviously restrict the freedom of their relations with each other. And since natural law is a declaration of the will of God, in the last resort it must be acknowledged that, whether we are concerned with Locke's . . . empiricism, his individualism, or almost any other aspect of his thought . . . there is always a point beyond which he will not pursue an argument: that is the point where no further concession can be made to a thorough going secularism (Simon 1951: 392).

When Locke taught at Oxford he would have faced a group consisting solely of male Anglicans. When the authors of this book step in to a lecture theatre we are faced with a multicultural audience of men and women of many faiths and none. Characteristically, contemporary political theory avoids the justification of moral and political principles by reference to religious ones. So what are we to make of Locke's position? Here, as you approach Locke for the first time, we would suggest that you suspend judgement. Treat Locke's language as a product of its time. Doing so allows us to engage with a masterpiece of modern political thought and we can work, together and individually, on the question of the ultimate foundation for morality as we continue to delve into the riches of political theory.

John Locke was at the centre of the political as well as the intellectual movements of his day. His life, the details of which you can find in most books dedicated to the study of his work, reads like a mini-history of the period from the Civil War up to the Glorious Revolution. His work outraged both the authorities at Oxford and King Charles II (who eventually terminated his academic appointment at Christ Church) and took a bold stand on matters of religion, philosophy and politics. The text that we are going to focus on is a clear argument against the defenders of absolute monarchical authority, an innovative defence of the responsibility of government to its citizens and a declaration of the rights of men. Locke's *Two Treatises of Government* is, as the title suggests, divided into two parts. The first is subtitled *An Essay Concerning False Principles* and is a refutation of Sir Robert Filmer's argument in favour of the 'Divine Right of Kings'. The arguments in this treatise form an important context for Locke's own political thought that finds its expression in the *Second Treatise* or *An Essay Concerning the True Original, Extent and End of Civil Government*. Our goal, however, is to get an introductory and conceptual grasp of Locke's position as worked out in the *Second Treatise*. Our task here can be helped if we think of Locke's position as arguing against that of Hobbes.

> The general pattern of Locke's *Second Treatise*.
>
> 1. A conception of the state of nature. *Importantly this incorporates*
> 2. An account of the natural law. *This is shown to be inadequate by*
> 3. An account of why life in this state of nature is imperfect. *This leads Locke*
> 4. To make a clear distinction between natural liberty and social and political liberty *and*
> 5. To emphasise the origin of property rights. *This in turn leads to*
> 6. An account of the origin of legitimate authority *and*
> 7. The origin of political authority *and*
> 8. An account of the limits of political authority.

There is some scholarly debate about whether Locke had Hobbes in mind when he wrote this tract and about the relative importance of Filmer's thought to a solid grasp of Locke. It is a fascinating debate and a fascinating period of history. However, ours is a normative project and our focus will be on grasping the basic elements of Locke's state-of-nature argument. Therefore, as with Hobbes, let us begin with a conceptual outline of Locke's argument. (See box on page 85.)

In this section our goal is to understand how points 1, 2 and 3 lead to point 4. We also need to gain an introductory grasp of point 5. The key, once again, is to gain a critical understanding of the conceptual tools that Locke uses to make his case. With that in mind let us turn to the text.

Locke begins the *Second Treatise* writing:

> To understand political power aright, and derive it from its original, we must consider what estate all men are naturally in, and that is a state of perfect freedom to order their actions and dispose of their possessions and persons as they think fit, within the bounds of the laws of nature, without asking leave or depending on the will of any other man. (Locke 1989: II, §4.)

Locke's state of nature is a state of perfect liberty and equality but this part of his theory could not be further from Hobbes's description of the state of nature. The crucial clause here is 'within the bounds of the law of nature'. To contrast Locke's understanding of natural liberty with that of Hobbes, we can usefully think in Locke's own terms. Our natural condition, Locke argues, is a state of 'liberty' and not of 'licence'. Hobbes's natural right to everything is a typical state of licence. However, for Locke, even in the state of nature, we are governed by a moral law.

> The state of nature has a law of nature to govern it, which obliges everyone, and reason, which is that law, teaches all mankind who will but consult it, that all being equal and independent, no one ought to harm another in his life, health, liberty or possession; for all men being the workmanship of one omnipotent and infinitely wise Maker; all servants of one sovereign Master sent into the world by His order and about His business; they are His property, whose workmanship they are made to last during His and not one another's pleasure. (Ibid.: II, §6)

There is a lot to think about here. We have already dealt, to a small extent, with the religious aspect of Locke's law of nature. So let us turn instead to the clause that leads us into the question of how we come to know what the law of nature is. 'Reason,' writes Locke, 'which is that law, teaches all mankind who will but consult it.' It is here that Locke's modernism makes its strongest appearance. Locke is perhaps most famous (outside political thought) for his epistemology (his theory of knowledge). In *An Essay Concerning Human Understanding*, he argues that humans do not have any innate ideas and that we certainly do not have natural access to the moral law. We are, famously, to be thought of as a blank sheet of paper or *tabula rasa*. We learn everything through reason and experience, including morality. This epistemological stance was highly 'modern' and highly critical of reactionary religious doctrine (such as that of Filmer) that argued that certain individuals (in Filmer's case divinely sanctioned kings) had the innate ability to dictate principles to the people (White 1989: 78). The moral or natural law could be learned by reason 'in the light of nature' and, although it was ultimately given its justification by virtue of the fact that it comes from God, every possessor of reason (that is everyone except madmen and children, to whom we owe a parental duty of care (Ibid.: II, §60)) is equally free in relation to other humans and obliged to obey this law because it is naturally knowable. This does not mean that all sensible people will automatically come to the same conclusions about the nature of morality. It must be theoretically possible, but knowing precisely what God intended is very difficult for mere humans. This is important because this problem is one of the 'inconveniences' of the state of nature that impels us towards political society. However, it does not affect the moral force of Locke's argument. The structure of Locke's epistemology is not our concern here. It is, however, important to appreciate that Locke was doing something far more innovative than merely appealing to God to support his case. That said, the fact that the natural law flows from God is what gives it is deontological character. We must use instrumental reason to find a way to obey the natural law and 'preserve' God's creation (Ibid.: II, §6, §16) but our duty to do so is absolute. (For a useful discussion of this see Simmons 1992).

It is not uncommon now, still less when Locke was writing, for humans to think of themselves as morally 'special'. Often it is our capacity to reason, or to participate at a higher level in the universe, that is thought to give us this distinction. Morality is thus thought to be a peculiarly human category. For some this is a prime example of the anthropocentric arrogance of humanity. For many others, for a variety of reasons (religious and secular), it makes a lot of sense to think this way. How do you react to this thought? It is some debate. As one very influential commentator put it, 'if Locke minus God equals Hobbes, then Hobbes plus God equals Locke' (Gauthier 1999: 74). The difference between Hobbes's vicarious account of natural liberty and Locke's moralised account turns on this point and it makes a huge difference to the political theory that is to be constructed out of a state- of-nature argument.

Knowing the law of nature is difficult and so is knowing how to act upon it. Locke notes:

> Every one as he is bound to preserve himself . . . ought as much as he can to preserve the rest of mankind, and not unless it be to do justice to an offender, take away or impair the life, or what tends to the preservation of life, the liberty, the health, limb or goods of another. (Locke 1989: II, §6)

The existence of the law of nature and the equality of humanity means that all, equally, have what is known as the 'executive power of the law of nature' (Ibid.: II, §7). The moral law is as actionable in the state of nature as it might be in political society (Ibid: II, §12). Indeed, the force of Locke's argument would be lost if this were not so. To this end anyone who renounces reason and offends against the law of nature

> hath, by the unjust violence and slaughter he hath committed upon one, declared war against the whole of mankind, and therefore may be destroyed as a lion or a tiger, one of those wild savage beasts with whom men can have no society nor security (Ibid.: II, §11).

If the state of nature is a state of perfect freedom and equality, and if there is a moral law to govern it, then why would we ever want to be a political society? It is here that Locke's depiction of the state of nature, which could not be much more different from the picture Hobbes gave us, slips into something very much like the war of all against all.

The real problems of life in the state of nature are described, in a rather understated fashion, as 'inconveniences' (Ibid.: II, §13). The crucial issue is that, although we have criteria by which to judge right from wrong, people have to be judge, jury and executioner in their own cases. This is almost certain to result in partiality. There is the very real possibility that we would judge too favourably in the case of ourselves and our friends. We may also go too far in punishing others (Ibid.: II, §13). In political society (such as ours) it is often the case that a claim to have executed 'natural' justice (thought of in Lockean terms as retributive justice such as an eye for an eye, more often a life for an eye) seems to be clearly unjust. Vigilante punishments, retribution and revenge may be termed 'swift justice' but we often think that the very reason we have independent police forces and law courts is to ensure justice for all. In a pre-political condition natural justice is all there is. We would not have much trouble agreeing with Locke that this may be rather inconvenient. This is an important point. Locke's account of human nature in a moral state of nature does not make us out to be angels. There is no innate, and so no uniform, knowledge of the law of nature. There is a significant problem of impartiality and proportionality. We may also lack the power to enforce the moral law. As a consequence we slip quickly from a moral state of nature to a 'state of war' that is strikingly similar to the one Hobbes describes.

> Men living together according to reason without a common superior on earth, with authority to judge between them, is properly the state of nature. But force, or declared design of force upon the person of another, where there is no common superior on earth to appeal to for relief, is the state of war. (Ibid.: II, §19)

Later Locke shows that the state of war is an almost inevitable consequence of a lack of 'common superior on earth' (Ibid.: II, §21). Life in the state of nature, even with a moral law, would be awful.

It seems that Locke has gone an awfully long way to end up agreeing with Hobbes. However the very fact that there is a moral law underpinning the pre-political condition changes everything. For even if we fail to live up to its requirements it is still there. We have a normative scale by which to judge our condition. A person who in trying to subject me to their will enters a state of war with me is not merely in a state of war with me. They are, in moral terms, *wrongly* so. This is vital. As was the case in Hobbes's conception of the state of nature, we have good pragmatic or instrumental reasons to establish politics. But in Locke's version of the story we have a moral, as well as an instrumental, goal – the effective rule of the law of nature. Until this moral goal is reached, and unless it is maintained, we are not in a legitimate society. Our natural liberty, argued Locke, is to be free from any superior. This means that Locke distinguishes natural from social and political liberty in the following way:

> The natural liberty of man is to be free from any superior power on earth, and not to be under the will or legislative authority of man, but only to have the law of nature for his rule. The liberty of man in society is to be under no other legislative power but that established by consent in the commonwealth, nor under the dominion of any will, or the restraint of any law, but that which the legislative shall enact according to the trust put in it. . . . Freedom of men under government is to have a standing rule to live by, common to every one of that society, and made by the legislative power erected within it. (Ibid.: II, §22)

The full implications of Locke's moralised state of nature become clearer as we come to examine the social contract and his conception of political legitimacy in the next chapter. However, we can begin to get a full grasp of what this entails as we turn briefly to the next step in Locke's argument, his theory of property.

The natural law establishes natural liberty. We are morally free and *nothing* (especially not force) can change that. This is a vital point and is the core of Locke's thought. But, as we have seen, our natural freedom is beset with such practical difficulties that we end up living a rather Hobbesian existence in the state of nature. It seems that our moral condition is rather empty, rather intangible. In fact, as we shall see in the next chapter, Locke's moral theory does a huge amount of work in his political theory. However, at this point in the text Locke turns his attention to the idea of property rights. For some commentators this section is a digression in the main argument (albeit an interesting one). For others it is the core of his work, the argument that gives life to his natural-law argument. It is certainly possible to get both readings from Locke but it is impossible to deny the impact that his focus on property has had on contemporary liberalism (see Chapter 7). Here we will look at his argument on property as that which makes his moral theory tangible. We also intend to use this part of his theory to help us to compare the consequences of his state-of-nature argument with that of Hobbes and, in the next section, Rousseau.

In Hobbes's state of nature, just as there was no justice or injustice, there is no 'mine or thine'. There is no right to property except in so far as everybody has a right to everything, which, as we saw, was ultimately a very empty right indeed. In Locke's state of nature the moral injunction to 'preserve God's creation' takes concrete form in his account of property. Practically speaking, we need the means to live freely and equally. God, argues Locke, gave the world to men in common,

> yet being given for the use of men, there must of necessity be a means to appropriate them some way or other before they can be of any use, or at all beneficial, to any particular men. The fruit or venison which nourishes the wild Indian, who knows no enclosure, and is still a tenant in common, must be his, and so his – *i.e.*, a part of him, that another can no longer have any right to it before it can do him any good for the support of his life (Locke 1989: II, §26).

The law of nature dictates that we can have ownership of the food we need to survive. If it did not we simply could not fulfil our duty to survive. In the most basic analysis we have a claim on that which we take to feed and clothe ourselves provided, and this is important, there is 'enough, and as good, left in common for others' (Ibid.: II, §27). But Locke does not stop here. In fact he envisages the development of a complex economy, supporting enclosure and wage labour, even the invention of money, in the state of nature and under the natural law. We are naturally free to enclose land, provided the upshot of this is that we make it more productive by 'mixing our labour' with the natural resources at our common disposal. Locke argues that 'ninety-nine hundredths' of material wealth is down to labour rather than nature and that this is demonstrable by noting that the lifestyle of a day-labourer in England is far more luxurious than that of a king in a less developed economy such as that Locke imagined the native Americans to enjoy (Ibid.: II, §§40–41). Property rights and a complex economy are thus part of the state of nature and a concrete example of our natural liberty under the moral law (an argument that would have bemused Hobbes and sent Rousseau into an incandescent rage). We have moral rights to property and wealth even before political society is instituted. It is a necessary part of our natural freedom and provided we do not offend the law of nature no one has a right to take it from us.

Of course, our natural right to property suffers the same fate as the rest of the natural law in the state of nature but it does have clear implications for a liberal understanding of economy and we will explore this in the next chapter. Before we turn to yet another competing account of the nature of freedom it is worth pausing to compare Hobbes's view with that of Locke. It is quite normal in contemporary western society to think of individuals as bearing certain natural, human rights. Locke's theory expresses this well and his politics flows from this idea. Hobbes's view of natural liberty, which often garners a more enthusiastic response from the new reader, denies this moralised view of human nature outright. Which do you think is more plausible? Before you decide let us turn immediately to our third exploration of the idea of freedom.

Jean-Jacques Rousseau

Jean-Jacques Rousseau is also a key figure in the history of politics and political thought. Writing in the mid-eighteenth century his work was to be the inspiration of the Jacobin revolutionaries such as Robespierre and Marat (who used to read from *The Social Contract* on street corners to stir the social conscience of the Parisian people). Rousseau was sharply critical of Hobbes and Locke. He argued that they had misunderstood the nature of freedom and the nature of man and thus the principles of politics. His views on the natural condition of mankind inform his most famous work, *The Social Contract* (1762), the first chapter of which begins with the immortal line 'man is born free, and he is everywhere in chains' (Rousseau 1968: 49: ch. 1). It is a huge claim. We are by nature free but our political existence is one of subordination and slavery. This is an argument that shook Paris during the French Revolution and it is one that even now we must take very seriously. The first four (very short) chapters of *The Social Contract* provide only a brief overview of Rousseau's position on natural freedom. However, an earlier work, known as Rousseau's *Second Discourse* or more properly as *Discourse on the Origin and Foundations of Inequality among Men* (1755) gives much fuller expression of his state- of-nature argument. Rousseau attached a quotation from Aristotle's *Politics* to this essay, which is particularly appropriate. Quoting from Book 2 he wrote, 'not in depraved things but in those well oriented according to nature, are we to discover what is natural' (Rousseau 1987: title page). This quotation is appropriate for several reasons. First, it is appropriate because it prefigures one of his main criticisms of Hobbes. He thought that Hobbes had artificially placed 'corrupt' or 'depraved' social man in the state of nature and had thus built his political edifice on false foundations. Second, it is appropriate because Rousseau is often associated with anti-modern tendencies and thought of as a champion of the 'liberty of the ancients'. To some extent this is true. He did think of the historical development of modernity and the Enlightenment as corrupt and corrupting. However, this was not a knee-jerk reaction. His state-of-nature argument is intended to show that the modern values of individual independence (seen as a social goal) relied upon mistaken accounts of natural liberty and a misunderstanding of the nature of morality, and that it was this account of freedom that was the root cause of social conflict. Tied to this is a stirring critique of the kind of individual property rights championed by Locke. In a very famous passage Rousseau declared:

> The first person who, having enclosed a plot of land, took it into his head to say *this is mine* and found people simple enough to believe him, was the true founder of civil society. What crimes, wars, murders, what miseries and horrors would the human race have been spared, had someone pulled the stakes or filled in the ditch and cried out to his fellow men: 'Do not listen to this impostor. You are lost if you forget that the fruits of the earth belong to all and the earth to no one!' (Ibid.: 60)

Exploring Rousseau's state-of-nature argument offers far more than just a critique of Hobbes and Locke. It is itself an insightful treatment of the nature of freedom. Rousseau's ambition was to 'consider if, in political society, there can be any legitimate and sure principle of government, taking men as they are and laws as they might be' (Rousseau

The general pattern of Rousseau's political thought.

1. A picture of the state of nature taking 'men as they are'. *This leads to*
2. A dynamic conception of freedom and morality *and therefore to*
3. A depiction of natural liberty *and*
4. A description of corrupt and true social liberty. *This in turn leads to*
5. A critique of modern political society and the idea that it could be legitimate. *This sets up*
6. A description of the only legitimate social contract *and*
7. The idea of society under the general will. *But this also includes*
8. A troubled account of how we might regain freedom.

1968: 49: intr. to bk I). His plan is based on the key thought that, provided we work within the bounds of a true understanding of human nature, we can make politics suit us. It is an important thought. If politics is the product of the artifice of man we should tailor it to our benefit and not accept anything less. On that positive thought let us turn to the general pattern of Rousseau's argument. (See box on page 93.)

Our aim here is to get a critical overview of points 1–5.

Rousseau begins his account of the state of nature expressing real doubts about the ability of the empirical sciences to give us an adequate or accurate portrayal of humanity's original condition and about the accounts of the state of nature provided by earlier philosophers. It is not that he was methodologically anti-science (except when prudently pointing out that historical accounts of the state of nature run contrary to the Book of Genesis). It is rather that he thought the evolutionary sciences so underdeveloped that we could not 'prove' anything this way. Rousseau instead hopes to offer us a picture of the state of nature based on 'hypothetical and conditional reasonings' that are 'better suited to shedding light on the nature of things than on pointing out their true origin' (Rousseau 1987: 38–9). This is an interesting thought itself. Obviously, empirical areas of study, such as anthropology, have developed considerably in the 250 years since Rousseau was writing. Have they developed enough to provide a solid scientific basis for a state-of-nature argument? Does it matter if they have or not? Is a state of nature a scientific claim about the nature of man or a hypothetical tool to aid the demonstration of complex points (a 'device of representation' as John Rawls, a modern-day social-contract theorist puts it)? In any case Rousseau's intention was to offer us a picture of natural man that would be more believable than those offered by other philosophers (particularly Hobbes) who spoke about savage man but depicted civil man (Ibid.: 38). Rousseau's real concern was this last one. *Natural* man is just that:

> I see an animal less strong than some, less agile than others, but all in all, the most advantageously organized of all. I see him satisfying his hunger under an oak tree, quenching his thirst at the first stream, finding his bed at the foot of the same tree that supplied his meal; and thus all his needs are satisfied. (Ibid.: 40)

It is a simple picture. But Rousseau's point is far from simplistic. There is nothing beyond the base 'facts' of existence that is natural in this peculiar sense. This generates a fierce individualism. In nature man is free. This is not a normative point because the normative force of 'freedom' would not have existed. It is a brute fact. Man is independent by nature. This does not necessarily mean he lives a solitary life but it does mean that those interpersonal relations that do exist naturally do not establish moral relations or obligations. The most natural social arrangement is the family but that does not mean that anyone is obliged to be a part of it. Children need care but beyond that any arrangement (such as the leadership of a family group by the head of the family) depends, Rousseau insists, on consent or choice. Natural freedom is simple independence (Rousseau 1968: 50: Bk I, ch. 2).

What then is the difference between Rousseau's account of liberty and the one offered by Hobbes? Physically speaking the answer is not very much, although Rousseau denies Hobbes's claim 'that man is naturally intrepid and seeks only to attack and to fight' (Rousseau: 1987: 41). Why, he wonders, would man bother? And what about natural compassion or pity? However, when Rousseau turns away from physical man to metaphysical man (to consider him from a moral point of view) his depiction of natural man becomes remarkably distinct from that of Hobbes.

From a moral point of view natural man is a non-entity.

> Men in that state, having among themselves no type of moral relations or acknowledged duties, could be neither good nor evil, and had neither vices nor virtues. . . . Above all, let us not conclude with Hobbes that because man has no idea of goodness, he is naturally evil; that he is vicious because he does not know virtue. (Ibid.: 52–3)

Moral relations, Rousseau insists, are not part of nature. But what of the war of all against all? What if someone forces you out of your independence? Rousseau's answers to these questions really set the scene for the rest of his theory.

Rousseau does not think that natural man has the characteristics that would lead to a war of all against all. He does not deny that you can find such characteristics in contemporary man but he thinks that these are the products of a corrupted process of socialisation. This is one of the keys to understanding Rousseau. We have the potential to change. Our perception of ourselves as members of society is very different to the animalistic or unsophisticated perception of ourselves that we may have had in the state of nature. This ability to develop is both our making and our undoing. It is our making because it marks the move from the animalistic 'savage' of Rousseau's state of nature to the rational and moral being we often associate with the dignity of humanity. In fact the potential to leave the state of nature and to become moral and social beings is the greatest characteristic of humankind. However, the danger here is that we would not make this move properly but that instead we would develop the characteristics of pride and envy, of 'competition, diffidence and glory', that stoked Hobbes's war of all against all.

The key idea is this: somewhere along the road to moral maturity our progress was hijacked and corrupted. Contemporary society is the product of this corruption and is thus subject to stringent criticism. Let us take this step by step because if you understand this aspect of Rousseau's work you have the foundation for all that is still to come.

Our natural condition is amoral and characterised by 'love of oneself' (*amour de soi*). However, in his own notes to the *Second Discourse* Rousseau makes a vitally important point.

> We must not confuse egocentrism with love of oneself, two passions very different by virtue of both their nature and their effects. Love of oneself is a natural sentiment which moves every animal to be vigilant in its own preservation and which, directed in man by reason and modified by pity, produces humanity and virtue. Egocentrism is merely a sentiment that is relative, artificial and born in society, which moves each individual to value himself more than anyone else, which inspires men in all the evils they cause one another. (Ibid.: 106)

For Rousseau love of oneself does not cause conflict. In the state of nature our crude independence is such that we have no cause for quarrel. It is quite literally a pre-social condition and such contact as there is between humans is irregular and simple. However such a condition does not last for long. We leave the state of nature not by choice but by necessity.

> I assume that men reach a point where the obstacles to their preservation in the state of nature prove greater than the strength that each man has to preserve himself in that state. Beyond this point, the primitive condition cannot endure, for then the human race will perish if it does not change its mode of existence. (Rousseau 1968: 59: bk I, ch. 6)

An increasing human population meant that we could not continue to live a simple and independent life. However, in this move lay the potential of humanity. Harnessing the two most important natural features of humankind, reason and pity (or compassion), we had the opportunity to develop into truly virtuous beings. For Rousseau morality is nothing other than the ability to see oneself through the eyes of others and act appropriately (*amour propre*). This is a fascinating description of morality. Learning to live with others *is* the essence of morality. Humans have the capacity to act morally but it is not natural in the sense of being fully fixed in all humans from birth. It is a capacity that has to be developed, educated and nurtured. Learning to live with other humans and to blend self-interest with reason and compassion is our task and a task that should be supported by politics (see Chapter 4). We have, Rousseau argues, no option but to leave our base independence. The move out of the state of nature is irrevocable. Natural independence has been made impossible and we thus have to 'change our mode of existence'. The questions are: how do we change and to what?

As we can see this is a very different story to that of Hobbes. However, there is a twist in this tale: 'emerging society gave way to the most horrible state of war' (Rousseau 1987: 68). With an increase in population comes scarcity of resources. With scarcity of resources come ownership, property rights, and economy. With ownership comes inequality and with inequality comes subordination and competition. As this process unfolds so our *amour propre* becomes corrupted and, Rousseau believed, we become the egoistic individuals that Hobbes would have recognised. Society and economy are both essential parts of human life. But developed badly, as Rousseau believed they were, they become the forge and substance of our chains. Hobbes took these characteristics of humans corrupted by society and read them back into nature, thus perpetuating the idea that we are naturally selfish and competitive. Locke is no less blameworthy for seeing property as natural rather than something to be managed carefully. With the struggle for economic advantage and satisfaction of selfish pride now reified as virtues mankind, Rousseau argued, 'ran to chain themselves, in the belief that they secured their liberty, for although they had enough sense to realize the advantages of a political establishment, they did not have enough experience to foresee its dangers' (Ibid.: 70). If the potential of man was equality and social freedom born of natural compassion and reason it would have been something worth trading our natural liberty for. However, corrupt *amour propre*, vanity and egoism necessarily led to subordination and slavery. Is there anything we can do about it?

Rousseau's take on the state of nature and the relation of natural liberty to social freedom is certainly novel. It gives us a series of insights into what morality should be and a chilling critique of those things we take to be justice and morality now. Existing governments and distributions of wealth are the product of chance, force and bad planning (except on the part of the powerful and wealthy!) (Ibid.: 70). None of these things can establish *legitimate* societies. Subordination is a fact of life but it is not natural. If it were established by force it would not be legitimate (despite what Hobbes thinks – see Chapter 4) and

> as soon as man can disobey with impunity, his disobedience becomes legitimate; and as the strongest is always right, the only problem is how to become the strongest. But what is the validity of a right which perishes with the force on which it rests? (Rousseau 1968: 53: bk I, ch. 3)

For Rousseau a conqueror and the conquered always remain in a state of war and to talk of rights in this instance is to make all talk of rights absurd. Even if our current societies were established by consent they would not be legitimate. One cannot contract away freedom. It is against nature and the very act would nullify the contract (Ibid.: 53–5: bk I, ch. 4). Contemporary societies are then illegitimate, morally impoverished and corrupt. We cannot return to the state of nature and our natural liberty and so the task of politics, argued Rousseau, is vitally important. This task was expressed in the form of a mission statement by Rousseau:

> How to find a form of association which will defend the person and goods of each member with the collective force of all, and under which each individual, while uniting himself with the others obeys no one but himself, and remains as free as before. This is the fundamental problem to which the social contract holds the solution. (Ibid.: 60: bk I, ch. 6)

This is the subject of our next chapter. The real problem, which we will face there, is that we have over time learned to be corrupt. We generally do think of the satisfaction of individual desires as good. It has taken us an entire history to establish these tenets. Rousseau requires that we change our moral psychology and then society. This is, as he realised, a very difficult task – perhaps an impossible one. If, however, it is to recapture the potential of humanity it must be worth the effort.

Conclusions

These three arguments are famous parts of our history and each contains insights that still inform our lives. In the next chapter we will see how each conception of freedom plays out in the political world but before we do that you need to reflect on a number of the complex and profound issues that these thinkers have touched upon. Are humans naturally moral beings? Are humans naturally greedy and selfish and is this a brute fact or a moral criticism? Is natural liberty something we should fear or something we should cherish? Should we conceive of morality in instrumental or deontological terms? These are very difficult questions but they are central to the study of politics and in coming to terms with these three seminal arguments you come closer to being able to answer them to your own satisfaction. In the debates that rage between supporters of Hobbes, Locke and Rousseau lie the foundations of modern politics. They really are views that shaped the world.

Topics for discussion

1. What are the key differences between the state-of-nature arguments put forward by Hobbes, Locke and Rousseau?
2. Was Hobbes right to search for a value-free account of our natural equality and freedom or is there something inherently moral about the human condition?
3. Was Rousseau right to claim that Hobbes projects corrupt and so-called civilised man back into the state of nature?
4. Do humans have to learn to be moral or is it natural?
5. What, if anything, is the difference between the fact of independence and the value of freedom?
6. Hobbes, Locke and Rousseau all believe that humans can find themselves in a state of war with each other. What are the similarities and differences in their depictions of this state?

Critical glossary

Historicity	Historicity refers to the historical context, or historical situation, of ideas, beliefs and cultures. A sense of history is essential to an adequate grasp of politics.
Enlightenment	The Age of Enlightenment or the Age of Reason refers to the rationalist intellectual movements of seventeenth- and eighteenth-century Europe. Although Enlightenment political thought has been heavily criticised (in its own time and in ours) it forms an essential component of the history of modern and contemporary political thought.
Modernity	Do not confuse 'modern' with 'contemporary'. Modernity tends to be used as a synonym of Enlightenment but has broader terms of reference and can incorporate anti-rationalist thought and political movements. In broad terms the modern period gained momentum around the end of the Thirty Years War as the political power of independent states gained supremacy over religious rule, during the period of the English Civil War in the mid-seventeenth century, and during the period of the French Revolution in the mid- to late eighteenth century.
The social contract	The basic premises of political society explained in terms of a contract between citizens or between citizens and their ruler(s).
Freedom	Freedom is a contested term but is one of the most important concepts in politics. Most political theories argue for a specific account of freedom the maintenance of which requires specific political structures.

	At its most basic politics asks whether we need protection from the excesses of human liberty or whether we need to construct political institutions to enable human freedom.
The state of nature	The condition of human beings prior to politics. More often a conceptual 'abstraction' rather than an historical description, this device seeks to explain the basic reasons for politics.
Deontological (morality)	Deontological moral arguments claim that moral principles are right in themselves rather than for any benefit they may bring.
Consequentialist/ Instrumentalist (Morality)	Consequentialist/instrumentalist moral arguments claim that moral principles are good only in reference to their consequences. Thus morality has only instrumental value.

List of references/Further reading

There is a wealth of reading available to help you engage with these vital ideas. The next step in your reading should be these primary texts:

Hobbes, T. (1968), *Leviathan*, ed. C. B. Macpherson, London: Penguin.

Locke, J. (1989), *Two Treatises of Government*, London: Everyman. This is presented as one book; 'II' indicates that references are taken from the *Second Treatise*. Each treatise is divided into subsections in the original and these are uniform across the many editions of the text.

Rousseau, J.-J. (1968), *The Social Contract*, tr. M. Cranston, London: Penguin.

Rousseau, J.-J. (1987), *Basic Political Writings*, tr. D. Cress, Indianapolis & Cambridge: Hackett.

References

Aubrey, J. (1972), *Brief Lives*, ed. O. L. Dick, Harmondsworth: Penguin.

Gauthier, D. (1999), 'Why Ought One Obey God?', in C. Morris (ed.), *The*

Social Contract Theorists: Critical Essays on Hobbes, Locke and Rousseau, Lanham, MD: Rowman and Littlefield, pp. 59–73.
Hampton, J. (1986), *Hobbes and the Social Contract Tradition*, Cambridge: Cambridge University Press.
Simmons, A. J. (1992), *The Lockean Theory of Rights*, Princeton: Princeton University Press.
Simon, W. M. (1951), 'John Locke: Philosophy and Political Theory', *American Political Science Review*, 45, 2, 386–99.
Taylor, A. E. (1938), 'The Ethical Doctrine of Hobbes', in K. C. Brown (ed.) (1965), *Hobbes Studies*, Oxford: Blackwell, pp. 33–55.
Warrender, J. H. (1957), *The Political Philosophy of Hobbes: His Theory of Obligation*, Oxford: Clarendon Press.
White, M. (1989), 'The Politics of Epistemology', *Ethics*, 1, 77–92.

Secondary literature

There is an abundance of literature in the history of political thought and you should widen your reading to include specialist journals and books on this topic. At a more introductory level useful companion reading to an engagement with the primary texts can be found in:

Boucher, D. & Kelly, P. (eds) (2003), *Political Thinkers: From Socrates to the Present*, Oxford: Oxford University Press.
Constant, B. (1988), *Political Writings*, ed. B. Fontana, Cambridge: Cambridge University Press.
Forsyth, M. & Keens-Soper, M. (eds) (1992), *The Political Classics: A Guide to the Essential Texts from Plato to Rousseau*, Oxford: Oxford University Press.
Hampsher-Monk, I. (1992), *A History of Modern Political Thought: Major Political Thinkers from Hobbes to Marx*, Oxford: Blackwell.
Hampton, J. (1997), *Political Philosophy*, Boulder, CO: Westview Press.

CHAPTER FOUR

HISTORICAL

Hobbes, Locke and Rousseau II

CONCEPTUAL

The Social Contract and the Artificiality of the State

Fully armed with an understanding of the nature of freedom we are now equipped to examine the question of how we should construct our political world. For our three modern thinkers this question was of paramount theoretical and practical importance. For Thomas Hobbes, John Locke and Jean-Jacques Rousseau the question of constitutional **legitimacy** was one to face immediately, one to fight for and to die for. While the immediacy of this issue was exaggerated through the prism of the fall of absolute monarchical rule in Britain and the demise of the *ancien régime* in France there is no denying the fundamental importance of this question to us all. We are talking about *our freedom*. The worlds of Hobbes, Locke and Rousseau changed dramatically because of the force of ideas about freedom, ideas that you have had the chance to think through. If you found the idea of freedom important then thinking through how we should give institutional expression to our collective will to freedom is equally vital. It takes freedom out of the realm of ideas and makes it concrete. This, when you get right down to it, is what politics is all about.

Exploring the social-contract arguments of our three moderns offers us much. We learn about the nature of **legitimacy** and **obligation** (Why do we have states and on what terms are we obliged to obey them?); we learn about different forms of state (Why is **limited government** different from **absolute government**? Which is better? Is democracy the way to freedom?); we learn about the nature of political authority or power and its just limits (What is sovereignty and where does it lie? What makes laws just? Under what condition may we withdraw our co-operation?). Exploring these issues and forming our own opinion on the best answers to these questions is what gives us our political identity. It may not result in us wanting to tear down the existing constitution and start again, as was the case in the era that our moderns lived in, but it will leave us with a clearer impression of how we can work towards the goals of politics such as peace, freedom, stability and justice.

Building upon the three accounts of liberty from the last chapter we want to complete the circle by looking at the social-contract arguments of Hobbes, Locke and Rousseau. We want you to focus particularly upon how their very different accounts of freedom feed into their very different accounts of political obligation and constitutional construction. Here we are exploring the reason for certain different political views. Hobbes champions a very outmoded conception of **absolute** power. Unfashionable it may be but if you find any truth in his account of the nature of man then perhaps our error lies in supporting (or in believing that we have achieved) a more limited political authority. Locke champions just such a **limited government**. Preserving our natural freedom but establishing 'convenient' and practical ways to govern our collective lives is how Locke describes the role of politics. It is a fascinating description. It shows us the working parts of a limited conception of government and introduces us to a whole series of ways to think about our relationship to 'the powers that be'. Rousseau's social contract is different again. His strident criticism of contemporary society leads him to an account of **popular sovereignty** under the 'general will'. His emphasis is on social **equality** as freedom rather than the more familiar claim that the more independence we can retain the closer we are to freedom. All three **thinkers** can contribute something to our understanding of the core elements of politics and so let us return immediately to their thoughts.

Thomas Hobbes

First let us refamiliarise ourselves with the general pattern of Hobbes's political thought. (See box on page 105.)

In Chapter 3 we covered points 1–4. In doing so we began to grasp the basic building blocks of Hobbes's argument and explore their content. In particular we focused on his 'scientific' conception of human nature and freedom. We also examined his discussion on the relation between reason and passion and the laws of nature (those precepts of reason that could lead us out of the war of all against all) and his instrumentalist account of ethics (good, bad, just and unjust). You will need all these tools to help you reflect on Hobbes's political theory as it develops through his use of the social contract mechanism.

The General pattern of the basic argument of Hobbes's *Leviathan*.

1. A scientific method that leads to an enquiry into the basic elements of society. *This in turn leads to*
2. A description of individual men *(and)*
3. A description of these agents in a pre-social condition – the 'state of nature'. *These three elements lead to*
4. A picture of the laws of nature (precepts of reason that lead us to recognise the origin of politics). *This in turn leads to*
5. An understanding of the nature of political legitimacy and obligation. *And*
6. A realisation that sovereign authority must be absolute.

As we reached the end of our explanation of Hobbes's conception of the state of nature we came to the realisation that natural liberty and equality was the very cause of the war of all against all. Given this 'fact' about human nature reason dictates that we 'endeavour peace' by giving up the right to everything that is ours by nature. The only way that we can do this is to contract or covenant our right away. These points are the first three laws of nature. They are tenets of instrumental reason but they also represent the only way we can escape the horrors of natural freedom. It seems strange to think of freedom as generating such misery. However, the description of the anarchy of the state of nature is eminently believable. Beyond the atomistic state of nature of Hobbes's hypothesis we are aware that anarchical situations where the rule of law has broken down or is unenforceable, where 'justice and injustice have there no place . . . [where there is] no *Mine* and *Thine* distinct' (Hobbes 1968: 188), are terrifying. Let us pick up the story again where we left it in Chapter 3 with Hobbes's discussion of the third law of nature. This time we will take more of the passage on promise-making and -keeping.

> From that law of Nature, by which we are obliged to transferre to another, such rights, as being retained, hinder the peace of mankind, there followeth a Third; which is this, *That men Performe their Covenants made*: without which, Covenants are in vain, and but empty words; and the right of all men to all things remaining, wee are still in the condition of Warre.
>
> And in this law of Nature, consisteth the Fountain and Originall of JUSTICE. . . . When a covenant is made, then to break it is *Unjust*: And the definition of INJUSTICE, is no other than *the not Performance of Covenant*. And whatsoever is not Unjust is *Just*. (Ibid.: 201–2)

Promising to give up your right to everything is the only way out of the state of nature. Keeping your promise is the origin of justice because breaking your promise leaves us in the state of nature. Nevertheless (and here is where politics proper makes its debut) working out what constitutes justice is not enough to establish peace. This is because

> the Lawes of Nature (as *Justice, Equity, Modesty, Mercy*, and (in summe) *doing to others, as wee would be done to*) of themselves, without the terrour of some power to cause them to be observed, are contrary to our naturall Passions, that carry us to Partiality, Pride, Revenge, and the like. And Covenants, without the Sword, are but Words, and of no strength to secure man at all (Ibid.: 223).

Once again we come to the word that is scattered throughout *Leviathan*, 'Power'. This word is the real key to Hobbes's political thought. We need to establish the background conditions that make the observance of covenants possible. To do this we need to institute a power of such might that it can force our passions in line with our reason. We need to be more scared of not doing the rational thing than we are of others reneging on their promises. We need to have acting upon our long-term self-interest made a more attractive prospect than the satisfaction of immediate desire. Hobbes points out that

> the only way to erect such a Common Power as may be able to defend them from the invasion of Forraigners, and the injuries of one another . . . is to conferre all their power and strength upon

> one Man, or upon one Assembly of men, that may reduce all their Wills, by a plurality of voices, into one Will (Ibid.: 227).

This is the social contract.

The authority established upon this covenant is no mere administrative authority. The Leviathan has to have absolute power. The Leviathan is an **absolute sovereign**, the source of all justice and law. It has to form the will of the people to give them one voice and avoid the problems of conflicting wills. It must have the authority and power to deploy its citizens 'as he shall think expedient' for their peace and common defence. Only under these conditions can we escape the state of nature. Hobbes does not care if this power is one man or an assembly of men (a thought that would have won him few friends in the civil war); it just had to be absolute. Its word must be law. Anything the Leviathan declares is unjust *is* unjust, there is to be no debate. We are still free to do anything that is not proscribed by the Leviathan but as soon as the Leviathan decides that something is outlawed that is it. For Hobbes, our nature is such that anything less than this is too weak to end the state of war.

The core point is that we give up, or alienate (see Hampton 1986 & 1997 and the discussion of Locke below), our freedom to gain peace and stability. It seems like a drastic trade but if our nature is as Hobbes describes it then it is a sensible one. However, the words 'trade' and 'contract' give a slightly false impression. Hobbes is sure that no one is obligated to any political authority except by his or her **consent**. Indeed the first picture of the establishment of society that Hobbes provides us with sees a group of individuals explicitly choosing to make this trade. He even finds a form of words that they might use to 'authorise' this commonwealth (Ibid.: 227). However, Hobbes thought that, while this was a hypothetical possibility, it was more likely that actual commonwealths were instituted by 'acquisition' or conquest and that even if our consent was forced from us at the point of a conqueror's sword it was still binding. There is no difference between us getting together and choosing to enter society and losing to an invading army (Ibid.: 252). This seems to rob the notion of consent of all its power; it certainly does not make sense of the basic idea that voluntarism is the source of political authority. However, this key point tells us all about Hobbes and introduces us to a harsh but interesting notion of political obligation.

Whether we are simply choosing to set up political society or if we are being forced to swear allegiance to a conqueror we are making the same choice from the same motive. This motive is fear. At the point of contract our reason and our passions coincide and it is clear that our long-term interest lies in political society. But how can this sort of coercion yield a valid contract? The simple fact is that there is nothing else but covenant and, given human nature, sticking to these promises is our only hope of escaping the war of all against all. The stark message that runs through this account of the social contract is simple. Effective power and authority is everything. Any state that establishes peace is legitimate. Whether you got your state via the ballot box or as a result of conquest be grateful that you have one at all. You are obliged to obey its rules whatever they may be because it is always in your real interest to do so. This is the price of peace, stability and justice.

Hobbes's use of terms such as 'sovereignty', '**obligation**', 'justice', 'right' and 'political liberty' is unusual but this is the point of his argument. We are to think of these normative concepts in instrumental terms. Everything is about escaping the state of nature and establishing those things necessary to commodious living such as property rights and effective arbitration of disputes. The state of nature is thus the conceptual baseline of Hobbes's political thought. If, when the sword of our conqueror is no longer at our throat, we renege on our promise we return to the state of nature and a condition of war. Similarly, if we think the law isn't looking and decide to get rich quick we place ourselves in a state of war with the Leviathan. The origin of the Leviathan's right to punish us therefore stems from its right of nature. You may recall that the inalienable right of nature confirms our natural liberty to use 'all helps and advantages of warre' when we cannot find peace. The prospect of facing up to the Leviathan under these conditions has to be more terrifying than the prospect of surviving the state of nature for politics to work. It is for this reason that the power of Leviathan has to be absolute.

The total commitment we make to the state, and the power we authorise in it, can be demonstrated by looking at conscription. Recall that the Leviathan has the right 'to use the strength and means of them all, as he shall think expedient for their peace and common defence' (Ibid.: 228). This means that the sovereign has sole right to decide (for example) when to go to war and how to use the resources of society to win. If the Leviathan decides that public conscription is the answer then everyone called must go (although Hobbes does allow that weak and 'timorous' people who would hamper the effort may be excused if they can find a substitute). It may seem strange to think that people who covenanted themselves to society from fear of death should find themselves obliged to take the field of battle. But the point is that without this power there would be no Leviathan and without a Leviathan there would be no security, no peace and no commodious living. It is a rational choice (even if we are terrified by the prospect of war). Having chosen the Leviathan over the state of nature we are obliged to fight until such time as our state can no longer defend us and the war is lost, at which point we return to the state of nature anyway (Baumgold 1983: 43–64; 1988: 32).

Hobbes's reasoning proceeds in a series of straight steps from his claims about natural liberty all the way to his claim that we choose to be obligated to an absolute sovereign. Despite the fact that so many find his state-of-nature argument compelling, few champion Hobbes's political claims. We are more accustomed to limited governments which are obliged to respect our 'human rights'. We will turn to an important precursor to that claim shortly. For now let's have one final think about Hobbes's position. For some commentators (who often brand themselves 'realists') all contemporary talk about rights and liberties is either a danger to political authority or, more likely, a mask for the realities of power politics. It is an unpalatable fact but when you get right down to it Hobbes was right. When a state finds itself in crisis then whatever liberties it grants its citizens are forfeit if they get in the way of maintaining stability. Witness the speed at which freedom of speech and public assembly are swapped for propaganda and even internment in time of war. Note how private property may become a public resource if needed. This, we are told, is in the public interest and maybe this is true; Hobbes would certainly think so. But if it is true then talk about inalienable liberties or rights is just so much hot air. Hobbes's view is that we alienate our natural freedom to the Leviathan, thus passing sovereignty to that power. If this is what it takes then we should get out of the habit of claiming certain 'rights' against the state and recognise that our obligations are absolute and rationally and morally binding. Doing so would allow us to begin to think about justice, morality, freedom, sovereignty and political obligation in a clearer, more scientific and Hobbesian way. But before agreeing with the realists let us turn to an argument that supports the idea of limited government and natural rights and see what underpins the claims that we are more used to making on our governments.

Hobbes's claim that we should think of ourselves as obligated to an absolute authority is very engaging. This is partly because his description of political power seems to fit a pessimistic reading of the world and partly because his argument stands up so well to a first reading. Rather than deal with his theory in the abstract we want to turn immediately to an examination of a defence of limited government. This will allow us to begin to compare these two positions and give us a basic starting point for a critical analysis.

John Locke

Let us begin once again with a recap of the general thrust of Locke's argument.

The general pattern of Locke's *Second Treatise*.

1. A conception of the state of nature. *Importantly this incorporates*
2. An account of the natural law. *This is shown to be inadequate by*
3. An account of why life in this state of nature is imperfect. *This leads Locke*
4. To make a clear distinction between natural liberty and social and political liberty *and*
5. To emphasise the origin of property rights. *This in turn leads to*
6. An account of the origin of legitimate authority *and*
7. The origin of political authority *and*
8. An account of the limits of political authority.

In Chapter 3 we covered points 1–5, emphasising the moral characteristics of the state of nature. It is the moral features of the natural law that do all the work in Locke's defence of limited government. It is extremely interesting to contrast the mechanics of Locke's argument with that of Hobbes. The language is often the same but by focusing on the key differences that make Locke's social contract a defence of limited government as opposed to Hobbes's defence of absolute rule we stand to learn much.

Let us begin by returning to Locke's distinction between natural, social and political liberty. For Locke our natural liberty is to be 'free from any superior power on earth', our social liberty is to be 'under no legislative power but that established by consent' and our political freedom is 'to have a standing rule to live by . . . made by the legislative power erected within [society]' (Locke 1989: II, §22). This part of Locke's theory contains two vital aspects of his argument. First is the prominence of the idea of consent. This is something that has much greater significance for Locke than it did for Hobbes and we will return to it shortly. Second, note the peculiar way Locke divides freedom between natural freedom and social and political freedom. This prefigures one of Locke's most innovative arguments, the two-step social contract. For Locke, just as it was for Hobbes, politics and society are the product of the artifice of man. However, for Locke, the fact that we are moral beings in the state of nature means that we have to construct political society in a way that preserves this moral agency.

In Chapter 8, entitled 'Of the Beginning of Political Societies', Locke writes:

> Men being, as has been said, by nature all free, equal, and independent, no one can be put out of his estate and subjected to political power of another without his own consent, which is done by agreeing with other men, to join and unite into a community for their comfortable, safe and peaceable living, one amongst another, in secure enjoyment of their properties, and a greater security against any that are not of it. This any number of men may do, because it injures not the freedom of the rest; they are left, as they were, in the liberty of the state of Nature. (Ibid.: II, §95)

It is not, however, a contract between each individual and a ruler as Hobbes's agents made with the Leviathan. In the first instance it is a contract between individuals to form a community and who as a community agree to be bound by the will of the majority among them (Ibid.: II, §96). Only then does the second part of the social contract take place. At this point, guided by the majority, the community establishes a government. 'And this is that, and that only, which did, or could give beginning to any lawful government in the world' (Ibid.: II, §99). The key point is that each individual has to consent to be governed by the will of the majority first and then, on the establishment of this community, they can begin to work out how they will organise the institutions that will help them overcome the inconveniences of the state of nature. The move into society is a product of instrumental reason. That is, it is a practical way to overcome the inconveniences of the state of nature. However, Locke's deontological moral theory sets strict limits upon how the social contract can be made. The second step of this contract is more properly thought of as a trust. Sovereignty remains with the community formed in the first step, who then entrust their power to an administrative authority or government to enable it to take on certain responsibilities.

This is very different to Hobbes's account of the social contract, where sovereignty passes over to the Leviathan. One very useful way of thinking about this difference is to use a framework developed by Jean Hampton, who makes a distinction between an '**alienation** social contract' and an '**agency** social contract' (Hampton 1997: 41). For Hampton, Hobbes is the most famous example of an alienation theory of contract (individuals give up or alienate their natural liberty to the Leviathan) and Locke the most famous example of an agency theory of contract (individuals entrust a government as agents to act on their behalf but retain their moral freedom). Hampton's real target is the undesirability and impossibility of an alienation argument (Ibid.: 49–52). She is concerned (as we shall see shortly) that Locke's argument flirts with an alienation view but in the first place she offers a powerful criticism of Hobbes's apparent plausibility. In fact, Hampton argues,

> Hobbes sets out to defend the alienation argument, but his conception of who human beings are and why they want to create government forces him to accept that the creation and maintenance of authoritative rule is something that is always in the hands of those who are subject to it. . . . In a very real sense, Locke need look no farther than *Leviathan* for the outlines of his own political theory. (Ibid.: 52)

Hampton's claim is that because it is the people who ultimately decide when the Leviathan can no longer protect them from the war of all against all then Hobbes's alienation view of the social contract fails. Hobbes may give good reason to think of our state *as if* it were an absolute power (the appalling nature of anarchy etc.) but he cannot prove that the state should be absolute. This is a vital argument, for if political power is not absolute, if sovereignty remains with the people, then the way we view politics is radically different. In fact, if sovereignty remains with the people we are encouraged to view politics in a Lockean way. The issue of consent becomes more than the rather empty image it was in Hobbes and the possibility of seceding from government becomes the subject of much more serious discussion.

The issue of consent is, as Locke notes, key to a defence of a social-contract argument. Is the social contract *necessary* to political legitimacy? Do we have to explicitly give our consent to the community? We will return to this key issue shortly. For now, proceeding on the assumption that Locke's two-step contract is adequate, we want to look at the consequences an agency theory of contract has for our understanding of political obligation.

The two-step contract is vital because it means that we retain sovereignty.

> The community perpetually retains a supreme power of saving themselves from the attempts and designs of anybody, even of their legislators, whenever they shall be so foolish or wicked as to lay and carry on designs against the liberties and properties of the subject. (Locke 1989: II, §149)

The fact that the people retain this power is a function of the two-step contract, which is itself an expression of Locke's natural-law argument. We cannot alienate our God-given liberty. Hobbes's concern would be that this is dangerously unstable and means that we would be permanently flirting with a return to the state of nature. However, Locke argues that this is not the case. Indeed it is precisely because we first contract to form a community that secession or rebellion would not lead to a complete dissolution of society. There are times when we can reclaim the executive power of the law of nature temporarily and times when we may withdraw it permanently from a government that appears to be failing in its duty to the natural law. We may temporarily reclaim the executive power of the law of nature where our government cannot protect us. This is something that really seems to explain the notion of natural justice. If the law is powerless to protect us, say when we are threatened by a highwayman with a sword (or a mugger or burglar), we are technically in a state of war with that individual and we are within our rights to kill him in self-defence. This is only the case where we have no recourse to law. Locke emphasises his point by showing that even if we were defrauded out of a lot more money than our highwayman might have been able to get away with, we would not have the right to use force to get it back. The law could help us resolve the issue (Ibid.: II, §207). Beyond this the individual citizen is not in a position to simply decide which of the laws they think are adequate expression of their natural rights. This is because they have consented to be bound by the will of the majority. Here Hampton is concerned that this may push Locke towards an alienation account of contract (Hampton 1997: 57). If we cannot secede from civil society this has serious implications for Locke's account of natural liberty. If, however, we allow, as Locke seems to, that ultimately we all individually answer to God and that we can take our chances on His judgement if we feel strongly enough about something, it has serious implications for the stability of Locke's political theory.

Passing over this huge issue we turn to an even bigger one. General rebellion or secession from government is, for Locke, a real possibility where that government fails to live up to the demands of the moral law. This may be because it fails to enforce the common good or it may act beyond the limits of positive law. Above all any government instituted by usurpation or conquest is illegitimate. Now secession is not something that should happen 'upon every little mismanagement of public affairs' (Locke 1989: II, §225). Public administration is after all a complex business and Locke is keenly aware that stability is a key issue. Nevertheless Locke stresses that government is our servant and can be held to account by us. This, of course, is how we view the relationship now but when Locke was writing this was far from settled. Locke's theory really set the stage for contemporary liberal politics. Despite this, as we noted in the last section on Hobbes's theory, governments sometimes claim that 'rights' claims can undermine the effectiveness of rule. Which is more important, stability and effective rule or liberty? Deciding which of these must be sacrificed, or where to find the balance between them, is the core of politics.

Wherever a Lockean liberal thought to draw the line there is no way that they could favour the constitutional arrangement that Hobbes had defended. Absolute sovereignty is contrary to the natural law. The implication of Locke's argument, although it is probably the case that it never even crossed his mind, is that government should be either what he calls a 'perfect democracy' (i.e. a direct democracy) or else one (either a representative democracy, a constitutional elective or hereditary monarchy or an oligarchy) elected by a universal adult franchise (Ibid.: II, §132). In 1688 a universal adult male franchise was still a long way off, let alone a properly universal adult franchise (meaning all men and women of the age of reason). Nevertheless what we have in Locke is a stunningly modern, liberal conception of a constitutional state, acknowledging both the sovereignty of the people and the need to separate the legislative (law-making) and executive (law-enforcing) arms of the state (Ibid.: II, §143). The key to understanding Locke's argument here is to note that the first requirement (that the sovereignty remain with the people) is a product of Locke's moral theory and is absolutely necessary and that the second requirements (the form of the constitution and the separation of powers) are the products of instrumental reason, matters of practical efficiency.

Before we can conclude our examination of Locke there is one final big issue that we must examine. Does Locke's argument require that we actually consent to be ruled or can it be taken as a hypothetical demonstration of the moral basis for government? The simple answer to this question is that consent is absolutely required. Given the deontological character of the law of nature, the idea of consent is no mere explanatory tool as, for example, it was in Hobbes. Voluntarism is a necessary feature of political obligation. However, it is unlikely that there ever was an original contract that established society and even if there had been it could not be binding on us. Each of us individually would have to give our consent. Locke attempts to get around this problem by making a distinction between express and tacit consent. Express consent is the explicit making of promises or contracts. Tacit consent is the implied giving of consent. The question now becomes 'what ought to be looked on as tacit consent?' (Ibid.: II, §119) in this vital context. Locke is adamant that merely 'submitting to the laws of any country, living quietly and enjoying the privileges and protection under them, makes not a man a member of that society' (Ibid.: II, §121). Consent is too important to be inferred this way (and in any case this would make law-abiding visitors to a state its citizens). There has been much scholarly debate on what might count as tacit or express consent. Perhaps voting counts (but what about the disenfranchised?), perhaps holding or inheriting land counts (but what about the propertyless?), perhaps saying the prayers of intercession in the established Church of England counts (but what about those in non-established religions or of none?). In this tangled muddle we can see the discriminatory judgements of much of our political history. People such as women, the poor, or Catholics may not have had the franchise but one thing is certain: they were free under the moral law. Perhaps there is no such thing as legitimate political authority and we should merely consider Locke's argument as a demonstration of how we might think of our relationship to our state (Lloyd Thomas 1995: 53). In any case the relationship between freedom, voluntarism and political legitimacy was now established as a core focus for the future of liberal political thought.

Jean-Jacques Rousseau

Rousseau's answer to the problem of establishing a free society seems far more radical to the modern reader. At its core it involves swapping one's natural freedom for an equal stake in political society. Our independence is natural but, argues Rousseau, politics is inevitable and we cannot establish a just polity if we attempt to preserve individual freedom. As was the case with Hobbes and Locke much depends on the foundational premises of his theory. To refresh our thoughts on those premises let us recall the general outline of Rousseau's argument.

The General Pattern of Rousseau's Political Thought.

1. A picture of the state of nature taking 'men as they are'. *This leads to*
2. A dynamic conception of freedom and morality *and therefore to*
3. A depiction of natural liberty *and*
4. A description of corrupt and true social liberty. *This in turn leads to*
5. A critique of modern political society and the idea that it could be legitimate. *This sets up*
6. A description of the only legitimate social contract *and*
7. The idea of society under the general will. *But this also includes*
8. A troubled account of how we might regain freedom.

In Chapter 3 we covered points 1–4 and touched on point 5. An awful lot hinges on these foundational points. We were, Rousseau maintains, naturally independent. As the inevitable move to society took place we changed. We grew as a species and began to use the basic tools of reason and compassion to become moral beings. In this move lay the potential for humans to continue to be free at a higher level and in a social setting. However, we failed to live up to this potential and, in trying to preserve our individual freedom, our lost independence, we developed a corrupt, egoistic, envious and competitive view of our self-interest. This corrupt sense of freedom and the society that developed out of it was the subject of Rousseau's vitriolic attack in the *Second Discourse*. It is this that forms the focus of *The Social Contract*.

Rousseau, you will recall, began his treatise with a clear statement of intent:

> How to find a form of association which will defend the person and goods of each member with the collective force of all, and under which each individual, while uniting himself with the others, obeys no one but himself, and remains as free as before. This is the fundamental problem to which the social contract holds the solution. (Rousseau 1968: 60: bk I, ch. 6)

Rousseau wants to argue that there is only one legitimate form of social contract. It is voluntary but its form is given entirely by the conceptions of freedom he developed in his earlier arguments.

The core of Rousseau's argument is based on the idea that society is inevitable and so a system of organisation that manages the move from natural liberty to social liberty is necessary. Those who jeopardise the possibility of social freedom should be, in Rousseau's infamous phrase, 'forced to be free' (Ibid.: 64: bk I, ch. 7). Rousseau's claim is that people should be compelled to act in a way that is consistent with the possibility of social freedom. This may sound draconian but the basis for this claim lies in point 5 of our general outline. Contemporary societies, with massive inequalities in property and wealth, and with established political hierarchies, are not legitimate. The chances are that the current arrangements are the products of force, in which case, no matter how long that society has been in place, those societies have no legitimacy (Ibid.: 53: bk I, ch. 3). Even if contemporary societies were based on a contract that established hierarchy (such as Hobbes's covenant) they would still not be legitimate, because they would be against nature and of no moral significance (Ibid.: 55: bk I, ch. 4). The idea of being 'forced to be free' may seem paradoxical but any choice that is not part of the specific social contract that Rousseau has in mind is itself an attempt either to get more than one's fair share or to contract away one's freedom – something so absurd that it would be 'illegitimate, void, if only because no one who did it could be in his right mind' (Ibid.: 54: bk I, ch. 4). You will recall that it was, in Rousseau's opinion, the misguided search for independence or the satisfaction of self-interest in society that led to the corruption of society (see Chapter 3). For Rousseau, natural liberty and freedom in society are totally different things and we have to realise this and stop striving for independence and instead focus on social **equality** as our goal. Thus the social contract takes the following form: 'Each one of us puts into the community his person and all his powers under the supreme direction of the general will; and as a body we incorporate every member as an indivisible part of the whole' (Ibid.: 61: bk I, ch. 6).

In order to ensure that there is no subordination everybody has to alienate all their rights to the community and obey what Rousseau calls 'the general will'. The general will is the concept that drives Rousseau's theory. It aims to transform human relations, turning an aggregation of independence seeking individuals into an association of equal citizens. The general will *is* the common good. It is the expression of will that is totally uncorrupted by private interest. It is general in that it is the voice of all and it applies to all. Thus for Rousseau the general will is the definition of justice, as it has as its goal the common good and it is an articulation of **popular sovereignty**. For Rousseau all people, equally, must be sovereign if political power is to be legitimate. Freedom is our goal and in society 'obedience to a law one prescribes oneself is freedom' (Ibid.: 65: bk I, ch. 8). In one obvious sense the idea of popular sovereignty enshrined in the general will makes a lot of sense. If the people are sovereign they are all equally free and the sovereign power can have no interest contrary to the real or common interest of the people. However, the general will is also quite a strange idea. What is thinking in terms of the common good like?

> There is often a great difference between the will of all [what all individuals want] and the general will; the general will studies only the common interest while the will of all studies private interest, and is indeed no more than the sum of individual desires. (Ibid.: 72: bk II, ch. 3)

This distinction needs to be kept in the front of your mind when thinking about Rousseau's points. Are we more free when we obey our private will or our public, general will? Characteristically we think of ourselves as free when we act upon our own will and there is a space for this in Rousseau's thought. Just as we might think that our choice of what to have for lunch is not a political concern so Rousseau recognises that we only alienate that portion of our freedom that is concerned with the community. However, the background conditions to having an appropriate private will require that we live in a society governed by the general will in the common interest of all. Prior to this, in the state of nature, we were slaves to appetite. Here and now, without the general will we would be slaves to other humans.

The general will, as an idea, is the definition of justice. It is the common good, the object of political right. It is a beautiful solution to the problem of social freedom. Freedom requires equality, popular sovereignty and the general will. But how do we find out what the general will is? The problem is that

> individuals see the good and reject it; the public desires the good but cannot see it. Both equally need guidance. Individuals must be obliged to subordinate their will to their reason; the public must be taught to recognise what it desires. Such public enlightenment would produce a union of understanding and will in the social body, bring the parts into perfect harmony and lift the whole to its fullest strength. Hence the necessity of the lawgiver. (Ibid.: 83: bk II, ch. 8)

There are two important thoughts at work here. The first is that while the general will is the definition of justice and political right the deliberations of the people and majority opinion are only a more or less effective tool for realising political right. The people can be wrong. This factor is made all the more important when we consider the second idea. In his critique of established societies Rousseau argued that people had become habituated and corrupted to thinking of individual will as the object of freedom. This process had been going on since the dawn of human society. Theoretically it may be obvious that this was a gross moral error but how do you get people to see this? This conception of freedom, egoism and desire is inbred into our moral consciousness and forms our corrupt *amour propre*. It is at this point that Rousseau begins to falter. The task facing Rousseau and his contemporaries was massive. To change society was to change human nature (Rousseau 1968: 84: bk II, ch. 7). Rousseau, particularly in his writings on the *State of War*, was deeply concerned that this would be a task too bloody to contemplate (see Hoffman & Fidler eds 1991), a worry borne out by the Terror that followed the French Revolution. Such a huge change was possible. The change from natural man to social man, while corrupted, was itself an enormous development. How could we change for the better and what would be the catalyst? Here Rousseau turns to the rather unlikely figure of the lawgiver.

Rousseau admits that 'Gods would be needed to give men laws'. He realised that a corrupt humanity could not come up with an incorrupt politics (this would place effect before cause) and imagined, as a catalyst for change, the arrival of a figure such as the legendary Lycurgus, who gave laws to ancient Sparta. Rousseau envisaged someone incorruptible who understood the passions of man but did not feel them, someone of 'superior intelligence' who would not be sovereign or take a role in government but would make the people ready to rule themselves (Rousseau 1968: 84: bk II, ch. 7). In itself this hope is bizarre and it suggests that Rousseau's project cannot work. In part this hope stems from the fact that Rousseau himself seems very pessimistic about the prospect of retrieving human nature from the grasp of corruption and vice. However, we are not at all sure that it matters very much. Rousseau may not have been able to complete his story in a satisfactory manner but in its telling he made a series of vitally important points about the nature of freedom and the nature of politics. Later on revolutionaries, philosophers and political theorists were to pick up his project and try and make it work but we should not (at this stage at least) let the entrance of the lawgiver drive us away from Rousseau's theory. Even if Rousseau's project is unrealisable, and the present authors are not entirely convinced that this is the case, we are still left with a normative standpoint from which to evaluate contemporary society. We have a stunning critique of the illegitimacy of contemporary politics and morality and we have the core elements of a moral politics. The question that Rousseau's lawgiver begs, and the question we have to ponder if we agree with any of Rousseau's claims, is how do we realise these values in society?

For some Rousseau's moral egalitarianism is the core of an idealistic but truly free liberalism. His theory seems, in moral and political terms, more demanding than Locke's. Although Rousseau acknowledges the force of the two-step social-contract argument (Ibid.: 102: bk III, ch. 1) it is not enough to simply entrust your freedom to government. Freedom requires popular sovereignty. The people and not just an administration elected by the will of the majority must govern. Thus 'the moment the people is lawfully assembled as sovereign all jurisdiction of the government ceases; the executive power is suspended' (Ibid.: 139: bk III, ch. 14 see also bk. III, ch.16).

While Rousseau does not advocate direct democracy, where the public debate and vote on all political issues, he does think that the sovereign body (the people) should meet to make important judgements. Indeed the more powerful the government the more frequently the people should assemble (Ibid.: 137: bk III, ch. 13). Our freedom is too important to exercise it only once every four years. Rousseau had the political models of Sparta and the ancient world in mind when writing. He advocated small, close-knit communities capable of sustaining civic pride and a real general will. He recommended tying religion to the apparatus of the state to help sustain the unity of the citizens and, through offices such as the censorial tribunal, sought to establish civic pride and responsibility through peer pressure (Ibid.: 174–6: bk IV, ch. 7). The core message seems to be 'respect your fellow citizens and take pride in your political community for it is the source of your freedom'. This is a message that was to be taken up with some enthusiasm by the French revolutionaries, whose own cry, 'liberty, equality, community', closely echoed the core values to be found in Rousseau's work.

Yet for others Rousseau's theory laid the groundwork for the twentieth century's most oppressive regimes and political doctrines. The idea of being 'forced to be free' by obeying the univocal general will that could be taught to us by a charismatic leader smacks of totalitarianism (see, for a discussion of this, Talmon 1952, also Hampsher-Monk 1992). The idea of educating a public to be free comes through very strongly in the final books of *The Social Contract*, as does the identification of freedom with the state and the connected claim that 'the essence of the political body lies in the union of freedom and obedience so that the words "subject" and "sovereign" are identical correlatives, the meaning of which is brought together in the single word "citizen"' (Rousseau 1968: 138: bk III, ch. 13).

What are we to make of this tendency? Here it may be useful to reconsider the core claim of Rousseau's social-contract theory. Ultimately, he argues, 'these articles of association, rightly understood, are reducible to a single one, namely the total alienation by each associate of himself and all his rights to the whole community' (Ibid.: 60: bk I, ch. 6). There are two particularly important ideas at work here. The first thing you should have picked up is the idea that we should 'alienate' our rights to the whole community. As was the case in Hobbes's social-contract theory we need to give up our rights, our natural freedom, in order to establish society. There is one important difference in Rousseau's argument and that is the idea that we give up our rights to 'the whole community' rather than to a Leviathan. This plays a vital role in Rousseau's social-contract argument as it leads to strict equality and popular sovereignty under the direction of the general will rather than a hierarchical relationship between the absolute sovereign and the ruled. The very strict form of this alienation theory means that, for Rousseau, 'since each man gives himself to all, he gives himself to no one' (Ibid.: 61: bk I, ch. 6). There is also a sense in which Rousseau's 'alienation' thesis even goes beyond Locke's 'agency' theory, as it does not even allow voluntary subordination to the will of the majority.

Despite the brilliance of Rousseau's account of natural liberty and social freedom many people remain concerned about the plausibility and the desirability of acting upon his political prescriptions. In one sense this is because Rousseau's is not a social-contract theory at all. Rather it is a moral critique of contemporary morality and a theory of justice dressed up as a social-contract theory. There is plenty of mileage in considering how we might enact Rousseau's theory but the resources for it are not necessarily to be found in the pages of *The Social Contract.* Nevertheless the resources for considering whether we should think of politics as equality or independence are all there. Once you can recognise these resources the choice is yours.

Topics for discussion

1. How do the separate understandings of the nature of freedom found in the work of Hobbes, Locke and Rousseau affect their political views?
2. What key differences can be seen in the preferred constitutional forms of the social contract theorists?
3. What are the essential differences between an alienation theory of contract and an agency theory of contract?
4. Should the goal of politics be more independence or more equality?
5. Does the social contract have to be real to have any moral force?

Critical glossary

Legitimacy — The justification (or rightfulness) of a state's authority is usually expressed as its legitimacy. In the work of Hobbes, Locke and Rousseau the legitimacy of political power is explained by its origin in the articles of the social contract.

Obligation — An obligation is a moral duty to act or refrain from acting. The extent and limit of our obligation to a political authority is determined by its legitimacy.

Limited government A government or political authority can be limited either by its moral duty to uphold the moral law (for example a conception of human or natural rights) or by a constitutional arrangement of checks and balances that serve to effectively limit the functions of the branches of government (the executive, legislative or judicial arms). Locke's *Second Treatise* advocates both limitations.

Absolute government In contrast to the idea of limited government an absolutist argument denies the moral or practical case for limiting political authority. In Hobbes's argument the essence of political stability is found in the granting of absolute sovereignty to one man or assembly of men; nothing else can end the war of all against all.

Popular sovereignty Popular sovereignty refers to the idea that sovereignty (moral, legal and political authority) resides in the populace (the people). Both Locke and Rousseau argue that sovereignty remains with the people but the idea is captured more completely in Rousseau's claim that where the people are assembled the authority of the government ceases.

Equality Equality is one of those values that has to be qualified in terms of (for example) equality of 'wealth', 'political power', 'opportunity' etc. In this chapter equality (of political power) is contrasted with independence (freedom from the constraints of society) as the appropriate goal of political ethics.

Alienation theory Jean Hampton's description of Hobbes's social-contract theory (Hampton 1986,

	1997). It captures the idea that we give up our freedom, our sovereignty to establish political authority.
Agency theory	Jean Hampton's description of Locke's social contract theory, capturing the idea that we entrust (rather than give up) our freedom to establish political authority.

List of references/Further reading

There is a wealth of reading available to help you engage with these vital ideas. The next step in your reading should be the primary texts.

Hobbes, T. (1968), *Leviathan*, ed. C. B. Macpherson, London: Penguin.
Locke, J. (1989), *Two Treatises of Government*, London: Everyman.
Rousseau, J.-J. (1968), *The Social Contract*, tr. M. Cranston, London: Penguin.
Rousseau, J.-J. (1987), *Basic Political Writings*, tr. D. Cress, Indianapolis & Cambridge: Hackett.

References

Baumgold, D. (1983), 'Subjects and Soldiers: Hobbes on Military Service', *History of Political Thought*, 4, 43–64.
Baumgold, D. (1988), *Hobbes's Political Theory*, Cambridge: Cambridge University Press.
Hampsher-Monk, I. (1992), *A History of Modern Political Thought: Major Political Thinkers from Hobbes to Marx*, Oxford: Blackwell.
Hampton, J. (1986), *Hobbes and the Social Contract Tradition*, Cambridge: Cambridge University Press.
Hampton, J. (1997), *Political Philosophy*, Boulder, CO: Westview Press.
Hoffman, S. & Fidler, D. (eds) (1991), *Rousseau on International Relations*, Oxford: Clarendon Press.
Lloyd Thomas, D. A. (1995), *Locke on Government*, London: Routledge.
Talmon, J. L. (1952), *The Origins of Totalitarian Democracy*, London: Secker and Warburg.

Secondary literature

See Chapter 3.

CHAPTER FIVE

HISTORICAL	CONCEPTUAL
Owen and Marx	**Socialism and the Artificiality of Man**

We have seen that the Greeks had a vision of both man and politics as natural whilst the social contractarians saw man as natural but politics as artificial. In general, socialism has gone the further step to claim not just that politics is artificial but that man himself is artificial too. Human nature at any time is as much the result of 'artifice', the product of the ideas and actions of men and societies, as is their government. Man not only makes or constructs the state but also is in some sense self-constructing. Plato, Aristotle, Thomas Hobbes and John Locke have essentially *fixed* conceptions of human nature. Human nature is at all times and places the same, and stays constant and unchanged in the transition between life in the state of nature and life in the state. Jean-Jacques Rousseau has a *dynamic* conception of human nature in so far as he argues that man's nature changes. There was an original 'human nature', later superseded by other natures, but one that can still be referred to and accepted as man's 'true nature'. Human nature is thus not the same in all times and places but there is a privileged description available. The socialist claim is that human nature is *malleable*. There is no privileged description of human nature in the past, present or future. Ask yourself whether we can simply assume that people at all times and in all places have been fundamentally the same. For socialists, asking 'what is man's essential nature?' may not even be a sensible question. We should ask instead 'what is man's nature in these circumstances and at this time?'. Man may have a discernible nature at any one time but this is not fixed and may even be actively reconstructed. As we shall see in this chapter, the socialist conception of a *malleable human nature*, of human nature as something constructed, underlies both Karl Marx's historical materialism and Robert Owen's new view of society. It also underwrites the hope and optimism for a better future found in these thinkers and in the broader socialist movement.

Owen's new view of society

The two thinkers we shall focus on as exemplars of this socialist conception of a malleable human nature are Robert Owen and Karl Marx. We're sure that you would be expecting us to consider Marx; his influential position in socialist philosophy would make it strange not to. However, it is unlikely that many of you have even heard of Owen. He is not as central a figure as Marx, although he is an influential figure in his own right and his *A New View of Society*, published as four essays between 1813 and 1816, is the starkest available statement of this conception of human malleability. The central claim in *A New View of Society*, which underpins everything Owen wrote, was a principle that he regarded as self-evident: that

> any general character, from the best to the worst, from the most ignorant to the most enlightened, may be given to any community, even to the world at large, by the application of proper means; which means are to a great extent at the command and under the control of those who have influence in the affairs of men (Owen 1927: I, 16).

This principle contains within it the key elements of our discussion of Owen. Human nature is not fixed, it is malleable; it changes and can be changed. Character, for Owen, is created by circumstance and 'it is without exception universally plastic' (Ibid.: IV, 72). On this understanding it becomes clear that even though people exhibit traits of greed or selfishness, or engage in criminal activity, they cannot be blamed for this. The fault is not theirs and so they cannot be held to be culpable for the consequences that ensue. The defects in their character are the result of the circumstances of their upbringing or, as Owen might put it, the social system in which their character has been trained. As the manager and owner of factories in Manchester and Scotland Owen came into close contact with the working classes. He was horrified by their tendency to crime, their persistent drunkenness, their everyday acceptance of violence and what he regarded as their general moral degeneracy. He was equally horrified by the attitudes of the rest of society towards the workers. 'How much longer', Owen asks, 'shall we continue to allow generation after generation to be taught crime from their infancy, and, when so taught hunt them like beasts . . . ?' (Ibid.: II, 25). Had the early circumstances and education of the workers and the judges that sentenced them when caught been reversed then their lives would have been very different. The criminals would instead have been decent and law-abiding citizens, perhaps even judges passing sentence on the degenerate workers who would in other circumstances have been judges (Ibid.: II, 25). Owen suggests that individual character is determined by circumstance:

> The character of man is, without a single exception, always formed for him; . . . it may be, and is, chiefly, created by his predecessors; . . . they give him . . . his ideas and habits, which are the powers that govern and direct his conduct. Man, therefore, never did, nor is it possible that he ever can, form his own character (Ibid.: III, 45).

People have no real personal control over their needs, desires and opinions; in these they are determined by what has been impressed on their minds by their families and by the traditions and environment that shape their upbringing.

We must appreciate the radical nature of this doctrine. At a time when the state, wealth and property were still controlled by a largely hereditary aristocratic elite Owen is implicitly claiming that children are potentially able to grow into men of any class. This challenges the traditional hierarchical structure of society in favour of a vision in which all people are potentially equal. Traditional beliefs are also challenged. If circumstances change then children may learn to regard (and violently defend) as rights and virtues exactly the opposite of what their parents so regard (and defend) (Ibid.: IV, 72). What motivated Owen was his absolute belief that if human nature changes then it can be moulded. Even if men are currently as Hobbes describes them there is potential for managed change; mankind can be saved from corruption and degeneracy by the deliberate action of other men. If man's nature is formed for him by circumstance then bringing about a change in environment will speedily and directly transform human nature. 'Withdraw those circumstances that tend to create crime . . . and crime will not be created (Ibid.: II, 34).' Owen is convinced that in a well-governed state any people can live 'without idleness, without poverty, without crime, and without punishment'. Since these ills are 'all necessary consequences of ignorance' the well-governed state is the state that directs its attention to the formation of character; the best state is the one that has the best and most rational system of education, in effect 'a national system for the formation of character'. Owen is arguing that the transformation of society for the better is reliant on the state provision of intellectual and physical education for all children (Ibid.: II, 37). Through universal education and training the lives of the 'poor unpitied sufferers' can be transformed into happy and fulfilled lives (Ibid.: II, 25 & I, 20). People need only be taught a single principle for action, that individual happiness is attained through conduct that promotes the happiness of the community. Instead of the pursuit of individual happiness in competition with those around us, which leads to conflict, crime and misery, Owen argues that the co-operative pursuit of the general happiness contributes overwhelmingly to making each individual much happier (Ibid.: I, 17). The competitive individualism of Hobbes, Locke and liberalism in general leads to anti-social behaviour in the form of drunkenness, violence and crime since it undermines our sense of responsibility for each other's well-being. Altering the circumstances of upbringing in order to make co-operative engagements more likely will replace these old habits with habits of regularity, temperance, order and industry that will bring happiness in their wake. Through education human nature can be reconstructed and, consequently, human relations and human society can be vastly improved, if not perfected. With what he called 'A System for the Prevention of Crime, and the Formation of Human Character' Owen claimed he could save mankind from itself (Ibid.: IV, 70).

A common reaction to an initial encounter with Owen's new vision of co-operative societies is that it is pious and utopian and we're sure that this thought has occurred to you. Friedrich Engels, Marx's co-author of *The Communist Manifesto*, grouped Owen with utopian socialists in contrast to Marxist scientific socialism. It must be admitted that Owen was idealistic in many ways; however, he was a very practical man. From modest beginnings in Wales Owen became part owner and manager of some of the largest spinning mills in Britain, at New Lanark near Glasgow. Here, and later in attempts to set up Owenist communities in the United States and in involvement with the trade union and co-operative societies as well as in lobbying for factory reform, Owen made a concerted effort to put his ideas into practice. In his management of New Lanark he demonstrated his commitment to the idea that employers should not treat their workers simply as a means to increased profit. He paid his thousands of workers decent wages, ensured that they worked shorter hours than their compatriots elsewhere, provided them with good-quality housing and employed no children under ten (children as young as six commonly worked in factories at the time). Excellent schools geared to teaching through play were provided free of charge to all children between the ages of two and ten. The educational and leisure facilities were also available without charge to older children and to adults who were interested. Unlike other employers, Owen also organised a pension scheme for his workers that would see them provided with high-quality accommodation and regular monetary payments. Owen ran what was in effect not just a factory but a co-operative and humane community.

To the surprise of his contemporaries, the New Lanark mills were economically successful and furthermore seemed to vindicate Owen's theories, so much so that New Lanark was widely applauded and visited by European royalty, senior churchmen, ambassadors and scholars from many countries. This reinforced Owen's conviction that national and international society could be transformed through peaceful reform. In his *Address to the Inhabitants of New Lanark* he claims that revolution 'may be effected without the slightest injury to any human being' (Ibid.: 110). He hoped to lead by example, inspiring other industrialists to reform their factories and the government to enact laws encouraging the widespread adoption of Owen's practices. As he regarded his new vision as irresistible he thought that 'the commencement of the work will, in fact, ensure its accomplishment' (Ibid.: I, 17). The capitalist world would be transformed into a world of small-scale and peaceful co-operatives.

For us, the important thought to take from this brief examination of Owenism is the question posed to philosophers who rely on a fixed conception of human nature: why should we simply accept as definitive the account of humanity in its current conditions? Perhaps we are not necessarily, as Hobbes claims we are, self-serving egoists. It might be that we have the potential to be many things, unconstrained by the limitations imposed on us by our current nature. Philosophers such as Hobbes use an account of human nature to limit the range of legitimate political forms. As evidence that supports his claim against a fixed conception of human nature Owen points out that children can be trained to acquire any sentiments, beliefs, habits or manners. The evidence is that this has already been done; 'the history of every nation of which we have records abundantly confirms [this] . . . the facts which exist around us and throughout all the countries in the world prove . . . [a] demonstration' (Ibid.: I, 16). Owen appeals to the pluralism that so fired Plato's relativist concerns as evidence of the malleability of the human race. However, it is this seemingly unlimited plasticity that should concern us. If human society, unconstrained by fixed limits of nature, can take almost any form then how can we privilege one particular sort of community? Why, when faced with the pluralism found in human history, should we not reach the relativist conclusion that worried Plato: that in this variety there is no better or worse, just different? Although Owen claims we can attain a perfect society, by what standard can we judge one society to be better than another if we have no legitimate appeal to nature? If, in addition to political institutions, human nature itself is artificial there may be no standards that privilege Owen's co-operative vision of society over Hobbes' Leviathan. One way of approaching Marx is to see if he has the resources that enable us to privilege the co-operative socialist account of a constructed human nature over the many other possibilities.

Marx and Engels and *The Communist Manifesto*

Marx shares many of Owen's views about the malleability of human nature but understands this plasticity in ways that may provide standards for judgement. Like Owen, he is sceptical of the claims of the philosophers and economists of the social contract and the market. Against their claims that there is a human nature which makes certain forms of social organisation rational Marx argues that 'law, morality [and] . . . religion, are [just] . . . so many bourgeois prejudices', inseparably tied up with the system of **capitalism**, in which the **bourgeoisie** (property owners) and the **proletariat** (propertyless working classes) are the two main **classes** in society, fundamentally opposed to each other (CM: 1, 92). The bourgeois theorists, and here he would have included Hobbes, Locke and the utilitarians, transform what are historically situated social relations into 'eternal laws of nature' by claiming that the way things are now is the way that they have always been and will always be. Marx's communism on the other hand 'consciously treats all natural premises as the . . . [creation] of hitherto existing men . . . [and] strips them of their natural character' (GI: 86). He wishes to put capitalism in its place, in its proper place in history.

Capitalism, and the view of human nature as essentially selfish that goes with it, is just the present stage in a whole series of economic stages that can be observed in human history.

This understanding of changing human nature differs from Owen's in that rather than regarding such change as the free formation of nature by circumstance Marx believes that it reflects a certain train of historical development; the changes occur in a more or less orderly and progressive fashion. Marx refers to this idea of stages of development as **historical materialism**: historical because it proposes an evolutionary understanding of mankind and society, materialism because the driving forces of this evolution are not ideas or philosophies but material or economic forces. You are being asked here to think about human history in a way in which you may not have thought about it before. Instead of viewing history as the story of great men such as Caesar, Napoleon and Churchill, or as a history of nations punctuated by regular wars, Marx is trying to draw our attention to what he thinks is the deeper economic story that underpins these other histories.

Marx's doctrine of historical materialism outlines six eras in human history, each characterised by different economic 'modes of production' of which capitalism is but one example. Modes of production describe different ways of producing necessary and luxury goods in different societies. They are characterised by different ways of dividing up the work between groups of people or classes defined in terms of their role in that division of labour, and by the relations of exploitation and oppression that exist between those classes. Indeed, Marx regards the conflict of interests between economic classes to be of the utmost importance, claiming that 'one fact is common to all past ages . . . the exploitation of one part of society by the other' (CM: 2, 103) – so much so that 'the history of all hitherto existing society is the history of class struggles' (CM: 1, 79). The class is more important than the individual since an individual's interests and status are defined by their membership of a particular economic class. The six eras of human history are as follows:

1. A primitive or agrarian system, where a class of chiefs or priests organises and tithes the surplus from an agricultural village economy.
2. A slave-based urban economy (perhaps of the sort we found in the Greek *polis*), where a class of masters literally owns the people, who are then set to work producing an economic surplus for their masters.

3. The feudal mode of production where a class of serfs who are partly free are coerced and exploited by a dominant aristocratic class who own all the land and are supported by a small state.
4. Capitalist production, where private ownership of the means of production (factories, natural resources etc.) and a money economy allow a class of industrialists, the bourgeoisie, to exploit the mass of supposedly 'free' people who must sell their labour to survive, the proletariat. This bourgeois exploitation is supported by a strong and sophisticated state.

5.&6. These are the future socialist and communist modes of production and we will discuss these after we have discussed Marx's analysis of capitalism, the current mode of production. (CM: 1, 79–81; GI: 43–6)

Marx does not believe that the development of human history through these particular stages is accidental or arbitrary. Rather, progress through these stages is regarded as necessary and in some sense predetermined. Whereas Owen's change is open to almost unlimited possibility Marx's stages follow each other in a particular order; change has a route to travel and a direction in which to move. Marx's doctrine of historical materialism is a denial of a 'timeless human nature'; human nature varies as the mode of production varies. Through its labour and through human creativity mankind creates itself and its own nature. Any claim to attribute to humanity any fundamental motives, desires or drives, such as Hobbes's claims for fear, power and honour, is just to focus on one aspect of one stage of history and then to go on to claim that that aspect is universal. The philosophers and economists of capitalism and liberalism had been mistakenly treating bourgeois (capitalist) values as eternal values.

Historical materialism is not meant to be a normative assessment of history and its picture of historical development is not supposed to be based on value judgements about whether one stage is better than another or whether the evolution itself is a good thing. Instead, this story of history as a series of economic stages might be used to provide a non-arbitrary basis from which to explain forms of social and political life, and of religious and philosophical beliefs. This is often interpreted as an empirical claim, perhaps even scientific, about the way the world really works. Historical materialism is not an arbitrary story but a scientific account based on real premises about 'real individuals, their activity and the material conditions under which they live.... These premises can thus be verified in a purely empirical way' (GI: 42). Whilst Marx agrees with Owen that human nature is plastic, historical materialism is an attempt to impose a structure on that plasticity.

Marx asks, 'Does it require deep intuition to comprehend that man's ideas, views and conceptions, in one word, man's consciousness, changes with every change in the conditions of his material existence?' (CM: 2, 102). In order to understand the basic mechanics of this process, and therefore the implication of Marx's account of human development, we need to unpack the manner in which man's nature is dependent on the current material conditions. Marxist analysis of any mode of production identifies two key elements, its economic base and the institutional and ideological superstructure built on top of it. The economic base consists of a range of productive forces, which are simply the things used in production. These include labour power and the way it is used as well as raw materials and the technology and machinery used to process them. A second feature of the economic base is that these productive forces give rise to particular relations of production, and that different productive forces lead to different sets of relations. These relations between people (although Marx also includes here relations between people and objects) may at different times take the form of master–slave, landowner–serf or employer–employee for example. These relations each correspond to a particular stage of development of productive forces. The change in productive forces that was the harnessing of steam power altered the feudal milling industry from being a craft to being a large-scale industry and so precipitated a revolutionary development from feudalism to capitalism; workers were no longer tied to a particular plot of land and a mobile workforce was needed to man the mass mills wherever they appeared (Singer 1980: 36). These relations between people are always relations of classes of people with other classes. Simplified, each of these different historical stages is characterised by a different class structure. This structure consists at each stage of two main classes in conflict as oppressor and oppressed, masters and slaves, lords and serfs or the bourgeoisie and proletariat. Together the forces and relations of production constitute the economic base.

This materialist base is the foundation for the superstructure, the institutions of law, morality, politics and religion as well as the ideas that make up the common sense of the age. The form that these institutions take is determined by the level of development of the economic base. Thus, liberal politics with its laissez-faire attitude towards the market coupled with a legal system based on private property and a Protestant religious morality underpinning the capitalist work ethic is, *in some way*, a natural outcome of capitalism, natural in the sense that they are the forms that the superstructure takes when it is built on a properly industrialised economic base. A different economic base would correspond to a different superstructure of institutions, and does so at each of the historical stages. Change from one mode of production to another occurs when the technological development of productive forces outstrips the resources of current society's institutions and supporting ideas for accommodating change (CM 1, 85). The discovery or invention of new productive forces alters the mode of production that in turn alters the way people relate to each other. The social relations between the classes of oppressed and oppressors change their character as the mode of production changes. Thus 'the history of all hitherto existing society is the history of class struggle', where although the names of the classes and the personnel that make them up change, 'oppressor and oppressed [always] stood in constant opposition to one another' (CM: 1, 79).

Capitalism, like any mode of production, consists of two main economic classes, in this case the bourgeoisie (owners of the means of production) and the proletariat (wage labourers). The proletarian must sell his labour to the bourgeois factory owner, who purchases it at the minimum market value. As a consequence these classes have different interests and the conflict of interest between the classes leads to an actual conflict between the classes; the bourgeoisie and the proletariat confront each other as oppressor and oppressed (CM: 1, 80). This conflict of interests between the classes is not an even match. Whilst the proletariat has the advantage of numbers the bourgeoisie, as the dominant class, has the advantage of resources. This resource advantage enables the bourgeoisie to further its interests at the expense of the workers. The class that is dominant in economic relations, since the institutional and ideological superstructure is shaped by the economic base, becomes dominant also in that superstructure. This is a quite general point that holds true across each mode of production; 'the ruling ideas of each age have ever been the ideas of its ruling class' (CM: 2, 102; GI: 64). The ideas and institutions that accompany a mode of production directly serve the interests of the dominant class. For the proletarian, 'law, morality, religion are to him just so many bourgeois prejudices, behind which lurk in ambush just as many bourgeois interests' (CM: 1, 92). Bourgeois notions of freedom and culture serve the interests of bourgeois production and property whilst bourgeois jurisprudence is no more than the will of that class made into law (CM: 2, 99–100). Standing over each of these constructions is the state and in any age political power, for Marx, is merely the organised power of one class for oppressing another. It follows that 'the executive of the modern state is but a committee for managing the common affairs of the whole bourgeoisie' (CM: 3, 105 & 1, 82; GI: 80). Rather than fulfilling the function of a guardian of the rights of the people, or of an expression of mutual freedom or of a common power enabling each to live without fear, the state is a tool for oppression and for the protection of the interests of one class at the expense of another.

In Marxist analysis the state serves the interests of some and not, as many classical and modern philosophers have assumed, the welfare of all. Here capitalism is no different from any other stage in Marx's historical story; the content of the superstructure of ideas and institutions is determined by the current economic base. In this way man's self-image as expressed in the ruling ideas of an age is also dependent on the mode of production. The capitalist understanding of human nature as essentially individualistic, competitive and self-interested is a function of the way capitalist production isolates newly mobile workers from traditional social structures and sets them against each other in the pursuit of jobs and money. For human beings 'what they are, therefore, coincides with their production. . . . The nature of individuals thus depends on the material conditions determining their production . . . . Life is not determined by consciousness, but consciousness by life' (GI: 42, 47).

Marx's is a vision of human nature as plastic, as manmade and artificial, changing in response to changes in economic circumstances. As in the case of Owen, this opens up the possibility of transforming human nature and as a consequence human society by altering the economic circumstances that make human beings what they are today. Trying to understand why and how Marx intends to achieve this transformation leads us to briefly examine his critique of capitalism.

This critique is focused on two broad areas, a critique of the exploitation that capitalism perpetrates and a critique of its alienating properties. The **exploitation** critique focuses on the wage–labour relation. Marx has a 'labour theory of value,' where the value of an object is created by the labour that is invested in the production of that object. When a worker produces in return for a wage the wage she receives is equivalent to the resources necessary to keep her alive and functioning as a worker, in effect the minimum wage the market will bear. However, the labour that she expends at work and so invests in the product of her labour is worth more than the amount she receives in wages. The employer appropriates this 'surplus value' and so the fruits of the labour of the proletariat line the pockets of the bourgeois factory owners, further bolstering the resources they control and therefore the power that they exercise. In this way the workers are exploited by the capitalists. They do not receive the full value for their labour equivalent to the value that their labour has created. This is an issue concerning the just distribution of society's resources and discussion will be picked up in Chapter 7. In this chapter we can focus on the **alienation** critique.

The term 'alienation' and the related idea of 'species-being' are difficult to grasp in the abstract. By alienation Marx is referring to a process whereby human creative labour becomes external to humans and appears to dominate and oppress them. This is of vital importance because Marx believes that it is free creative labour that sets humans apart from the animals, it defines the 'species-character of man'. Whilst animals such as bees and beavers produce they do so because they are preprogrammed to do so in a certain way and produce only to ensure their survival. In contrast, human beings are instead capable of producing in many ways and to standards of their own creation such as the standard of beauty. They are also creative and productive out of more than necessity or survival in that they labour for luxury or for art. Indeed Marx goes further, to claim that when humans produce to meet their physical needs they are producing as an animal, suggesting that they only genuinely demonstrate their humanity in production freed from physical necessity. Creative production is the essence of human life; it constitutes their 'species-being' (EPM: 62–4). Alienation is a distortion of this free and creative human productive activity. Marx identifies four main ways in which humans are alienated under capitalism:

1. *Alienation from the product*: the proletarian worker is alienated from the product of her labour (what she makes in the factory) as it confronts her as something alien or external. This is firstly just because it belongs not to her but to her employer and so she is distanced from it. More importantly, the product escapes her control; in fact the product controls the worker. Face to face with the product on the production line it is the product that dictates her time and movements. The product and the labour value it represents also go into the capitalist's pockets,

deepening the worker's position of subordination. In effect the worker's labour creates and sustains the alien and hostile power of the bourgeoisie. Just as the monster created by Frankenstein escapes his control and threatens him so does the worker's product escape her control and threaten her (EPM: 59–61).

2. *Alienation from the activity of labour*: the capitalist mode of production alienates man from productive activity itself, capitalist factory labour is far from being the model of free creative expression. The worker is alienated from her labour in that she has no control over it. Having to sell her labour she becomes a wage-slave. She does not control what she is producing, how and when she is to produce it or the quantity she is to produce. She confronts her own labour as something alien and external. She has no control over her productive activity but must still work in order to survive. As a consequence labour is not liberating and expressive but stifling and forced (EPM: 61–2; GI: 54).
3. *Alienation from species-being*: if human species-being consists of free, creative labour then capitalism prevents the worker from engaging in her proper life activity. The worker labours not creatively but simply in order to earn a wage that barely meets physical needs for survival. Labouring only for survival is animal activity. In forcing the workers to degrade creative labour to merely a means for survival capitalism is subjecting the human to the animal (EPM: 63–4).
4. *Alienation of man from man*: just as a worker is cut off from his own humanity he is cut off from the humanity in other men. Since productive labour becomes a tool of domination and the power relation, other men become perceived as alien and hostile beings. We are either in competition with them for jobs and resources or they are actively coercing and dominating us as our employers. Other people come to be viewed as limiting the free exercise of our capacities, not as extending it. Under capitalism human beings fail to recognise their common humanity; instead they regard each other as instruments for furthering their selfish interests (EPM: 64–5).

This discussion of alienation shows us that it is the wage–labour relation, labour in the service of capital, that is the source of capitalist alienation. Private property, itself a human creation, dominates and stifles our creative activity. This applies as much to those who own property as to those who do not. The bourgeois capitalist is as alienated as the proletarian, although admittedly his lack of creative labouring is conducted in more comfortable surroundings. Bearing in mind the universality of alienation under capitalism helps us to understand that it is the capitalist mode of production that Marx is criticising and not individual capitalists, who should not be blamed for being well off.

So Marx claims that capitalist production both exploits the workers and alienates everyone. He also claims that just as other modes of production have developed and disappeared so too will capitalism. It is only one stage in the history described by historical materialism and, as have the other stages, it contains the seeds of its own downfall. Marx's economic determinism makes the fall of capitalism inevitable. How does capitalism undermine its own existence? Marx makes a number of claims that rely on the internal logic of the wage–labour relation and the private ownership of the means of production. Firstly, private ownership distributed across a number of individual factory owners means that those owners are in direct competition with each other in the open market. This leads to a sort of 'arms race' between capitalists where each is forced to increase production in order to avoid being pushed out of the market by competitors. If they are each doing this in an unplanned market then a crisis of overproduction is inevitable. Once existing markets are totally exploited the only way of solving these crises is to expand into new markets to take up unwanted production. New markets cannot always be found and there will come a point when overproduction crises cannot be averted in this manner (CM: 1, 86). Secondly, capitalism inevitably involves falling rates of profit. Competition between manufacturers encourages increased and continuous modernisation and mechanisation in the form of expensive capital investment. The mass production that results drives down the cost of each item produced (since more of the product is on the market and less value-imparting labour is invested in each item). The only way to maintain profits is to drive down costs but with the necessary capital investment manufacturers are faced with a problem. The only place to make savings is on workforce costs but wages can only be driven so low since the cost of keeping workers alive and healthy enough to man machinery is basically fixed. There comes a point when wages can fall no more and so profit rates cannot be maintained, whereupon capitalism hits a financial crisis. Finally, and most importantly, the effects of capitalism on its workforce are decisive. The proletariat is itself manufactured by the growth of capitalist production. Intermediary classes left over from the feudal era such as craftsmen, artisans and landed gentry are either able to mutate into members of the bourgeoisie or forced into the proletariat in an increasing polarisation into the two capitalist classes. As capitalism develops the numbers of workers required grows with it, swelling the ranks of the proletariat further. Capitalist production also requires these workers to concentrate in particular places whilst at the same time finding it necessary to drive wages as low as they can go. This has the effect of making it plain to the proletariat that they are exploited not individually but as a class, and that their class confronts the bourgeoisie as the exploiting class (polarisation means that these are the only two real classes left). The bourgeoisie also find themselves engaged in conflicts among themselves and with foreign bourgeoisie over new markets. They need to appeal to the proletariat for support in these battles and so drag them into the political arena. Capitalism politicises the exploited proletariat whilst making it conscious of its common interests as an exploited class. In effect capitalism revolutionises the proletariat, forcing it to recognise that it is not in competition with itself but with the bourgeoisie. 'What the bourgeoisie, therefore, produces above all, is its own grave-diggers. Its fall and the victory of the proletariat are equally inevitable (CM: 1, 94).' It is this inevitability that is important for us here. The fundamental claim of historical determinism is that there is an inevitable and one-way progress through history towards its communist endpoint. Capitalism is just one necessary stage in this history and its inevitable end is to come in the form of a proletarian revolution.

Robert Owen believed that capitalist society could be transformed peacefully. He actively campaigned to persuade governments and industrialists to legislate for and to support the creation of rational productive communities, with some limited success. Marx, on the other hand, believed that it would not be possible to talk the bourgeoisie into giving up the reins of power; you cannot persuade the rich to give up their wealth. Instead Marx insists that under almost all circumstances communist 'ends can be attained only by the forcible overthrow of all existing social conditions' (CM: 4, 120; GI: 95). It will take a violent proletarian revolution to bring about the end of capitalism just as each previous era had ended in violence of one sort or another. Revolutionary violence is both inevitable at the juncture between modes of production as well as necessary if the workers are to be released from their exploitation. Any radical who dreams otherwise is simply misguided by, as Leon Trotsky forcibly put it, 'priestly-Kantian, vegetarian-Quaker prattle about the sanctity of human life' (Dunleavy & O'Leary 1987: 222). Some individuals (perhaps a great many) will necessarily be sacrificed in the struggle between classes. You should take this opportunity to reflect on your attitude towards political violence. Do you think that Marx is right when he claims that real change will only be brought about by force? Do you think that this makes the use of violence legitimate or right? Do ends justify means? If not, must we just accept the status quo even if we think that it cannot be justified in its own right? You might want to bear in mind that the liberal democracy that we ordinarily think of as legitimate may have originated in the violence of the English, French and American revolutions. It is also the case that any state uses force, or at least the threat of force, itself in its everyday affairs. If this seems odd then think about what happens to you if you challenge the state by breaking the law: you are forcibly detained and may well be imprisoned. Marx claimed that this coercive power of the state was being actively used to oppress the proletariat. Perhaps the Marxist revolution is simply meeting violence with violence.

Whatever we think about these questions Marx does not believe that the revolutionary power of the proletariat can be stopped. He closes *The Communist Manifesto* dramatically and emotionally:

> Let the ruling classes tremble at a Communistic revolution. The proletarians have nothing to lose but their chains. They have a world to win. WORKING MEN OF ALL COUNTRIES, UNITE! (CM: 4, 120–1).

The capitalist era becomes transformed by revolution into the socialist. Here the proletariat seizes political power and the state apparatus in a sort of dictatorship of the proletariat. It does this in order to protect the revolution against hostile forces within the state (bourgeois insurgents) and outside the state (interfering foreign powers). Proletarian political power is also needed to centralise ownership of the means of production in the hands of the socialist state. This involves the immediate abolition of private property, and therefore competition, and the imposition of a sort of state-planned capitalism. However, whilst the proletariat becomes the ruling class it has no other classes to rule over since capitalism reduces the number of classes to two and the revolutionary proletariat gets rid of the bourgeoisie. The proletariat becomes a universal class, the only class, ruling itself. However, since classes are defined in opposition to each other, if there is only one class then there is really no class at all. Class distinctions disappear and we are left with a classless society. Since political power is the organised interests of one class against another then economic power will lose its political character and the state will cease to exist. When this has happened we will have made the final transition to communism and reached the end of history as we currently know it (CM: 2, 104–5). It is on this issue that socialism and **anarchism** part company. Many anarchists would share, in broad outline, the socialist analysis of modern capitalism, of the malleability of human nature and of the possibilities for a humane future society. However, anarchists do not accept that the transition from capitalism to communism must be mediated by a period of workers' control of the state. Anarchism rejects coercive authority in any guise in favour of a free and spontaneous co-operative order. Anarchists claim that the dynamics of political power in a proletarian dictatorship would not lead to the disappearance of the state. Instead the workers would become embroiled in the exercise of power and centralised organisation, and in the dehumanising bureaucracy that accompanies it. The revolution should not be just a revolution against capitalism; the true revolution is an immediate revolution against both capitalism and any form of political power. If it is not then the descent from revolutionary ideal to Stalinist oppression is the most likely outcome and the ideal communist future will not be realised. It is worth considering whether we can expect political power to be used to organise its own abolition or whether power corrupts these Marxist good intentions. On the other hand, it is difficult to see how the transition from capitalism to communism could proceed unmanaged and be successfully carried through under the shadow of internal and external threats.

About his vision of this future communism Marx tells us little although it is clear from his critique of capitalism that there will be no exploitation and that labour will be unalienated. Freed from the limitations of class conflicts, the full productive potential of man will be released and harnessed for the good of all. Human beings will reassert their control over the productive process, enabling them to be truly free. This rationalised production without the wastage produced by competitive markets will free humanity from physical necessity; each will produce according to their ability and receive according to need (CGP: 321). Freed from slavery to its animal nature mankind will be able to properly express its humanity in free creative activity. Instead of being limited, constrained and defined by one's role in the productive process, in communist society

> nobody has one exclusive sphere of activity but each can become accomplished in any branch he wishes, society regulates the general production and thus makes it possible for me to do one thing today and another tomorrow, to hunt in the morning, fish in the afternoon, rear cattle in the evening, criticise after dinner, just as I have a mind, without ever becoming hunter, fisherman, herdsman or critic (GI: 54).

This will constitute an end to alienation; free creative labour removes the experience of distance between the labourers, their labour and their product, enabling them to feel at home with themselves, their product, their fellow man and humanity in general. Communist society will be the first truly free society, 'an association . . . in which the free development of each is the condition for the free development of all' (CM: 2, 105). In contrast to capitalist relations, everybody reciprocally contributes to society and so everybody contributes to everybody else's well-being. Just as envisioned by Owen and contrary to the claims of the philosophers of human nature, the circumstances in which mankind lives are changed and this enables them to construct an idyllic and co-operative, free and equal way of life without competition and conflict.

Conclusions

Let's stand back a little and take stock of the arguments we have encountered in this chapter. Political philosophers such as Hobbes and Locke, with economic theorists such as Adam Smith, understand man and society in a way that tends to coincide with our received and 'common-sense' views. They seem to be in tune with everyday thinking when they regard human beings as individual pursuers of interests, self-serving if not plain greedy. It also seems natural that such individuals find themselves in competition with each other for the relatively scarce resources of the world. To cope with the conflict caused by scarcity the plausible claim underpinning social-contract theory is that it is rational for mankind to organise so as to better its situation, improving resources and security. Competition between selfish individuals is transferred to the economic sphere and something like a market economy becomes recognisable. This story regards the market as rational, as it does the market relations of producer and consumer, employer and employee. These philosophers and economists inform us that the various economic and political institutions that develop as a response to a mankind that is naturally self-interested and competitive are the only rational way to deal with such beings. These are the institutions of the state, law and morality (and perhaps religion). They are rational devices either for conditioning or constraining man's naturally competitive nature or for protecting the private property of such individuals. The socialist position we have found in Owen and Marx claims that this picture of natural man creating political institutions by artifice fails to grasp the important truth that mankind is capable of refashioning itself. There is no canonical interpretation of human beings in the world that fundamentally constrains the proper forms of political organisation. Instead man as well as politics is a thing of artifice. By remaking circumstances through revolution or education mankind itself is remade. One common argument you often hear against socialism (you may have come across it yourself) is that a socialist or communist society is perfectly fine in principle but can never work in practice because of human nature and man's inherent self-interest and corruption. Such arguments are usually followed by reference to the political regime of the Soviet Union as a demonstration that the world will always fail to live up to left-wing expectations. One thing this chapter does is to make it obvious that this is a misguided criticism of socialism. Socialists are quite aware that humanity may currently be self-serving and prone to corruption but they believe that the plasticity inherent in human nature makes a co-operative society possible.

The very malleability that makes socialism possible, however, poses for it a number of questions. We ended the section on Owen asking what standards could guide our judgement of possible institutions and societies if mankind can be remade in an infinite number of ways. Once we recognise human plasticity, free from the anchor provided by a fixed conception of human nature, why are we not just pushed to affirmation of a basic relativism where each remaking of man is as good as any other? Marx has offered us two interrelated but separable standards that can impose themselves on this variety.

Firstly, the doctrine of historical materialism, whilst affirming man's malleability, imposes an historical and developmental structure on change in our nature. That nature is determined by the current economic mode of production and will change as this mode of production is revolutionised and replaced by another. Historical materialism is an attempt to identify a progressive one-way direction to history and change that is in some way predictive; it holds out the vision of a future society organised rationally and co-operatively for the benefit of all. Societies can be judged more or less advanced through this process of development towards communism. Marx's particular materialist story has been largely discredited on a number of accounts. For example, the Marxist prediction that capitalism will run out of markets for expansion and so suffer from overproduction and falling profit seems untrue. Marx drastically underestimated the ingenuity capitalism has shown for creating markets through advertising, for example. Also, the confidence in the proletariat as a revolutionary class seems misplaced. In fact they have been peculiarly reactionary, largely content with liberal freedoms, democratic rights and some form of welfare state. Finally, where Marx predicted the growth of the proletariat into a class of overwhelming numbers conscious of their common interest we have instead seen the fragmentation of the proletariat. Today it does not seem likely that we can identify an economic and revolutionary underclass united by its members' perceived general interests.

As for the general idea of justifying particular societies, cultures or principles as the endpoint of a progressive history this Marxist attempt serves as a salutary lesson. Firstly, we must ask ourselves what evidence can be brought in support of such a claim. There seem to be plausible historical stories told by the social contractarians and by the Marxists, but history doesn't often provide simple answers or simple evidence on which to construct answers. Instead, we might be better off viewing these stories as competing interpretations of a limited fund of historical knowledge and hearsay. These interpretations are trying to tell a story that convincingly accounts for how we got to where we are today, and new interpretations of this history are always possible. It may be that if we want to justify a society, culture or principle then we cannot bypass straightforward normative argument about why one option is preferable to the others, giving reasons in support that are as good as are currently available.

The second standard for guiding judgement that Marx offers us is implicit in his conception of unalienated labour. Alienated labour is labour that is somehow less than human. It serves man's animal side in so far as it is about guaranteeing survival and is dehumanised as it is externalised, placing control of our lives in the hands of outside objects or people. It is fundamentally labour that is not in accordance with humanity's species-being. Communist society best liberates human potential for free creative labour, best realises our species-being, and so is the best form of human society. However, this is a claim to identify a standard based on that which is distinctively human, a capacity for free creative labour in accordance with our species-being. What can this claim be but the identification of quite a loaded account of human nature and a claim that this nature is privileged? Like Rousseau this appears to be a recognition that human nature is dynamic but at the same time a claim that one form of human nature is privileged above the rest. Owen too may be working with a conception of human nature as he has a definite account of man's co-operative potential united with the claim that humanity should realise that potential in a particular way. Perhaps appeals to nature are harder to do away with than either Owen or Marx suspected? You should think about this. Can we consider political institutions and decisions without making some assumptions about human nature? If not, does an account of nature determine or simply constrain the proper form of political institutions? So, both of the possible sources of standards for political judgement in the face of malleability that we have identified in Marx have proved problematic. Basic economic predictions of materialism have been discredited and the invocation of species-being simply reintroduces a conception of human nature.

We need also to take this opportunity to draw out some reactions to other aspects of the socialist positions we are now familiar with. Firstly, we should think about the vision of a possible future co-operative society where there is no conflict and so no state is necessary. We need to ask ourselves whether all conflict is at its base economic conflict. If it is then Marx's communist society and Owen's co-operative communities, since they remove the necessity for economic competition through increased production, may be conflict free. On the other hand, if national, religious, philosophical and moral conflict is not reducible to economic conflict then we have no reason to think that a situation of productive plenty would be free of conflict and so no reason to believe that political institutions for managing conflict would be unnecessary. In order for this reduction to take place economic class would have to be the fundamental identifier of people's status and interests. However, there is nothing in the basic argument for malleability that necessitates its economic basis. In fact this malleability may show itself most obviously in national, cultural and religious variety. The Marxist position has real trouble coming to terms with the possible non-economic basis of national, ethnic and multicultural conflict. You should think about whether common interests are shared more widely within economic class, within national boundaries, within ethnic or cultural communities, or within religious affiliation. The answer you come up with will make a great deal of difference to how persuasive you should find socialism, and to whether you believe a post-conflict situation is possible. Whatever our answer, though, the socialist conception of malleability coupled with the vision of a truly co-operative society should encourage us to question the status of liberal contract theory. We should question whether competition and conflict is man's natural state and whether this must be accommodated. If so, is this done best by market mechanisms and coercive political institutions? Acknowledging that conflict and competition is man's natural state is a recognition that there must always be losers in society. For some to do well others must do badly; this is the nature of competition. Human malleability encourages us to question the idea of natural losers. If man can be made into anything by changing circumstance then there are no natural superiors and inferiors, no natural winners and losers; there is no natural hierarchy and as such recognition of malleability may be a powerful argument for human equality. It may be considerations of this sort, not those of materialist economics or unalienated labour, that surprisingly constitute the best argument from malleability to socialism. The malleability of man's nature that seems to be central to a socialist vision highlights the morally arbitrary nature of the distinctions we have drawn among men and between men and women. As such it may generate the presumption in favour of basic equality that is necessary to socialism. Malleability underpins equality and so is absolutely central to socialist theory and practice.

We must also ask ourselves if there is a price to accepting at least some interpretations of malleability and whether this price is paid by accepting the downgrading in importance of the individual. Owen claims:

> THE WILL OF MAN HAS NO POWER WHATEVER OVER HIS OPINIONS; HE MUST . . . BELIEVE WHAT HAS BEEN . . . IMPRESSED ON HIS MIND BY HIS PREDECESSORS AND THE CIRCUMSTANCES WHICH SURROUND HIM. It becomes therefore the essence of irrationality to suppose that any human being . . . could deserve praise or blame, reward or punishment. (NVS: III, 53)

If human beings really are reduced to the product of their circumstances or education then there is no place for choice, freedom or individual autonomy. On Owen's conception our actions and opinions are, in some sense, not our own. Instead they are the result of our upbringing over which our 'will . . . has no power'. If our actions are not freely chosen then do you agree that we cannot be praised and rewarded for our good actions or blamed and punished for our bad ones? If you do then does this hold for all bad actions or are there some, the more extreme violent and sexual crimes for example, that you are unwilling to react to by recommending a different programme of early-years education and instead think deserve punishment? Perhaps we can recognise that social environment has a significant influence on character without having to accept that it determines our nature. There is a well-established link between poverty and certain types of crime, for example. However, we also seem to be committed to the belief that there is still a place for an act of will, that the criminal still has a choice to make about what to do in the same way that the saint does. Are you willing to give up this commitment and accept what Owen believes are the implications of malleability?

Finally we must think a little about a central achievement of the particular socialist visions we have examined in this chapter. This achievement is to break the obviousness of the link between nature and rightness. It seemed obvious to the Greeks that what could be shown to be natural was also therefore right. Likewise, it was clear to the social contractarians that, on the whole, it was only by properly understanding human nature that the right form of politics could be identified and constructed. An understanding of nature leads to comparatively easy answers for justice and politics, answers that can be 'read off' or deduced from nature. If, however, human nature is artificial then all these simple or easy answers are no longer available, or at least they can no longer be found and supported in the way they once were. If nature no longer privileges any particular set of institutions or values then in our justification of values we are left with the option of normative argument of the sort that claims that 'this is better than this because . . .' and with thinking hard about the sorts of reasons that could fill in that blank. Once we have recognised the importance of normative argument we should stand back and ask ourselves why the claim that something is natural has been taken to be a sign of rightness. There are all sorts of things that appear to be natural, ranging from natural disasters, through fatal diseases, genetic deformities and tribal warfare to hierarchical political structures. What is it about their status as natural that is supposed to make them good or right? Doesn't this list just go to show that we can only identify the right by the quality of the reasons that support it, not simply by making the lazy claim that it is natural? Socialism has done us a service, drawing our attention to this by undermining the assumed link between human nature and proper political organisation and therefore weakening the 'obviousness' of the link between nature and rightness more generally.

Topics for discussion

1. How far do you agree with the socialist that human nature is determined by circumstance? What are the implications of this, if you do agree?
2. Can socialism manage without an account of human nature?
3. Do you agree that law and morality are no more than bourgeois prejudices?
4. How important is the materialist understanding of human relations? Does it capture everything that is important about human interaction?
5. Are all conflicts class conflicts?
6. Is violence an acceptable and justifiable means of political action?

Critical glossary

Capitalism The stage of human history where the means of production are in the hands of private individuals and class relations are dominated by the bourgeoisie and the proletariat.

Bourgeoisie One of the two principal classes in the capitalist mode of production. The bourgeiosie are the owners of the means of production, a position they use to exploit the proletariat.

Proletariat The other major class within the capitalist mode of production. Commonly referred to as the working class, this class owns no property and so is forced to sell its labour to survive.

Class The fundamental unit of Marxist analysis. A person's class (and therefore their life prospects) are determined by their relation to the means of production.

Historical materialism An evolutionary (historical) understanding of human society. The driving forces of this process are understood not to be ideas or theories but economic structures.

State In Marxist theory the state is the institution by which the power of one class is organised for the oppression of another.

Exploitation The extraction of surplus value from the subordinate class in an economic relation. This is an inevitable part of the capitalist mode of production.

Alienation A process whereby human creative labour becomes external to humans and appears to dominate and oppress them.

Anarchism The idea that the state is necessarily illegitimate and that human flourishing would be better served without governmental authority.

List of references/Further reading

Primary Texts

CM Marx, K. & Engels, F. (1967), *The Communist Manifesto*, Harmondsworth: Penguin. This is divided into four short sections, reference is to section and then page to ease the use of the many different editions of this work that are available.

GI Marx, K. & Engels, F. (1974), *The German Ideology*, ed. C. J. Arthur, London: Lawrence and Wishart.

CGP Marx, K. & Engels, F. (1994), *Critique of the Gotha Program*, in K. Marx, *Selected Writings*, ed. L. H. Simon, Indianapolis: Hackett.

EPM Marx, K. & Engels, F. (1994), *Economic and Philosophic Manuscripts*, in K. Marx, *Selected Writings*, ed. L. H. Simon, Indianapolis: Hackett.

Owen R. (1927), *A New View of Society and Other Writings*, London: Everyman. This includes the *Address to the Inhabitants of New Lanark*.

There is also an edition of *A New View of Society* (NVS) on its own published by Woodstock (1991). NVS is divided into four short essays so all references are easily found in any edition. References take the form 'essay number, page number (edition)'.

References

Dunleavy, P. & O'Leary, B. (1987), *Theories of the State: The Politics of Liberal Democracy*, Basingstoke: Macmillan.

Singer, P. (1980), *Marx*, Oxford: Oxford University Press.

Secondary literature

Morton, A. L. (1962), *The Life and Ideas of Robert Owen*, London: Lawrence and Wishart.

SECTION III

CONTEMPORARY UNDERSTANDINGS OF POLITICAL THOUGHT

CHAPTER SIX

HISTORICAL
Bentham, Utilitarianism and Rights

CONCEPTUAL
How Do We Take People Seriously?

How should people be treated? How should their interests be taken into account given the fact that people often have very different interests? When should the interests of some individuals be sacrificed to those of others? Instead of outlining a range of competing accounts of what we should do to and for each other this chapter will take a look at the possible ground rules that may constrain any answer to these questions. It is important that we think about the sort of ideas that people often think of as appropriate considerations on this issue. We are, for example, familiar from everyday life with claims that people and their interests should be treated equally or that they should be treated impartially. The two basic positions we will explore are a utilitarian position and one that gives a central place to individual rights; they offer competing accounts of the ground rules for the ways that government and other people can legitimately treat us. Exploring these positions is not a matter of working out which one treats people equally or impartially. Instead we will find that both utilitarian and rights theories would claim to properly understand the nature of equal or impartial treatment. They agree that everyone counts, that everybody's interests need to be taken into account in our moral and political decision-making, but they understand this requirement in very different ways. We will be faced, therefore, with competing understandings of what equal or impartial treatment might entail. One role of this chapter is to enable you to think about what issues any judgement that we might make between the two positions should consider.

To those with some familiarity with the history of political theory it will be clear that we have departed somewhat from the broad chronological sweep of this book by discussing utilitarianism after Marxism. Whilst *The Communist Manifesto* was published in 1848 the main text we will be considering here, Jeremy Bentham's *An Introduction to the Principles of Morals and Legislation*, was published in 1789 and was itself an attempt to systematise ideas that already had a long history. Bentham's utilitarianism is also very firmly a central part of the bourgeois morality that Marxism opposes as it is individualist, almost certainly capitalist and profoundly unhistorical. On the other hand, John Stuart Mill's *Utilitarianism* was published in 1861 in full awareness of socialist positions. More importantly, John Rawls claims that 'during much of modern moral philosophy the predominant systematic theory has been some form of utilitarianism' (Rawls 1999: xvii). The central concerns of utilitarianism are live issues, as attractive and controversial as they have ever been, and we shall consider them in contrast with contemporary understandings of rights. It is utilitarianism that is the point of departure adopted by both Rawls and Ronald Dworkin and taken seriously by Robert Nozick, three of the most important rights theorists of recent years. This chapter places utilitarianism and these rights theorists in opposition to each other and it takes a noticably more adversarial tone than previous chapters. By the end of the chapter you should be equipped to understand what is at stake in this debate and perhaps to make a preliminary judgement about which side of the discussion you consider more compelling.

Bentham's utilitarianism

In moral and political philosophy Bentham had little regard for what had gone before. He thought of it as a series of vague and conflicting generalisations that cloak personal opinion in metaphysical claims, rob philosophy of solid foundations and thus lead to interminable and inconclusive discussion (PML: II, 14 n. d; OB: 85). In contrast, Bentham's utilitarianism is to enable us, in principle, to calculate the right course of action or the moral thing to do in any situation. He does this by founding all of morals and legislation on the greatest-happiness principle, where 'it is the greatest happiness of the greatest number that is the measure of right and wrong' (FOG: Preface, 2). The basic utilitarian claim is that law, morality and politics are all fundamentally concerned with the happiness, welfare or utility of human beings, and that these institutions should all be driven by the aim of making our lives go better and, if possible, as well as they can go. Many people find this simple thought very appealing and utilitarianism is an attempt to systematise this concern with our welfare and to lay out in a coherent theory what might be necessary to ensure that this concern is actually underpinning law, morality and policy. For utilitarians the concept of **utility** has come to signify many things, happiness, benefit, good and preference satisfaction amongst them, as well as including the absence of their opposites. Bentham effectively reduces these concerns to those of pleasure and pain, which he thinks are the grounds of these other feelings (PML: IV, 7). As Mill puts it, describing both his own position and Bentham's,

> Utility, or the Greatest Happiness Principle, holds that actions are right in proportion as they tend to promote happiness, wrong as they tend to produce the reverse of happiness. By happiness is intended pleasure, and the absence of pain; by unhappiness, pain, and the privation of pleasure. . . . Pleasure, and freedom from pain, are the only things desirable as ends; and . . . all desirable things . . . are desirable either for the pleasure inherent in themselves, or as means to the promotion of pleasure and the prevention of pain. (Util: 257)

Indeed, pain and pleasure are the two 'sovereign masters' that 'govern us in all we do, in all we say, in all we think' and 'it is for them alone to point out what we ought to do' (PML: I, 1). Bentham is claiming two things here. Firstly, the only things that actually motivate people are considerations of utility. The pursuit of pleasure and the avoidance of pain are the only reasons any of us really have to explain our desires or actions, despite every protest we may make to the contrary. Secondly, since morality must recognise that utility is the only end of human action Bentham regards utility as providing the only possible standard of right and wrong; utility, he claims, is 'the only right ground of action' (PML: II, 19). As the foundation of utilitarianism, the principle of utility 'approves or disapproves of every action whatsoever, according to the tendency which it appears to have to augment or diminish the happiness of the party whose interest is in question . . . to promote or to oppose that happiness.' Bentham goes on to claim that this principle applies to 'every action of a private individual' and to 'every measure of government' (PML: I, 2).

Before we take a look at what implications these claims might have for morality and politics we have to think about the *scope* of morality, about whose utility counts. It is clear that Bentham is committed to including all human beings equally within the scope of morality. All human beings suffer pain and experience pleasure and so the pain and pleasure of each should be taken into account without concern for social status. Bentham is also aware that he, and other utilitarians, may have every reason to extend the scope of morality beyond the limits of humanity to our animal relations. He asks what it is that sets humans apart from animals. Is it the number of legs, the texture of the skin or the capacity for reason or language?

> But a full-grown horse or dog, is beyond comparison a more rational, as well as a more conversible animal, than an infant of a day, or a week, or even a month, old. But suppose the case were otherwise, what would it avail? The question is not, Can they *reason*? nor, Can they *talk*? but, Can they *suffer*? (PML: XVII, 4 n. b)

This highlights the importance of Bentham's focus on utility: since animals experience pain just as we do why should their utility not be taken into account? Utilitarians may have trouble accounting for our understanding of morality as a fundamentally human concern. It is not that we usually think that we should have no moral concern for animals, just that they should not count for as much as humans when we make moral decisions (after all, most of us eat animals). We are less interested here in questions about how we should treat animals, although you might want to think about this yourself, than we are in what this says about the utilitarian attitude towards people. It may be that people are not themselves of prime importance for utilitarians other than as experiencers of pain and pleasure. Instead it is the experience of pain and pleasure that is of central importance, not who or what experiences it. We should bear this in mind as we explore the broader utilitarian position.

Setting aside for now the question of who counts we can move on the question of how they should count. Bentham is clear that the principle of utility must somehow take into account the utility of all but how is it to do this? At the individual level the utilitarian method is simple and intuitive and reflects the deliberations we all undertake when deciding what to do. In deciding between two courses of action Bentham instructs us to

> sum up all the values of all the *pleasures* on the one side, and those of all the *pains* on the other. The balance, if it be on the side of pleasure, will give the *good* tendency of the act . . . with respect to the interests of that *individual* person; if on the side of pain, the *bad* tendency (PML: IV, 5).

This is an instruction to weigh up the pros and cons of any action, just as we often do before making up our minds. Once we have done this for both possible actions we will be in a position to decide between them. The process is much the same at the level of the community. Since Bentham understands the community to be the sum of its members then the utility of the community is 'the sum of the interests of the several members who compose it' (PML: I, 4). Bentham is clear that in arriving at an account of the utility of the community, 'each is to count for one and nobody for more than one' (PML: xlvi–xlvii). Every individual's interests are to be taken into account in our communal deliberation by repeating the above process of individual deliberation for each person and then adding up their totals for good and bad tendencies. The resulting balance of good and bad is the utility of the action under consideration for that community of individuals (PML: IV, 5). Two things are important to note about this process. Firstly, utility has come to function as a sort of common denominator into which we can convert all the good and bad tendencies of any action in order to compare the rightness of actions. This is important as it enables us to consider different people, who appear to desire all sorts of different things, and to reduce those desires to amounts of utility, thus enabling us to make decisions between the desires of different people. In this way, the subjective desires of many are accounted for in the single objective value of utility. When faced with a difficult decision such as choosing between state support for opera or diverting those resources to health care we have, in principle, a method for deciding between these courses of action: which action produces the more pleasure balanced against the pain caused by not performing the other action? Secondly, whilst utilitarian calculation takes everybody's interests into account equally it does so by aggregating those interests. Aggregating interests throws them into a common pot and blends them together. This may seem like the obvious way of taking everybody's interests into account but, as we shall see when we consider rights theories, it is not the only way.

This process of calculation as aggregation makes possible the judgement of states of affairs. Any state of affairs can be judged by reference to the standard of maximised utility. Pleasure and the absence of pain is good and we should promote that state of affairs where this good is realised to the greatest extent. Bentham is defining right action as that action which has the consequence of promoting the state of affairs where this good is maximally realised. For this reason utilitarianism can be thought of as a form of **consequentialism**, whereby the rightness of actions is judged in terms of their consequences for the realisation of some previously identified good state of affairs. Utilitarianism is a type of consequentialist theory, the one that measures good and bad consequences in terms of pleasure and pain. Alternative consequentialist positions might judge consequences by reference to economic efficiency, the greater glory of the state, the health of the community or the production of cultural masterpieces, for example. Any form of consequentialism will tell us that we ought to perform the action that has the best consequences, that it is right that we do so. Bentham's claim is that in this way utilitarianism gives moral terms such as '*ought*, and *right*, and *wrong* . . . a meaning: when otherwise, they have none' except as a reflection of the opinions of those who used them (PML: I, 10). Moral terms only have meaning and content by reference to their consequences for the production of good. Consequentialists regard **the Good as prior to the Right**. They identify the good (greatest utility) and claim that the right can only be identified by reference to it. Right action aims at the goal of producing good states of affairs. Since antiquity this understanding of morality has often been referred to as a teleological theory (see Chapter 2).

This conception of morality also underpins Bentham's understanding of law. Much of *An Introduction to the Principles of Morals and Legislation* is concerned with cataloguing the various offences and punishments that should form the content of law. These painstaking, and often tedious, passages are throughout informed by Bentham's belief that the legislator should be guided by the principle of utility.

> The happiness of the individuals, of whom a community is composed, is the end and the sole end which the legislator ought to have in view (PML: III, 1). The general object which all laws have, or ought to have, in common, is to augment the total happiness of the community; and . . . to exclude, as far as may be, everything that tends to subtract from that happiness (PML: XIII, 1).

The legislator's job is to pass laws that put in place punishments or sanctions that prevent by 'terror' the performance of 'mischievous acts' that diminish the general welfare (PML: VI, 45). Coercive laws and the fear of punishment that accompanies them are justified because the disutility of fear and coercion is outweighed by the utility of preventing bad things from happening. We have property laws which are used to imprison and punish thieves because allowing anybody to help themselves to the possessions of others would lead to widespread unhappiness. Each law must be justified by explicit reference to the general welfare and the punishment for law breakers must be just as much as is necessary to form an effective deterrent (PML: XIV, 1–28). This is a theory of legislation with very radical potential since it also implies that any law (or, by extension of this utilitarian understanding, any policy, principle or institution) that does not increase the general welfare is unjustified. The extent to which current law (policy and institutions) meets this utilitarian standard is an open question you might like to think about.

For our purposes Bentham's theory of legislation is important as it embodies a slightly more sophisticated approach to the consequentialism that is at the heart of utilitarianism. We can draw a distinction between **act utilitarianism** and **rule utilitarianism**. So far in this chapter we have been exploring a basic act utilitarian position whereby we assess the consequences of each act to be performed. However, if we each did complex utilitarian calculations before acting we may very well get round to doing nothing at all. Bentham recognises this and admits that 'it is not to be expected that this process should be strictly pursued previously to every moral judgement' but that it must be 'always kept in view', perhaps embodied in rules of thumb that we have found generally have good consequences (PML: IV, 4). Mill also recognised that secondary principles of this sort would be required in order to apply the fundamental principle of utility (Util: 276). Rule utilitarianism can be seen as a development of this approach. Instead of calculating the utility of the consequences of each act, a process that might actually have bad consequences (think of the time wasted and the possibility of individuals making poor judgements), it is possible to identify rules that, if generally observed, would tend to produce more utility than if there was no such rule at all. The usual example is a rule about promise-keeping. It is better (in the consequentialist terms of utility maximisation) to have a rule that everybody keep all their promises than not to have such a rule. If each of us were to calculate when it would be best to keep a promise then none of us could ever be sure that the promises made to us by others would be kept. As a result promise-keeping as an institution would break down and no promises would ever get made. Bentham's theory of legislation can be seen as a form of this rule utilitarian approach to calculating consequences. The legislator calculates whether the consequences of having a rule backed by the coercive power of the state would be better than allowing individuals to undertake their own utility calculations about the matter at hand. In this way we are likely to end up with rules or laws concerning promise-keeping, property and violence but not concerning what colour we paint our bedrooms or how long our hair can be. Rule utilitarianism is an attempt to capture the basic and intuitive appeal of the utilitarian concern with the actual consequences of actions for human welfare within a conception that recognises the most obvious time and resource constraints that we all act under. Following rules that are themselves justified by the principle of utility saves each of us the excessive time and superhuman effort that would be involved if we tried to calculate the consequences every time we made a decision. A rule utilitarian approach enables us think about maximising utility *indirectly* through the medium of what appear to be non-utilitarian rules, principles or laws. Most importantly, these seemingly non-utilitarian rules are themselves *directly* justified by the appeal to utility that Bentham claims should ultimately underpin every justification.

Utilitarianism has had a fruitful existence since its formulation by Bentham, with many theorists suggesting modifications or improvements to this basic utilitarian position. These modifications have focused on issues such as refining the definition of utility, on developing aspects of the act/rule or direct/indirect distinctions, on questions of the distribution of utility and on explorations and justifications of the extent to which utilitarianism matches or departs from conventional law and morality. Some of these later modifications will be broached at the appropriate points in the rest of the chapter, but it is enough for our purposes to recognise them as variations on a consequentialist theme rather than radical departures. Utilitarian ideas have been prominent for so long because the basic position has so many attractive features. As moral and political theories go it asks little of us in the way of basic assumptions. We are not asked to accept the existence of God or of Platonic Forms, nor that history culminates in a utilitarian society. Instead we can reflect on our own experiences and those of others and recognise that the experience of pleasure and pain is something real for all of us. Whilst not everyone accepts the same God or the same account of metaphysical reality everybody understands what it is to feel pain and pleasure. Utilitarianism removes the need to make unsubstantiable claims that go beyond human experience and which Bentham believes rest on no more than personal opinion. In contrast the utilitarian remains firmly within the constraints of human experience and holds out the possibility of humanity putting its own house in order. Good and bad consequences are reduced to their positive and negative utility values, which enables us, in principle, to calculate answers to moral and political questions. By identifying utility as a common denominator, standing for the pleasure and pain that everyone experiences, utilitarianism provides a counterpoint to concerns about relativism. Utility functions as an objective good since everyone values pleasure and the absence of pain. As such it provides an objective and universal standard for making moral and political decisions.

These decisions are made by reference to the balance of probable consequences of an action. The consequences may be taken into account on each occasion (act utilitarianism) or, perhaps more realistically, in the formulation of general rules that produce good consequences on the whole (rule utilitarianism). Either way, this consequentialism means that moral, legal and political decisions are made on the basis of their real impact on the lives of real people. Any rule or principle that makes people's lives go worse than they need go is illegitimate. One effect of this is that in any decision there will be a better and a worse course of action. Since utilitarianism directs us to always pursue the better consequences, and since one option will always be better than the other, for the utilitarian there will always be a right thing to do. There is always a right and rational answer to a dilemma, exchanging 'interminable discussion' for 'precision of thought' (OB: 85 & 91).

Human welfare and human interests are the foundation and driving force of utilitarianism. Those interests are taken into account impartially and equally. In calculating consequences we are directed not just to take into account our own utility but to impartially assess the impact of our actions on utility generally. Nor does utilitarian calculation recognise distinctions of status. Everybody's happiness is treated in the same way; in utilitarian calculations the pleasure and pain of the poorest and most marginalised members of society counts for as much as that of the richest and most important. No one person or group of persons occupies a privileged position in the calculative process and so utilitarianism can be viewed as the embodiment of impartial concern and the equal treatment of the interests of all. At this point you should take a moment to think about this basic utilitarian position. On an initial reading do you find it intuitively attractive?

Problems with utilitarianism

Despite the attractions of a utilitarian approach to moral and political questions it has encountered a great deal of criticism. These criticisms have been of two broad sorts; the first group centre on claims that utilitarianism underestimates moral complexity and the importance of pluralism whilst the second focus on the issue of moral boundaries. We can think about each of these in turn. There are a number of ways in which utilitarianism underestimates the complexity of moral issues. Firstly, there are problems with making the necessary interpersonal comparisons. Is making comparisons of utility between persons really as easy as utilitarianism claims? How do we know that when Jack claims to be very happy (that he is experiencing x amount of utility) he is feeling the same as when Holly claims to be similarly happy (she also is experiencing x rather than y units of utility)? We commonly speak of some people having lower pain thresholds than others. Is this because they experience the same pain but handle it differently or because they experience the pain differently? It may be that there is no metric for utility that applies across persons, no simple scale against which different people can reliably compare happiness. Beyond this there is the further concern with whether Jack and Holly, when engaged in the same activity, experience the same kind of pleasure. Is the sort of experience Holly has when eating her favourite food the same as Jack has when eating his, let alone the same as Jack has when playing his favourite music?

The basic utilitarian focus on pleasure also comes in for criticism. It might already have occurred to you that some pleasures may be better than others in ways that reflect more than just the quantity or intensity of the experience. Is the pleasure of watching soap operas, eating burgers or drinking large quantities of alcohol every weekend the same sort of pleasure as is derived from viewing great works of art, engaging in philosophy or bringing up happy children? Don't pleasures differ in their quality as well as their quantity and aren't better quality pleasures worth more? Bentham certainly didn't think so and famously claimed that pushpin (the eighteenth-century equivalent of pool or ten-pin bowling) was as good as poetry. This has seemed implausible to many people, including Mill. He argued that there are higher and lower pleasures, roughly equivalent to intellectual and physical pleasures, and that 'competent judges' that have experienced both consistently prefer the higher sort (Util: 258–61). This is because people value the exercise of their complex intellectual faculties over the experience of animal pleasures.

> It is better to be a human being dissatisfied than a pig satisfied; better to be Socrates dissatisfied than a fool satisfied. And if the fool, or the pig, are of a different opinion, it is because they only know their own side of the question (Util: 260).

Whether or not there is a coherent distinction to be drawn between types of pleasure, utilitarians face a strong challenge to the very claim that pleasure is what is important to us and is the 'spring of action' that Bentham describes. Robert Nozick asks us to imagine a machine into which we could be plugged that would directly stimulate the pleasure centres of the brain whilst we float in a tank (Nozick 1974: 42–5). Given that we are supposed to be motivated by the pursuit of maximised pleasure we must ask ourselves whether we would sign up to spend our entire lives in such a 'pleasure machine'. Would you choose to live your life in this way? Do you think many people would? Perhaps it is not pleasure that is of fundamental importance but something else, perhaps the experience of the activities from which pleasure is derived? Note that even making this move is a radical departure from Bentham's or Mill's utilitarianism (higher pleasures are still pleasures after all). But even this move may not help. Perhaps more sophisticated scientists invent an 'experience machine' that could reproduce in your brain the experience of doing whatever you choose. This machine could allow you to experience swimming with dolphins, walking on the moon or dating celebrities in ways which are indistinguishable from the experiences and memories of the things you have actually done. Would this make a difference? Would you now choose to spend your life in such a machine, blissfully happy and with a life more full of wonderful experiences than anyone has ever lived? Perhaps some of us would choose this life, though it is more likely that some of us might choose it for a holiday from time to time. Either way, it is probable that most people would resist this choice. The utilitarian has to face the problem that it does not seem that pleasure as such, or even the broader category of rewarding experiences, is what we regard as most important or valuable. Even more recent attempts to modify the utilitarian understanding of utility in terms of preference satisfaction rather than pleasure may be vulnerable to arguments featuring more sophisticated machines. Just as became clear when we discussed interpersonal comparisons, people's interests may resist reduction to any single common denominator. They may instead reflect a plurality of concerns that require a more complex approach to moral and political questions. People may just value a whole load of different things and it may not be possible to account for this pluralism under the umbrella of a single value, however utility is defined.

These problems are compounded by our second set of criticisms, those focused on consequentialism and the question of moral boundaries. Though the prime concern of utilitarianism is human welfare many critics have pointed out that this concern shows itself in strange ways. Utilitarian calculations seem capable of justifying a whole range of actions that strike us as immoral or unjust. Imagine that there is a vicious serial killer on the streets of a major city, bringing terror to the lives of thousands of people and proving difficult to catch. The police may be justified, in utilitarian terms, in picking up an innocent vagrant, rigging a trial and executing him, rather than continuing to fruitlessly pursue the real killer. The pleasure that thousands (perhaps millions) feel as a result of their belief that they are more secure may outweigh the pain of the vagrant. Likewise, the shortage of organ donors could be met by using the organs of people that no one will mourn. Each childless criminal or unwanted orphan may nobly save the lives of many others. Perhaps these others are important cancer researchers, or children at the heart of large and loving families. Especially if the practice were hidden from public view, this course of action may very well increase overall utility. General utility may also be increased in other counter-intuitive ways. Perhaps the happiness of the overwhelming majority could be maintained at a higher level if the minority were viciously exploited as slaves, allowing the majority to live a life of luxury. Or, in a state ethnically divided between one large and one small ethnic group, utility may be maximised if the state apparatus is used to systematically discriminate against the minority culture. What makes these examples particularly telling is the way that utilitarianism does not take these decisions with regret but, as they maximise utility, would seem to celebrate the sacrifice of innocents and the persecution of minorities as the morally right and just thing to do in each situation. Utilitarianism faces further problems when we realise how it treats certain sorts of experiences. We would normally disregard as irrelevant to moral judgement the pleasure that a torturer gets when torturing their victim or that the rapist gets from their assault. We normally think of these pleasures as illegitimate preferences. However, the utilitarian is committed to counting them on the positive side of any calculation, treating them in the same way as they treat the pleasure you might get from eating ice cream. Whilst the utilitarian would think that the pain of the victim outweighs the pleasure of the attacker something still does not seem right with this. Should the attacker's pleasurable sensations be thought to mitigate the badness of their crime in any way? Especially if you think about how the sums might balance if the torturer invites enough of his bloodthirsty friends round to watch, thus adding to the positive utility of the act.

The utilitarian response to these sorts of criticisms has most often been to point out that a rule utilitarian calculation would not give these results. Rule utilitarianism would justify rules against violence, the execution of innocents and the persecution of minorities on the grounds that, if generally performed, these acts would diminish utility. However, we must remember that the justification of the rule itself is the maximisation of utility. If for any given action it could be shown that breaking the rule in this case would maximise utility but not endanger the rule's general support (perhaps it could be broken in secret) then the utilitarian has to acknowledge that the rule should be broken. In fact instead of a rule such as 'always do *x*' the utilitarian would support a new rule, 'always do *x* except when circumstances are such as to make not doing *x* the better option'. This is equivalent to doing what will maximise utility for each action. If pushed, rule utilitarianism appears to collapse into act utilitarianism. They appear to be the same thing, and so equally vulnerable to the criticisms we have raised. If we can show the rule utilitarian that executing an innocent man would maximise utility on this occasion, and assure them that it could be done secretly so that no one loses faith in the judicial system, then they would have to think execution justified. Alternative utilitarian strategies such as maximising the average utility across a population rather than the total utility fare no better. Average utility might easily be increased by persecution of a small minority; if the benefits to the majority are large enough this would pull the average up even if some fare badly. These criticisms point to what may be a general problem for consequentialist theories. Any theory that bases moral judgements *solely* on the consequences of an action will make judgements that we feel uncomfortable with. For consequentialists the ends literally justify the means. Since Bentham in particular, and consequentialists more generally, define moral terms by reference to the good then conventional morality can place no limitations on the pursuit of that good. If you find consequentialism attractive you will just have to bite the bullet here.

Utilitarianism is an individualist theory. Individuals experience pleasure and pain, they undertake utilitarian calculations and societies are regarded as collections of individuals. As an individual calculates their own utility they weigh one pleasure against another or decide whether to endure a sacrifice now for the benefit of greater future pleasure. This is all very well, we each perform this balancing act between pains and pleasures every day, but utilitarianism seems to treat the community as if it can do likewise. It is as if the community calculates what balance of pains and pleasures is good and acts accordingly.

> But there is no *social entity* with a good that undergoes some sacrifice for its own good. There are only individual people . . . with their own individual lives. Using one of these people for the benefit of others, uses him and benefits the others. Nothing more . . . Talk of an overall social good covers this up. (Nozick 1974: 32–3)

When an individual accepts a loss now in order to achieve a gain then the same individual loses as gains. But there is no social entity to lose and gain for the utilitarian. As an individualist they must accept that when one person loses out so that another person can gain then different entities are affected. If society is just a collection of individuals why should some be sacrificed for others?

The central problem here, and with the anti-intuitive consequentialist results we noted earlier, is that utilitarianism appears to license trade-offs, the sacrifice of one person for the benefit of another. Utilitarianism blurs what we ordinarily think of as important moral boundaries between people. In aggregating the interests of everybody, mixing them into one big pot, the fact that they are the interests of different people is forgotten. In this way everybody's interests are taken into account but in the processes of aggregation and maximisation individuals are treated not as the originators of interests but as vessels for utility. What matters is not whether decisions are in all our interests but how to maximise the experience of pleasure. If this means sacrificing some for others then so be it. Critics claim that utilitarian decision-making ignores the 'separateness of persons', 'that there are different individuals with separate lives' and that the life of one should not be outweighed by the interests of others (Nozick 1974: 33; Rawls 1999: 25). Rights theorists draw attention to what they claim are moral boundaries between people in order to demonstrate that what is wrong with utilitarianism is that it lacks any proper conception of individual **rights**. Whilst Mill does have a theory of rights, it is justified consequentially by general utility and may not escape the criticisms of rule utilitarianism made above (Util: 309). The concerns outlined in this section might lead us to conclude that utilitarianism is an inappropriate method of taking people's interests into account and that what is needed is a theory that will safeguard the moral boundaries between people. Uneasiness with the possible outcome of utilitarian calculation points us in this direction. It is not that utilitarianism has any sort of predisposition towards acts that we would usually regard as immoral transgressions of boundaries between people, just that there is nothing within the theory that rules such actions out. This is the role that individual rights are supposed to fulfil.

Rights as boundaries

Individual rights are the most common and important way of understanding boundaries between people. They are thought of as boundaries that limit both other people's actions in pursuit of their interests as well as the legitimate actions of government. Rights have been conceived of as 'trumps', special cards held by individuals that overrule or 'trump' concerns of the common good, general welfare or government policy (Dworkin 1977: xi). Rights therefore depend on a conception of right action that directly opposes the basic consequentialist claim of utilitarianism, that right action aims at the good. Recall that, for Bentham, right action was defined as that which maximised utility. However, the moral complexity we have already briefly considered provides support for the claims of rights theorists that there is not one single thing called 'the good' that all action should aim at. Instead there is a plurality of different people who want different, and perhaps incompatible, things. Instead of attempting to reduce everybody's interests to a single interest in utility or pleasure, theories of rights recognise that these interests constitute a plurality of goods, each of which is likely to be pursued in different ways by different people. By denying that there is a single good that should be the focus for social concern theories of rights undercut the consequentialist justification of trade-offs between people, where the experience of the good of some is sacrificed for a greater experience of that good by others. Whilst utilitarian individuals are regarded as the means through which the end (utility maximisation) is pursued rights theories, inspired by Kantian terminology, regard human beings as 'ends in themselves' and not as merely the means to some other end. This means that individuals, and not just their experiences, are the object of moral concern, and that individual integrity is paramount. It is because each individual is a separate object of moral concern that rights theories have such a high regard for the 'separateness of persons' and are focused on the moral boundaries that prevent trade-offs between individuals. For theories of rights, individuals matter as individuals and not as vessels for the experience of the good.

Denying that there is a single object of moral concern and recognising that there are many individuals in the world, each with their own conception of the good, rights theories are all about securing for them the space in which to pursue that good. Each separate person is conceived of as having, consciously or unconsciously, a conception of the good that may be personal or may be shared with many others (as in the case of Catholicism for example). That is, they each have an understanding of the social and natural worlds around them, of their place in those worlds and of the appropriate moral, religious or philosophical beliefs to hold. Rights are the way in which the boundaries between people are conceptualised so as to make the space for individuals to act on their conceptions of the good. In this way rights theories reverse the consequentialist understanding of the relationship between the right and the good. Instead of the good being prior to the right, which is then defined in terms of that good, theories of rights generally regard **the Right as prior to the Good**. Right and wrong actions are defined in reference to individual rights which constrain the pursuit of the good. Individuals are regarded as free to pursue their good, and governments the common good, in so far as they do not infringe on the rights of others. The consequentialist categorises actions as only either right or wrong. Any particular action either maximises the good and is right or doesn't and is wrong. We are obliged at all times to act rightly so as always to maximise the good. Theories of rights also recognise the categories of right and wrong action. Right actions are those we must perform in order to *respect* rights, such as taking care where I throw my knife. Wrong actions are those that *violate* rights, such as putting my knife into the back of someone who annoys me. However, theories of rights also recognise a third category of action, permitted actions. Permitted actions are neither right nor wrong as they are not necessary to respect rights but they do not violate rights either. As an individual in pursuit of her good Holly is free, or permitted, to do all sorts of things such as attend religious ceremonies, go shopping, play in a rock band or take a job teaching philosophy at university. In these decisions Holly is free to make her own choices, constrained only by the rights of others and not by a never-ending obligation to maximise the common utility. In his most famous work, *On Liberty*, Mill shared this vision of individuals pursuing their own interests within a sphere of liberty, free from the interference of government or other individuals (OL: 137–8). However, since this is justified on consequentialist grounds (OL: 136) the existence of this sphere of liberty is contingent on considerations of maximal utility. If Mill conceives of these moral boundaries around individuals as constraints beyond any violation that is justified by considerations of general utility then his theory ceases to be utilitarian at all. In fact Mill is clear in *Utilitarianism* that rights are indeed justified by general utility and, as such, they are vulnerable if circumstances change and the calculations work out differently, no matter how rarely he thinks this will happen (Util: 309, 314, 318–21). In contrast Nozick characterises rights as side-constraints on action. Instead of the consequentialist understanding of rights, 'do not violate constraint C unless the consequences justify it', Nozick argues that rights take the form 'don't violate constraint C' (Nozick 1974: 28–9). 'Individuals have rights, and there are things no person or group may do to them (Ibid.: ix).' Rights should not be violated, whatever the benefits of doing so on this particular occasion. Likewise, Ronald Dworkin claims that rights 'trump' consequentialist reasoning (Dworkin 1977: xi, 368). Theories of rights are therefore non-consequentialist and also **deontological** as they prioritise the right over the good. Rights provide a *framework for liberty* and choice that is supposed to be impartial between individuals and neutral between conceptions of the good. Instead of aggregating people's interests together and satisfying as many as is possible, theories of rights recognise certain fundamental interests we all have, in personal security for example, and accordingly distribute protective rights to each of us. Because of the separateness of persons interests are not aggregated but instead the means of pursuing our interests are distributed to each of us equally in the form of rights.

Having briefly outlined the broad conceptual contrasts between utilitarianism and rights we can now talk a closer look at rights themselves. One way to help us think about rights is to consider their relationship with obligations. My freedoms to use a phonebox, to swim in the sea and to get my hair cut can be thought of as rights but no one is under an obligation to meet those rights. Ordinarily, no particular person is obliged to cut my hair, vacate a phonebox for me or take me to the seaside. As we saw in Chapters 3 and 4, Thomas Hobbes thinks that all rights are like this. For Hobbes we have a right to everything but no one is under any obligation to respect these rights, they are liberty rights that everyone has with no accompanying or *correlative* obligations in others. Most rights theorists disagree with Hobbes and identify rights to which there are correlative obligations. Recall that John Locke, for example, believed that my right to life is partnered with a moral obligation on every other individual not to murder me. We usually think of rights in this way as identifying obligations in other people to behave in certain ways towards me, or to provide me with certain services. My right to have my salary paid imposes an obligation on a particular employer to pay me, my right to a fair trial imposes obligations on the judicial system to provide legal representation and a jury of my peers and my property rights impose obligations on each and every other person in the world not to sleep on my front-room floor without an invitation. To complete the picture, there may also be obligations that are not correlative to rights. For example, many people feel under an obligation to give to charity but this does not establish a right in any particular person or charitable organisation that the money be given to them. These obligations are often referred to as 'imperfect obligations', in contrast to 'perfect obligations' that are correlative to rights.

The question of exactly what particular rights individuals have is a complex one. We have seen that for Locke, and the same goes for Nozick, we each have rights to life, liberty and property. The US Declaration of Independence recognises inalienable rights to life, liberty and the pursuit of happiness. A number of philosophers, Rawls and Dworkin amongst them, would include a right to at least adequate resources such as income and health care. The United Nations, in their Universal Declaration of Human Rights, outlined the basic rights anyone should be entitled to have respected. The UN also went on to adopt several specific conventions regarding, amongst other things, rights against torture and genocide as well as covenants detailing civil and political rights and economic, social and cultural rights. Chapter 7 will examine economic rights whilst Chapter 8 will explore the hotly contested question of whether groups or cultures, as well as individuals, can be bearers of rights. Why not take a moment to think about the range of basic rights that you think people have and that you would claim for yourself before you read these chapters? Perhaps the arguments addressed will cause you to reflect on, and modify, your initial thoughts.

Here we have only the space to briefly explore several important and related distinctions concerning broad categories of rights. One of the most important distinctions is between legal rights and moral rights and these are distinguishable in terms of their justifications. Legal rights are identified and justified by their pedigree. Jack can be said to have a legal right if a law, having passed through the appropriate legislative process, confers that right on him. In this way Jack might have the right to vote in regular elections or the right to paid holidays from work. Moral rights are rights that people should have whether or not they are generally recognised and, as we shall see, they have been justified in a range of different ways. Obviously, many legal rights, such as the right not to be attacked, are also widely regarded as moral rights. Likewise, with the increasing focus on rights in international law and, for example, European law many moral rights are gaining a legal status. Still, the idea of a moral right helps to make sense of the thought, behind anti-apartheid, civil-rights and gay-rights movements for example, that the law may be unjust as it fails to recognise rights that we ought to have. Cutting across this distinction is another, between general and special rights (Hart 1967). General rights are those that everyone has and are often referred to as natural or human rights. They are abstract and universal rights. Special rights are those that we have only because we are in a special relationship with particular people. Legal rights are overwhelmingly special rights. We have them against specific people and a particular state as a result of living in a particular jurisdiction and of our relationship to those other people as fellow citizens. Some moral rights are also special rights. Special moral rights may be created when Jack makes a promise to Holly. This gives Holly a specific moral right against Jack that he fulfil his promise. Similarly we may each derive special moral rights from contracts entered into or as a result of being born, the correlative obligations falling on our parents. Special rights are rights against particular people or groups of people and are therefore always local and particular rather than universal.

Whilst some moral rights are conventional, deliberately created by human beings through promises and contracts, others are thought to stand in need of further justification. We have already seen that Locke thought our rights ultimately derived from God's creation of us and the natural law that governs our actions. There are also arguments in Locke, likewise attributed to Nozick, that base our human rights on our self-ownership. As I have property rights in my own body (who else would have them) then, just as with any other piece of property I own, only I am entitled to decide what happens to it. From this foundation moral rights protecting life and liberty can be derived. Hobbes finds our rights in nature, where we have no superior to create and enforce law, justice or morality. As a consequence no one can legitimately deny that we have a right to everything. Rights might also be thought of as rational constraints on action given the circumstances of pluralism, or as guaranteeing the conditions in which the autonomy necessary for individuals' freedom to pursue their interests can flourish. More recently, John Rawls has argued that rights are constructed as part of a hypothetical contract. He asks us to imagine a situation, he calls it the 'original position', where a group of people attempt to agree on the principles that will govern their social co-operation. In order to eliminate bias and ensure fairness Rawls places the contractors behind a 'veil of ignorance' that prevents them from knowing morally arbitrary facts that would enable them to unfairly tailor the principles to their own benefit. For example, the contractors would not know whether they were rich or poor, male or female, black or white, intelligent or stupid. In this original position of equality Rawls claims that the contractors would at least agree to a range of equal civil and political rights and liberties. That these are the rights that would be agreed to by all persons in a position of fairness and equality is a strong reason for us to regard them as moral rights held by each of us (Rawls 1999: 10–19).

Whatever the most appropriate justification of moral rights, Dworkin claims that 'anyone who professes to take rights seriously . . . must accept one or both of two important ideas'. The first of these is the 'vague but powerful idea of human dignity'. Drawing on the Kantian claim that people are ends in themselves and not means to the ends of others Dworkin claims that the idea of human dignity 'supposes that there are ways of treating a man that are inconsistent with recognising him as a full member of the human community, and holds that such treatment is profoundly unjust' (Dworkin 1977: 198). The second idea that may underpin rights is the idea of political equality. 'This supposes that the weaker members of a political community are entitled to the same concern and respect . . . as the more powerful members (Ibid.: 198–9).' These ideas of basic human dignity and political equality embody the further idea of a fundamental moral entitlement to equal concern and respect due to each and every person 'not by virtue of birth or characteristic or merit or excellence but simply as human beings' (Ibid.: 182, 368). These are powerful ideas. If treating everybody with equal concern and respect involves treating them as if they have rights then this would constitute a very strong support for rights.

Problems with rights

Just as we explored an attractive utilitarian position only to find possible flaws so we must look closely for flaws in theories of rights. Firstly, theories of rights, like utilitarianism, face a problem when it comes to identifying the scope of moral concern. Recall that utilitarianism seemed to have too *inclusive* a scope so that it had trouble capturing the human character of morality. Since pain and pleasure are the only ground of moral concern, and animals suffer in the same way as people, surely animal welfare is on a par with human welfare? Rights theories that regard rights as something we have simply by virtue of our humanity have a similar problem explaining why humans should be singled out for special treatment. Most theories of rights, however, are potentially too *exclusive*, ruling out people we usually think of as rights bearers. This is because they justify rights in terms of human autonomy or rationality, for example. The potential exclusivity becomes clear when we realise that newborn infants, the senile, people in a coma (or perhaps just asleep) are not capable of autonomous or rational action, or of exercising reciprocal moral respect. In this way they may slip through the net of moral concern and end up being regarded as a part of the non-human animal kingdom.

Secondly, and more importantly, Bentham acknowledges that there may be legitimate rights but points out that these can only be legal rights, not natural or moral rights. He is clear that law can create rights but also believes that law is the *only* creator of rights. If there was a state of nature in prehistory then there was 'no government, consequently no rights' since rights are dependent on a judicial system. Any appeal to '*natural rights* is simple nonsense . . . nonsense upon stilts' (AF: 405). Bentham is clear that a lack of government and rights would lead to great unhappiness and that therefore

> a reason exists for wishing that there were such things as rights. But reasons for wishing there were such things as rights, are not rights; – a reason for wishing that a certain right were established, is not that right – want is not supply – hunger is not bread (AF: 405).

Since all rights are legal rights that depend on law, and this argument aims at any non-legal understanding of rights as moral rights, the only rights we have are those that we are given by the state. This is not to say that utilitarians do not recognise prior moral claims of the form '*x ought* to be a right.' Utilitarianism can accept that where there is no right there should be one, and that such a right is morally justified. However, the moral reasons that justify the creation of a right are themselves based on considerations of utility. In this way there can be both legal rights and moral reasons explaining why certain legal rights should be created, but not moral rights themselves.

This utilitarian understanding of rights as based on moral claims that derive from utility is open to the objections raised above concerning the way such rights can be legitimately overridden in trade-offs. Because rights are simply instrumentally justified as means of maximising utility they lack an absolute character. We have so far treated this as a problem but are things this clear? If rights are absolute then they are also inflexible. Bernard Williams asks us to imagine that a number of Indian villagers are to be shot by a firing squad but, since Jim is an honoured guest, if Jim shoots one Indian himself then the others will be released as a mark of respect (Smart & Williams 1973: 98). If Jim regards as absolute the right of the single Indian not to be killed by him then the other Indians will die. We may regrettably accept this outcome if the total number of Indians is two or three, agreeing that Jim should not violate rights. However, the Williams example has twenty Indians involved and what if the numbers are greater? Should Jim refuse to violate the rights of one person even if this results in the death of one hundred, or one thousand, or ten thousand? The utilitarian point (although Williams is not arguing in favour of utilitarianism) is that if rights are absolute then no matter how large the number of deaths that result Jim should never shoot the Indian. Surely, utilitarians argue, this is just stubbornness taken to absurd lengths. There must be some number of deaths for which it would be the right thing to do to shoot the Indian. If human beings are important then surely our moral theories cannot be this inflexible. The absolute character of rights would result in more violations of the very rights that are supposed to be absolute. Instead, rights must be treated flexibly, enabling us to minimise rights violations by occasionally sanctioning a violation of rights if this is morally justified. Some theories of rights recognise that rights should not always triumph over concerns of utility (Dworkin 1977: 191–2). However, once we admit that if we could avert a thousand deaths we should cause one then the utilitarian can seize on this. If a thousand for one is justifiable then why not a hundred for one, or ten for one, or two for one? As Bentham notes, 'there is no right which, when the abolition of it is advantageous . . . should not be abolished'

(AF: 405–6). Surely if we can avert moral disasters then rights must be violated and rules broken; what, then, is wrong with trade-offs in those circumstances when standing on rights seems unjustifiable? . . . Smart goes so far as to claim that

> the chief persuasive argument in favour of utilitarianism has been that the dictates of any deontological ethics [e.g. theories of rights] will always, on some occasions, lead to the existence of misery that could, on utilitarian principles, have been prevented (Smart & Williams 1973: 62).

There is no easy answer here. Assuming that we have rights, the question of whether and when they should be violated is a difficult and complex issue. You should consider whether and where you might draw the line, and then try to work out what that might mean in different circumstances.

As well as there perhaps being a problem with trade-offs there may also be reason to think again about the utilitarian treatment of minorities. Recall that utilitarianism was accused of not treating people properly as it might allow the majority's interests to outweigh the minority's, that the interests of one per cent might be sacrificed for the benefit of ninety-nine per cent. The utilitarian response would draw attention to the way in which, when rights block consequentialist reasoning, the interests of the majority are sacrificed to the minority. Theories of rights sacrifice the interests of ninety-nine per cent of the population for the benefit of one per cent. How is this justifiable if people's interests are to be taken seriously? Rather than allowing minorities to sabotage the common good, utilitarianism might be seen as the moral equivalent of democracy. Just as in democratic processes, each person's interest/vote is aggregated together, the majority decision carries the day and the minority, who enter the process knowing that they may not get their preferred option, should accept the will of the majority. A vote, like utility, is a common denominator into which people's interests are converted. Each individual is then equally counted as one and only one and so each is shown equal concern and respect. Why then should the outcome of this aggregative process not be generally accepted? Why should some individuals' interests weigh disproportionately heavily so as to block the outcome that meets the interests of most individuals? Surely, so the argument goes, it is utilitarianism and not theories of rights that take the individual seriously?

Conclusions

Utilitarianism and theories of rights understand the relationship between the good and the right in different ways. The utilitarian understanding is consequentialist: the good is prior to the right. Right actions, indeed standards of right and wrong in general, are identified and justified by reference to a predefined understanding of the good. For utilitarians this good is utility, usually understood in terms of pleasure and pain, and the proper consequentialist response to this good is to maximise it. Utilitarian rights are therefore instrumental in the pursuit of maximised good. As such they are always provisional, potentially overridden by consequentialist reasoning depending on circumstances. Rights are recognised and respected only 'so long as it is upon the whole advantageous to . . . society' (AF: 405–6). Theories of rights reverse this understanding: the right is prior to the good. Rights are not instrumentally justified and are instead defined separately from the good, which itself is usually understood as a plurality of conceptions of the good pursued by different individuals. Rights are understood to frame our individual and communal pursuits of interests and thus to constrain consequentialist reasoning. Theories of rights do not deny that there is a place for consequentialist reasoning in, for example, the formation of government policy where general welfare is an important concern. It is just that such policy deliberations have to take as given the rights that individuals legitimately hold and formulate policy that respects rather than violates rights (Dworkin 1977: 90–1). Theories of rights usually embody a conception of limited government. Recognising that almost all government action is ultimately coercive, rights delimit a sphere of legitimate government action. Government must work within the framework of certain constraining principles. This is, in the opinion of advocates of rights, 'the one feature that distinguishes law from ordered brutality. If the Government does not take rights seriously, then it does not take law seriously either' (Ibid.: 205).

For the utilitarian, on the other hand, rights cannot be ultimately considered as limits on legitimate action but only as rules of thumb that tend to coincide with maximising utility. As such, utilitarianism appears to adopt a conception of unlimited government, where neither right nor law itself can stand in the way of maximising utility. Of course, utilitarians can and do argue in favour of limited government. They might do so on the grounds that governments are, on the whole, far more efficient at preventing pain than they are at producing pleasure, or that pain weighs more heavily than pleasure in utilitarian calculation.

This sort of *negative utilitarianism* concentrates on limiting the ways in which governments and people can impact negatively on the general welfare. In principle, however, these limits cannot be absolute; if the consequences for welfare look to be good enough any limit, right or law can be set aside.

Competing understandings of the relationship between the right and the good underpin two competing understandings of concepts such as individualism, equality, and impartiality. These combine into two opposing answers to the question 'how do you take people seriously?'. People and their interests are conceptualised in competing ways, as is the proper response to their interests. Should we regard all interests in the same way so that taking people's interests seriously involves a process of aggregation? Every individual is treated equally and impartially in this process. Everyone counts as only one and no one's interests have a privileged status. Everybody has the same input into moral decisions and those decisions reflect the status of all individuals as equal objects of moral concern. Alternatively, are there certain things that it is always immoral to do to anyone, ways of treating people that are inconsistent with regarding them as fully human and protection from which should be enshrined in a theory of rights? Rights depend on an understanding of interests at odds with utilitarianism. Instead of all interests being reducible to the same sort of thing, certain interests that we each have should be regarded as fundamental and in need of protection. These are the interests that inform the idea of the 'separateness of persons', interests of security, liberty and the individual's pursuit of her own and distinctive conception of the good. These interests are fundamental to a proper understanding of the importance of individuals and should not be outweighed by any combination of less important concerns.

This chapter is not supposed to provide you with the answer to questions about what taking people seriously involves. Instead we have only been able to explore two of the most important recent understandings of the form such answers must take. In reading this chapter you have hopefully had to stop and think several times about what approach you find convincing. It may be that you have changed your mind as the chapter progressed, perhaps more than once. This is as it should be. These are complex issues and answers are not straightforward. We explored a range of strong criticisms of utilitarianism that highlight the ways in which trade-offs it licenses clash with our ordinary understanding of morality. You need to consider whether to bite the bullet at this point. Perhaps conventional morality is wrong?

After all, if it could give us clearly acceptable answers we would have no reason to think critically or philosophically about morality. Utilitarianism is a systematic and normative account of morality whilst conventional understanding may be nothing more than a combination of custom, superstition and religious feeling. What, after all, is so obviously wrong about trade-offs? Surely it is right to sacrifice one to save a thousand and utilitarianism provides us with the resources to make these difficult moral decisions. Alternatively, you could take conventional moral misgivings about utilitarianism as pointers towards a more adequate moral theory of rights. Most of us think that we have rights, and are certainly ready to claim them when our persons or interests are threatened. Should we then be arguing about what rights we have and what those rights entail rather than whether we have rights in the first place? You should now be able at least to think in an informed way about how to make a judgement between a theory of rights and biting the utilitarian bullet.

Topics for discussion

1. Is it possible to reduce all human interests to a single currency?
2. Is it ever right to trade off the interests of some against those of others? If there are times when it is not right to do so, why not?
3. Are all rights special rights?
4. Are all rights important? Are some more important than others? You might like to look at the United Nations Universal Declaration of Human Rights, the International Covenant on Economic, Social and Cultural Rights and the International Covenant on Civil and Political Rights in this discussion.
5. How wide is the scope of morality? Does it include only humans? All humans?

Critical glossary

Utility — Literally those things that are of use to human beings. In utilitarianism it usually refers to pleasure, happiness or preference satisfaction.

Consequentialism	The view that all actions can be considered right or wrong by reference to the value of their consequences.
The Good as prior to the Right	The idea that principles of justice are identified by reference to a general account of the good (value) or the good life for human beings.
Act utilitarianism	The political theory that claims that each and every act must be assessed in terms of its consequences for the maximisation of utility.
Rule utilitarianism	In contrast to act utilitarianism, the theory that utility maximisation is better served by the institution of general rules of conduct that constrain individual action, themselves justified by reference to utility.
Rights	Constraints on conduct that are based on an understanding that there are ways of treating a person that can never be justified and are therefore always unjust.
The Right as prior to the Good	The claim that right principles of justice can be identified independently of any conception of the good life. This claim is generally part of a deontological view.
Deontological	Deontological views hold that moral conduct is justified without reference to its consequences, either in terms of the satisfaction of individual interest or of the realisation of a greater good.

List of references/Further reading

Primary texts

AF Bentham, J. (2001), *Anarchical Fallacies*, in *Selected Writings on Utilitarianism*, Ware: Wordsworth Editions (first published in 1843).

FOG Bentham, J. (2001), *A Fragment on Government*, in *Selected Writings on Utilitarianism*, Ware: Wordsworth Editions (first published 1776). References are to chapter and paragraph.

OB Mill, J. S. (1962), *Essay on Bentham*, in J. S. Mill, *Utilitarianism, On Liberty, Essay on Bentham*, ed. M. Warnock, Glasgow: Fontana (first published in 1838).

OL Mill, J. S. (1962), *On Liberty*, in J. S. Mill, *Utilitarianism, On Liberty, Essay on Bentham*, ed. M. Warnock, Glasgow: Fontana (first published in 1859).

PML Bentham, J. [1789] (1982), *An Introduction to the Principles of Morals and Legislation*, ed. J. H. Burns & H. L. A. Hart, London & New York: Methuen. References are to chapter and paragraph.

Util Mill, J. S. (1962), *Utilitarianism*, in J. S. Mill, *Utilitarianism, On Liberty, Essay on Bentham*, ed. M. Warnock, Glasgow: Fontana (first published in 1861).

References

Dworkin, R. (1977), *Taking Rights Seriously*, London: Duckworth.

Hart, H. L. A. (1967), 'Are There Any Natural Rights?', in A. Quinton (ed.), *Political Philosophy*, Oxford: Oxford University Press, pp. 53–66.

Nozick, R. (1974), *Anarchy, State, and Utopia*, Oxford: Blackwell.

Rawls, J. [1971] (1999), *A Theory of Justice*, Oxford: Oxford University Press.

Smart, J. J. C. & Williams, B. (1973), *Utilitarianism: For and Against*, Cambridge: Cambridge University Press.

Secondary literature

Jones, P. (1994), *Rights*, London: Macmillan.

Scarre, G. (1996), *Utilitarianism*, London: Routledge.

CHAPTER SEVEN

HISTORICAL

Rawls, Cohen, Nozick and Walzer

CONCEPTUAL

Distributive Justice

Is it right that some people are so badly off when others are very well off? Why should some people have more than enough resources to meet their needs whilst others are struggling to meet theirs? Even more to the point, why should some people have enough to buy a yacht, keep four cars on the road, eat in exclusive restaurants or have cosmetic surgery whilst others cannot afford a house, the bus fare to the supermarket, nutritious food for the family or essential medical treatment? Questions like these have motivated a large number of both political theorists and political activists. It is likely that these questions have occurred to you at some time, although you may have dismissed them with an answer like 'that's just the way things are'. However, when great disparities exist between rich and poor it is difficult not to either question the justice of the situation or feel that we have to offer reasons in justification of such inequality. Perhaps there are not enough resources to go round and if only things were different then everybody could have as much as they wanted and no one need go without. Some answer of this sort is implicit in the vision of a future communist society that we encountered in Chapter 5. Karl Marx believed that the revolution would free up man's true productive potential and scarcity would no longer be a problem. In this post-scarcity situation resources would be plentiful, distributed according to need, and everyone's needs would be met. Is 'there is not enough to go round' the only type of answer available to us? Might it not be that we do not live in conditions of absolute scarcity (after all, some people appear to have more than enough)? Instead we may be faced with relative scarcity, a situation where, although there are not enough resources for everybody to have everything they want, there are adequate resources to ensure that everyone has enough. If this is the case then the rich person suggesting to his poor neighbours, as a reason for their deprivation, that there is not enough to go round may rightly be regarded with suspicion. Whether better reasons for inequality are available, or whether no such justification can be given, will be explored in the course of this chapter.

Living together in societies produces benefits for the members of a society but also creates burdens for them. Benefits include amongst other things the increased production that social co-operation makes possible, greater security, increased community and companionship and access to legal and political institutions. Burdens include limiting our actions so that we do not impinge unjustly on fellow citizens, obligations to society (e.g. jury service) and payment of taxes. Questions of **distributive justice** are questions about how we should distribute the benefits and burdens of social co-operation across society. Some theorists, for example John Rawls, believe that currently the poor have more than their fair share of the burdens whilst the rich have the lion's share of the benefits. Other theorists such as Robert Nozick claim that there is nothing necessarily unjust about poverty whilst redistribution to combat that poverty would place illegitimate burdens on the wealthy. These questions are important political questions rather than just economic ones for two reasons. Firstly, they are political because the distribution of resources concerns the state. Not only is the state often the agent that distributes benefits and burdens in the form of education, health services, police and courts and taxation, but the property rights and entitlements this distribution creates are backed by the coercive power of the state. Anyone who claims that inequality in resources is justified is usually also claiming that the state should protect the unequal property rights through the police and judicial system. Anyone who claims that a redistribution of resources is necessary in the cause of equality is usually also claiming that the state should tailor its taxation and spending plans to achieve this. Secondly, this is not just a question of economics, because the impact of inequality can be devastating for people's lives. Poverty leads to immense suffering and the knowledge that society is standing by and letting you suffer may also encourage you to think of yourself as a second-class citizen. On the other hand the redistribution of resources may involve large-scale restrictions on the rights and freedoms of those whose resources are being redistributed. Either way these are issues that are unavoidably political. It is not true that the poor are simply poor and the rich simply rich and the state does nothing but react to this fact. Politics and political institutions form the frameworks within which people become rich and poor. The political environment shapes the economic and social lives of its citizens. Questions of distributive justice very quickly become questions of what sort of state is justified, or of what sort of state we want. Do we want a state that limits freedom so that it can control the production and distribution of resources in order to ensure **equality**? Or do we want a state that protects property rights even against the starving? Between these extremes are any number of possible forms of state. It is important that we recognise that what we think about equality is going to influence what we think about the state.

But things are not as simple as this. Neither the state nor the economy *cause* the rich to be rich and the poor to be poor. Sometimes people are well off because they have made sacrifices and worked very hard. Likewise, some people are not so well off because they have been lazy or did not do well at school. Perhaps they invested badly, spent instead of saved or lacked necessary entrepreneurial skills. If Holly works hard and watches the pennies whilst Jack is lazy and spends everything he has on going to the theatre then perhaps Holly deserves the benefits she accrues. It may be that people should take responsibility for their place in society instead of blaming others or looking to the state for help. People make choices and Jack's choices have led to him being in the position that he is in. We ordinarily regard people as responsible for their choices. That is why we ask them for reasons to justify their behaviour or attitudes; we assume that they could have behaved differently and hold them responsible for choosing the course of action that they eventually followed. Instead of always buying the best seats in the house Jack could take cheaper seats, go to the theatre less often or take up an inexpensive hobby. His poor position is influenced by his choices and he should accept responsibility for that fact.

However, choice isn't the only factor that influences one's economic position. Some people who are badly off have just been unlucky. Perhaps their investments failed for reasons that they could not have foreseen: they lost their job through no fault of their own or they fell ill and can no longer work. What should we think about these people, whose position is not a result of choices for which they bear responsibility? One particularly far-reaching way in which luck influences your position in society is in your starting point in life. We do not start life on a level playing field. Some people are born into wealthy families that can buy them the best education and protect them from financial hardship whilst others are born into families that struggle to put food on the table and a roof over their heads. Some people are lucky enough to be brought up in family and social environments that encourage academic achievement, others unlucky enough to find themselves growing up in environments where learning is not valued or is even ridiculed. As a matter of luck some people benefit from great social advantages and others suffer social disadvantage. To what extent should arbitrary luck be allowed to influence people's life-prospects?

Utilitarianism provides one way of addressing all of these concerns but, since we have already had a good look at utilitarianism and it answers distributive questions in much the same way it answers any questions, we shall not focus on it. Instead, this chapter will introduce you to four important and distinctive contemporary answers to the questions concerning distributive justice that we have raised. These are the liberal view of Rawls, Nozick's **libertarianism**, the socialism of Gerald Cohen and the **communitarianism** of Michael Walzer. It will become clear that each of these thinkers is concerned with equality in one way or another. Although they disagree with each other about what equality is, they all reject the idea, which we encountered most strongly in the ideas of Plato and Aristotle, that there is a natural ranking of human beings. Since this ranking is absent there is no natural aristocracy, no group of people who just are, and must be, regarded as superior to all others and singled out for special treatment. It is possible to treat each of the positions we will examine as expressing a different way of understanding the political implications of accepting this basic equality. Each of these positions will answer the central concerns of distributive justice in ways that will help you to understand what thinking hard about just distributions involves, whilst exploring them should help you to work out what you think too. It will also become apparent that each of these thinkers is clear that questions of distribution cannot be addressed independently of broader discussions of principles of justice and just political organisation. Since each of the other thinkers tells us what they believe by showing us how they think Rawls goes wrong we will explore Rawls's ideas first.

Rawls and the liberal conception of 'justice as fairness'

Rawls's *A Theory of Justice* is arguably the most important work of political thought of the twentieth century. Whereas, for example, Plato conceived of justice as harmony and John Locke as the non-violation of natural rights, Rawls thinks that justice is *fairness*, where 'no arbitrary distinctions are made between persons' by important political, social and economic institutions (Rawls 1999: 5). Together these major institutions, consisting of the political constitution and the principal economic and social arrangements such as the market, make up the *basic structure* of society. This basic structure will 'define men's rights and duties and influence their life prospects. . . . The basic structure is the primary subject of justice because its effects are so profound and present from the start' (Ibid.: 6–7). As it has so much of an influence on the way our lives pan out it is very important that the basic structure of society is just, so that each of us gets a fair go in life. Justice for Rawls, like order for Thomas Hobbes and efficiency for utilitarians, is the 'first virtue of social institutions' (Ibid.: 3). A well-ordered society is one in which these social institutions are generally regulated by principles of justice and where everyone accepts those principles (Ibid.: 4).

Instead of directly telling us what he thinks the principles of justice are, Rawls takes an indirect approach. He is concerned to work out a process by which principles of justice can be arrived at. The simple thought is that a fair process will lead to a fair outcome. If Rawls can show how, if they are placed in a fair 'original position', everyone would agree on certain principles then the fairness of that original position would ensure the fairness of the principles agreed upon. What would this original position of fairness look like? Rawls claims that there are commonly shared presumptions about fairness that are widely accepted and can help us to understand what the original position ought to be. Firstly, threats are not fair arguments. If I say 'agree with my proposed principles or else' then, if I am big enough or have enough large friends, I may be able to secure agreement but I would not do so fairly. A process is not fair if I can influence its outcome by threatening my fellows. Nor, secondly, would the process be fair if it allowed me to tailor principles of justice to favour my own case. Suppose I were to suggest the principle that all white males over six feet tall, or all persons whose first name begins with P, should be privileged in any distribution: this seems obviously unfair. I am proposing principles of justice that might as well name me personally as someone with a special status. The same goes for principles that are based on a particular conception of the good. For example, if principles are suggested that single out a particular religious faith for special treatment then this too would be unfairly tailoring principles to suit my own case. Finally, Rawls claims that it seems unfair for anyone to be 'advantaged or disadvantaged by natural fortune or social circumstances in the choice of principles'. The choice of principles of justice would be unfair if it allowed such accidents of birth, matters of luck beyond a person's control, to influence the outcome (this will become very important in the further discussion below). The problem for Rawls is how to lay out the original position so that it embodies these fair and reasonable constraints on the choice of principles (Ibid.: 16–17). He does this by imagining the people in the original position behind a 'veil of ignorance'.

This veil of ignorance deprives the inhabitants of the original position of a range of knowledge that might make the position unfair for the choice of principles of justice. Behind the veil,

> no one knows his place in society, his class position or social status, nor does anyone know his fortune in the distribution of natural assets and abilities, his intelligence, strength, and the like . . . the parties do not know their conceptions of the good. . . . This ensures that no one is advantaged or disadvantaged by the outcome of natural chance or the contingency of social circumstances. Since all are similarly situated and no one is able to design principles to favor his particular condition, the principles of justice are the result of a fair agreement. (Ibid.: 11).

This veil prevents the choice of principles on the basis of considerations that are 'arbitrary from a moral point of view' (Ibid.: 14). The parties in the original position are effectively denied knowledge of their personal circumstances and so cannot choose principles on the basis of how they will themselves be affected. Because they do not know their place in society the parties are effectively required to make their choice on the understanding that they could be in any place in society, the best off or the worst off economically, or a member of a religious or political minority, perhaps. This means that they have to take everyone's position into account in their choice of principles.

The hypothetical original position is a very abstract idea but this should not put you off. It is not a situation that could ever exist, nor does Rawls claim that it can. Instead he asks us to imagine people in an imaginary situation and to think hard about what choices these people can make. We have already encountered this type of argument, Hobbes's state of nature is an imaginary situation inhabited by imaginary people, and we are also familiar with everyday examples of hypothetical reasoning. We ask hypothetical questions every time we ask questions that begin 'what if . . . ?' or 'what would it be like if . . . ?'. The question 'what would it be like if everyone behaved like that?' asks us to imagine a hypothetical situation and invites us to think about the moral implications of our imaginings for our choice of behaviour in the real world. Rawls's original position is the same sort of argument. We are asked to consider what principles hypothetical people behind the veil of ignorance would choose to govern their social interaction once the veil is lifted and they return to society. They are asked to choose unanimously for a closed society entered only by birth and left only by death so that everyone's interests must be taken into account over their whole lives. The principles they choose will be principles governing the distribution of *primary goods* throughout society. Primary goods are 'things that every rational man is presumed to want', whatever else they may want. Whatever their conception of the good it is assumed that they will need the primary goods of rights, liberties and opportunities, income and wealth, and the social basis of self-respect (Ibid.: 54). Rawls argues that as the parties in the original position are all situated equally then we can assume that they would choose an equal distribution of primary goods, unless an unequal distribution makes *everyone* better off (Ibid.: 54–5). From a position of equality no one would choose inequality unless it made even the worst off in society as well off as they can be (remember that because of the veil no one knows whether or not they will be the worst off). Rawls also argues that the parties have a special interest in protecting certain civil and political rights and liberties (they would want to take no chances with freedom of speech and expression and the right to vote, for example) and so he concludes that the parties would choose the following two liberal principles of justice as fairness, giving priority to the first (Ibid.: 266).

- *First principle*: Each person is to have an equal right to the most extensive total system of equal basic liberties compatible with a similar system of liberty for all.

The priority of this principle means that its requirements have to be fulfilled before we can move onto the second principle. In effect there are to be no utilitarian trade-offs between these rights and liberties and the financial concerns of the second principle.

- *Second principle*: Social and economic inequalities are to be arranged so that they are both: (a) to the greatest benefit of the least advantaged [the difference principle], and (b) attached to offices and positions open to all under conditions of fair equality of opportunity.

The second principle, which includes the difference principle (so called because it justifies inequalities or differences), is designed to provide equality of opportunity by making sure that any inequalities are in everyone's interests, especially those of the worst off. Injustice is the opposite of this, inequalities that are in the interests of only a portion of society. It is important to bear in mind that Rawls's position is underpinned by a basic presumption in favour of equality, with departures from equality needing to be justified. If a departure from equality makes evervone better off then preventing it in the name of equality, thus making the worst off even worse off than they need be, seems like little more than stubbornness.

You have probably found nothing remarkable in these two principles; commitments to democracy, rights and equality may even strike you as banal. However, Rawls endorses an understanding of equality of opportunity that makes his second principle potentially very radical indeed. The easiest way to understand this is to think through what we might mean by equality of opportunity (Ibid.: 57–65). The most natural reading of equality of opportunity is a formal one where there are no legal barriers stopping anyone from attaining any privileged social position. All careers and offices are open to everyone provided they have the talent, and the political and legal systems are organised to protect these equal opportunities. However, this interpretation does not take into account background social and economic conditions. People have different starting points in life. Some are born into wealthy families who may provide them with the best education and significant financial support, whilst others are born into poorer families who are unable to provide them with these advantages. On a formal reading these initial inequalities in starting points become translated into inequalities of life prospects; a talented person from a disadvantaged background is likely to do worse than an equally talented person from a more privileged background. Liberal politics has long recognised this problem and has worked out ways to ensure *fair* equality of opportunity. Instead of formal equal opportunity to attain any social position, the liberal commitment is to a *fair* chance to attain those positions. Those with similar abilities and skills should have similar life chances, *whatever their starting points in society*; their prospects should not be affected by social class since class is arbitrary from a moral point of view (Ibid.: 63). Class is, in an important sense, contingent. I could have been born into a different social class, so why should class make a difference to how my life goes? Fair equality of opportunity might be achieved through the state provision of education for all, for example.

Rawls is clear that this is an improvement on our initial and purely formal understanding, but still thinks it is defective. Whilst working to eliminate social contingencies this liberal reading still allows the distribution of wealth and office to be determined by natural contingencies. Economic distributions will still be influenced by the natural distribution of talents and abilities – the more talented you are the better your life prospects. But surely our natural starting points are as arbitrary and contingent as our social ones. I am in no way responsible for my talents; they are the result of my good or bad luck in the natural lottery. I may be lucky enough to be intelligent, charismatic and strong but I could easily have been less fortunate. Why should my luck in the natural lottery of starting points be any more able to influence my life prospects than my luck in the social lottery? If we have moral reason to try to stop social contingencies from influencing life prospects then we have the same moral reason to prevent the influence of natural contingencies. To model this thought the veil of ignorance screens out our natural abilities as well as our social positions. If people do not know their talents and abilities then they will not permit inequalities simply to mirror the distribution of talents. As the second principle implies, all inequalities, even those that result from differences in talent, are only permitted if they benefit the worst off. Perhaps it is better for everyone if the most talented people take the most important positions in social and legal institutions, but this is justified only under conditions (perhaps taxation conditions) where benefit accrues to the untalented.

At the heart of justice as fairness is the claim that society is just only when no one is advantaged or disadvantaged by their place in the natural and social lotteries, when no one is unfairly treated on the basis of factors that are arbitrary from a moral point of view. If any inequalities must benefit the worst off then Rawls's vision of society regulated by the two principles of justice as fairness is one where the worst off do as well as it is possible for them to do.

> Once we decide to look for a conception of justice that prevents the use of the accidents of natural endowment and the contingencies of social circumstance in the quest for political and economic advantage, we are led to these principles. They express the result of leaving aside those aspects of the social world that seem arbitrary form a moral point of view. (Ibid.: 14)

Just as the original position is designed to remove sources of bias from the choice of principles of justice (so placing everyone on an equal footing in this choice) the difference principle is designed not to be biased towards the poor but to compensate the worst off (as naturally and socially unlucky) by levelling out the playing field in the name of greater equality.

Cohen's socialism

Socialists are not convinced by Rawls's claim to be an egalitarian. Instead of aiming for equality they argue that the difference principle is all about legitimising inequalities; after all, there are still groups of people referred to as the best off and worst off in society. If Rawls is truly committed to equality why should he be unconcerned with these inequalities? Many socialists, and we will look at Cohen in particular, think that the distinction that Rawls draws between the basic structure of society and society as a whole masks the existence of real inequalities of power (Cohen 2000: 139). The rich are still powerful and the poor still weak. Marx recognised that the structures of bourgeois legality and formal equality mask oppressive and exploitative social and economic relations. Cohen is concerned that Rawls's focus on the basic structure may do the same.

Cohen is equally concerned, however, that 'history has shredded each of [Marx's] . . . predictions' (Ibid.: 104). Marx thought that communist revolution was inevitable but capitalism has not produced its own gravediggers as the predicted growth and self-awareness of the industrial proletariat as a revolutionary force has not materialised. Nor does it seem that the Marxist optimism about ever-increasing production and greater technology banishing problems of scarcity was justified (see Chapter 5). Rather than waiting for the inevitable tide of materialist history to fix things for us, Cohen argues that socialists have to fully engage in political and philosophical argument and fix things themselves. They can continue to affirm the task that Marxism set itself, 'the task of liberating humanity from the oppression that the capitalist market visits upon it', but they must do so by engaging with the justifications of that capitalist order (Ibid.: 180). Cohen does so by confronting Rawls, perceived as the most important justification of a liberal politics, and does so by confirming the continued importance of the socialist conception of a malleable human nature. Cohen (ibid.: 120) argues that, contrary to Rawls's concern to limit political argument to the basic structure, he has become increasingly convinced that 'for inequality to be overcome, there needs to be a revolution in feeling or motivation'. It is a key conclusion of socialism, as identified in Chapter 5, that such a revolution in human nature is possible.

Cohen supports his claims by considering Rawls's justification of inequality through the difference principle. Rawls argues that since the talented do not deserve their talents, as they have them as a matter of luck, then they should only benefit from them so long as the untalented (worst off) also benefit. The best off only get lots so long as the worst off also get some. We need to look closely at this argument for inequality. We need to ask why the talented or hard-working should be rewarded for what they have done by being allowed unequal economic benefits. Did they exercise their talents in order to enrich themselves? If so, then why should this self-interest command a high reward? Or did they do so in order to benefit others? If so, then to reward them with resources that others could have received instead contradicts their own aim (Cohen 1994: 13). Cohen argues that the best off either affirm justice as fairness and the difference principle or they do not. If they do not then Rawls's claim that in the just and well-ordered society everyone affirms the same principles of justice is contradicted and so the society, complete with its inequalities, is necessarily unjust in Rawls's terms. If the best off do affirm the difference principle as necessary for justice, complete with its concern that the worst off should be as well off as they can be, why do they need extra economic rewards to work to relieve inequality? Perhaps the rewards are necessary incentives in order to motivate the talented to work harder for the benefit of the worst off. But if this is the case then the talented, by their own choice, make rewards and inequality necessary as they effectively decide to produce less if the extra rewards are not available. It is their unwillingness to work for ordinary rewards that makes inequality necessary and results in the worst off doing as badly as they do. High rewards and inequality are therefore only necessary because of the self-interested choices of the talented, who cannot, in that case, be properly motivated by the justice of equality and the difference principle. (The argument of this paragraph is a paraphrase of Cohen 2000: 126–7.) It seems that the focus on structure cannot prevent the personal choices of some from making others worse off than they might otherwise be; justice and injustice therefore cannot be solely a matter of structure but must also be concerned with the choices people make within structures. 'If justice relates to structure alone . . . it might be necessary for the worst off to occupy their relatively low place only because the choices of the better off tend strongly against equality' (Ibid.: 135).

The reason for Rawls's focus on basic structure is the great impact these institutions have on people's lives. If, as Cohen argues, people's choices have a similar impact then we also have to take seriously the justice of those choices; continued emphasis on the basic structure seems arbitrary. Does Cohen's conclusion, that the self-interested choices of people undermine the supposed justice of the basic structure, leading to inequality, mean that we cannot achieve justice and equality at all? Do the constraints of market motivation, of maximising self-interest, place severe and necessary limits on the level of equality we can justify? We need to recall here the socialist conclusion that human nature is malleable and that therefore 'a maximising ethos is not a necessary feature of society' (Ibid.: 144). People need not affirm the capitalist market ethic of unbridled self-interest. If we are to have a just and equal society we need to effect the 'revolution in feeling or motivation' necessary to bring about 'an *ethos* of justice that informs individual choices' (Ibid.: 128). The personal choices of people's everyday lives must reflect their commitment to the difference principle and to the ideal of equality that it embodies. Capitalist markets have encouraged an ethos in which other people are seen either as threats or as sources of enrichment. Other people are conceived of instrumentally as the means by which we satisfy our self-interested ends. Cohen invites us to recognise that this is a 'horrible way of seeing other people' and that, as seeing people this way is what the market requires, then it may be that 'the market is intrinsically repugnant' (Cohen 1994: 9–10). Instead of asking what we can get out of other people Cohen encourages socialists to foster, as a matter of justice, an ethos of community whereby I serve you because you need my service, not because I think it may benefit me (Ibid.: 9). When we affirm and act on this ethos we properly regard others not as tools to get what we want, but as equals that deserve our respect. A society that reflects the ethos in which each of us recognises and affirms that others are our equals, and that we should work so as to realise this equality in society, will be a just society. Cohen is insistent that once we recognise that people are not necessarily self-interested, that high levels of reward are necessary only as a result of the choices of the talented, then it is not clear that any inequalities are necessitated by the difference principle; motivated by an alternative ethos, why will the talented need to be rewarded in order to benefit the worst off? A just society, in which the members accept and act on the difference principle as a principle of justice, will be radically egalitarian; 'justice requires (virtually) unqualified equality' (Cohen 2000: 209, 124).

Nozick's libertarian entitlement theory

Nozick shares many basic liberal concerns with Rawls, including commitments to individualism, freedom and pluralism and a common cause against utilitarianism. Their competing interpretations of what these commitments entail bring to the fore the debate about what kind of state we want to have, about what we think the job of the state is. Nozick opposes both socialism and Rawlsian social democracy with a libertarian vision of a **minimal state** that exists only to uphold our rights. Injustice exists whenever our rights are violated. This means that, in Nozick's account, poverty and extremes of inequality may not be unjust whilst redistribution to alleviate poverty almost always is. According to Nozick, 'almost every suggested principle of distributive justice is patterned' (Nozick 1974: 156). A patterned principle judges a distribution of resources to be just when it matches a certain pattern: to each according to need, merit, effort or contribution, for example. Rawls's justice as fairness is patterned; a distribution is just when the worst off under that distribution are better of than they could be under any alternative distribution. Cohen's socialism promotes a pattern where a just distribution is the one that most approaches absolute equality. Whilst most theories are patterned it is not obvious that they should be. Why should we seek to fill in the blank in 'to each according to his _______'? Against patterned theories of justice, Nozick argues that this assumes that resources are like 'manna from heaven', belonging to no one and awaiting distribution. Instead, Nozick is adamant that the history of objects is important as 'things come into the world already attached to people having entitlements over them' (Ibid.: 160). Nozick comes to a theory of distributive justice of his own, the historical entitlement theory, by exploring the source and consequences of these entitlements.

The argument for entitlements starts with rights. 'Individuals have rights, and there are things that no person or group may do to them (without violating their rights)' (Ibid.: ix). These are rights to life, liberty and property and all individuals have them equally and are entitled to the equal enforcement of those rights. The whole of *Anarchy, State, and Utopia*, Nozick's main work of political theory, is dedicated to working through the implications of these statements. If you recall the last chapter, Nozick conceives of these rights as absolute 'side-constraints' on action that can never be legitimately violated. He also appears to regard these rights as negative, rights only to non-interference and not to the services of others. For example, our right to life is a right not to be killed, not a right that someone provide us with everything that we may need to continue living. These rights are also natural, as we have them independently of our membership of any social or political institution. Indeed, 'so strong and far-reaching are these rights that they raise the question of what, if anything, the state . . . may do' (Ibid.: ix). In fact, a minimal state *is* justified in order to protect against the force, theft, fraud and breach of contract that constitute the violation of our rights, but this is the limit of legitimate state action, any more extensive state will violate those rights (Ibid.: ix, 149). This minimal state provides maximum freedom and protection for individuals; a more than minimal state will violate rights and infringe on individual freedom.

The minimal state protects our rights to life, liberty and property. Nozick's entitlement theory of distributive justice is shaped by his understanding of these property rights and the role of the state in protecting them. The entitlement theory consists of three principles (Ibid.: 150–1, 178):

1. The principle of justice in acquisition: a person has a legitimate property right in a previously unowned object if their owning of it makes no one else worse off (Nozick 1974: 178).

Since the world and most of the objects in it are now owned the second principle becomes more important.

2. The principle of justice in transfer: a person has a legitimate property right in an object if they are given it freely by someone who has a legitimate right in that object.

The voluntary nature of exchange, perhaps as a gift or in return for services or money, passes the right from one person to the next. Some transfer of this kind occurs every time you buy something from a shop. Finally,

> 3. The principle of justice in rectification: 1 and 2 are the only legitimate methods of acquiring property rights. If property is acquired in other ways, through theft for example, the state should rectify this injustice.

It is important to recognise that any distribution, no matter how unequal, that arises through the proper exercise of the principles is just. 'Whatever arises from a just situation by just steps is itself just' (Ibid.: 151). The role of the state is not to guard financial equality, it is to provide the security services necessary to protect my rights to life and liberty and to guard property rights from theft and fraud and non-fulfilment of contract – that is all. Other services such as health and education provision, transport infrastructure and utility supply are to be provided by private organisations through the free market and private insurance. The state cannot legitimately provide these services, nor redistribute in the name of greater equality, since doing so would require the infringement of liberty and property rights in the form of taxation. This is clearest in Nozick's four main arguments against Rawls (and against any patterned principles of justice).

Firstly, Nozick argues in the following way that *Liberty upsets patterns* (Ibid.: 160–4):

1. Principles of justice that justify redistribution are patterned principles (the reason for redistribution is always to bring the distribution closer to an ideal).
2. The free exercise of liberty upsets patterns.
3. Patterns are therefore unstable if liberty is permitted.
4. We therefore face a choice between the pattern and liberty.

We need to look closely at the claim that liberty upsets patterns. Nozick asks us to imagine a society that embodies our ideal distribution, perhaps one where everyone has an equal share. Now imagine that the famous basketball player Wilt Chamberlain is in great demand and so signs a contract with his team that guarantees him 25 cents of every ticket price. This is made clear to the paying fans, who on entry buy their ticket as normal and drop an extra 25 cents into a box with

Wilt's name on it. Because so many people are willing to pay to see him play, by the end of the season Wilt has $250,000, which is far higher than the equal share everyone started with. Is this new distribution just? We started with a just distribution and every step in the process was wholly voluntary so why should it not be just? Either this new distribution is just or the state must interfere with people's free choices, either to return Wilt's money to the fans or to prevent them from spending it in the first place. In fact, every free transfer of resources, from giving gifts at Christmas to buying something from a shop, will lead to deviations from the pattern. As such, any pattern is upset by liberty and so any theory of justice is faced by a choice between the pattern and liberty. State redistribution of resources, such as would be necessary in support of the difference principle or socialist equality, will lead to significant and continual interference with liberty. Nozick thinks that any theorist, especially a liberal one like Rawls, would have trouble giving up on liberty and so must give up on the pattern and on redistribution instead.

Nozick's second argument against redistributive theories is that *taxation equals forced labour*. This is a fairly straightforward argument (Ibid.: 169–70). Assume a 25 per cent taxation rate:

1. If I work 40 hours in a week for total earnings of £100, then I pay £25 in tax and take home £75.
2. Without taxation I would have to work only 30 hours to take home £75.
3. Taxation means that, if I need £75, I have to work 10 extra hours.
4. Paying taxes is compulsory and backed by coercion (try not paying them).
5. Therefore, because of taxation I am coerced into work for 10 hours a week and taxation is equivalent to forced labour.

Nozick is claiming that using the taxation system to redistribute wealth to the worst off involves subjecting people to a regime of forced labour, once again an infringement of their liberty.

The third argument, that *redistribution makes the state my owner*, builds on the second (Ibid.: 172):

1. Having a property right in an animal or object means that I control it and make decisions about what is to happen to it.
2. If taxation is forced labour then the state is directly exercising

control over my time and actions for that extra 10 hours a week.
3. Redistribution supported by taxation gives the state a property right in me, making the state my part-owner.

Rawls's difference principle for example, which uses taxes to redistribute wealth in order to compensate for a lack of natural talent, is effectively a 'slavery of the talented' in which the state uses the talented as a resource to benefit the untalented. Redistributive theories use us as means to satisfy the ends of others.

These arguments are designed to show that redistribution and the taxation needed to enact it are illegitimate infringements upon our liberty and our property rights, no matter how great the inequality between rich and poor. They also show that taxation to finance state support of anything other than the police and courts necessary for the protection of rights to life, liberty and property is illegitimate. Nozick has a vision where everybody's equal rights are respected equally by the minimal state in which everyone is equally free, but this is all the state can legitimately do. All other services such as education, welfare and medical services would be supplied privately through the market. Relieved of the burden of taxation both individuals and industry would flourish and people could purchase the exact services they require and avoid paying for those they do not. To critics worried about the worst off in society, who may not be able to afford health and unemployment insurance or schooling for their children, Nozick replies that our rights only rule out the state enforcement of aid in these cases. Just as many people feel they have obligations to God but not that the state should enforce them, we may feel that we have all sorts of moral obligations to the worst off in society, obligations of compassion or of charity, but that it is not the job of the state to force us to be either compassionate or charitable. This is effectively Nozick's answer to Cohen's call for an egalitarian ethos. If there is such an ethos then state involvement is unnecessary; if there isn't then state involvement is illegitimate. If we feel that we have these obligations then Nozick's minimal state maximises our freedom to be compassionate. If we do not recognise these obligations then we need not fear that we will be coerced into fulfilling them. The minimal state provides us with the freedom to live as we choose and to take responsibility for our choices. Indeed, and this is the fourth argument against redistribution, *unlike redistributive institutions the minimal state avoids* ***paternalism*** by treating us as responsible adults and not as children who have to be guarded against the consequences of their decisions.

> The minimal state treats us as inviolate individuals, who may not be used in certain ways by others as means or tools or instruments or resources; it treats us as persons having individual rights with the dignity this constitutes. Treating us with respect by respecting our rights, it allows us . . . to choose our life and to realise our ends and our conception of ourselves, insofar as we can, aided by the voluntary co-operation of other individuals possessing the same dignity. How *dare* any state or group of individuals do more. Or less. (Ibid.: 333–4)

Walzer's communitarianism and complex equality

Michael Walzer takes an altogether different approach to questions of distributive justice. He is concerned about the presumption of each of the approaches that we have looked at so far that distributive justice is a single thing, that it is the same thing everywhere. This Platonic presumption is that when we think about justice we should 'walk out of the cave, leave the city, climb the mountain' in order to attain an objective standpoint from which to judge the terrain below. Walzer's thought is that in seeking this general standpoint you find yourself so far away that you cannot see clearly, so much of the detail is lost and blurred and to that extent it is difficult to make sense of what you see. The universalist approach to justice that asks the question 'what is justice?' at this level of abstraction fails to take proper account of the complexity of the world. Instead Walzer's 'radically particularist' approach doesn't attempt to distance itself from the social world we live in with a veil of ignorance, original position or state of nature. Walzer is trying to 'stand in the cave, in the city, on the ground . . . to interpret to one's fellow citizens the world of meaning we share' (Walzer 1983: xiv). The role of political thought is not the abstract one it has traditionally had but an interpretative one, starting in the particular communities we live in and together making sense of our commitments to one another.

Against the individualism and universalism of liberal thought (exemplified in Nozick and Rawls), the basic communitarian idea is that human beings can only make sense of themselves as citizens, persons and moral agents through the concepts and standards bequeathed to them by the practices and traditions they inhabit. Instead of the separateness of persons, as a communitarian Walzer thinks in terms of the interconnectedness of persons. We understand our identities and make sense of who we are not by thinking in abstract terms but by looking at our place in a web of particular and interconnected social relationships, the roles we inhabit and the community that makes those roles available to us. We think of ourselves specifically as (amongst many other things) parents, loving children, committed to particular religions, fiercely loyal to particular countries and members of certain clubs and associations. This is who we are and it makes no sense to claim that we can be separated from these things by something like a veil of ignorance and remain ourselves, able to choose appropriate principles of justice. Indeed, it may be that the very meaning of words like 'justice' make no sense outside of particular communities. Meaning, like language, is social. Meanings are inherent in and dependent on the understandings, traditions and practices of communities of people. The meaning of a cross, for example, differs greatly between Christian and non-Christian communities. The meaning of work as paid employment equally open to all citizens that Rawls uses is very different to the meaning of work we encountered in Aristotle's Greece, where work was something that slaves did and was considered beneath citizens. It is not clear that there is any essence of 'cross' or 'work' that makes one of these views the right one (Ibid.: 7). The meanings of moral terms are also social meanings. Ideas of right and wrong have differed widely, and still do as the communities in which they are used differ. Why should we think that there is any one privileged understanding of right and wrong, the essence of morality, any more than we think that there is a privileged understanding of what is polite conduct? The role of political thought is interpretative; it is to help us to characterise and to make sense of our social understandings. If Walzer is right about this then we should not, with Plato, Aristotle, Rawls, Cohen and Nozick (amongst others) ask 'what is justice?' but should instead ask 'what is justice here and now in this community?'. 'Justice is relative to social meanings' in the same way as anything else (Ibid.: 312).

Walzer also claims that the universalism, and abstraction that it entails, of Rawls and others has led them to misunderstand equality and the nature of the goods that distributive justice is concerned to distribute. The best example of this is Rawls's use of the 'primary goods' that every rational man is supposed to want. Walzer argues that, since meanings are social and relative to context, then there can be no universal list of primary goods (Ibid.: 8). People will want and need all sorts of different goods in all sorts of different circumstances and contexts. Missing this important insight has led to a fundamental misunderstanding of the nature of equality. Liberals and socialists are generally proponents of what Walzer calls *simple equality*. That is, they identify the privileged or dominant good, rights or wealth perhaps, and argue that this good should be distributed more equally. Money is often regarded as a dominant good: if you have lots of it then you can get whatever goods you want. When this sort of dominant good is monopolised by a small section of society they can use this monopoly to exploit the dominance of money and so get the best of all goods, including power. The monopoly of a dominant good in the hands of a few leads to tyranny, where unequal distribution of one good leads to an unequal society generally. Proponents of simple equality propose breaking up the monopoly and so combating tyranny (Ibid.: 10, 13–14). However, Walzer, in an argument similar to Nozick's that liberty upsets patterns, argues that this sort of equality would 'require continual state intervention' to maintain, and that then state power itself would become the dominant, monopolised and tyrannical good (Ibid.: 15). Walzer's solution is to target not the monopoly of goods as liberals do, but to undermine the dominance of any one good in particular. This would lead away from simple to *complex equality*.

The idea of complex equality relies on two claims about goods that we have not yet examined and which build on the idea of political thought as interpretative. Firstly, Walzer argues that the proper criteria for distributing any good are intrinsic to the social meaning of that good and that political philosophy should help us to tease out the intrinsic principle of distribution (Ibid.: 8–9). For example, it is intrinsic to the social meaning of Olympic gold medals that they be distributed to the sportsmen and women who perform best in their event. A just distribution of a good is one that matches its intrinsic distributive criteria; it would be obviously unjust if the medals were handed out on the basis of height, wealth or colour of skin. Secondly, Walzer argues that if different goods have different social meanings, and therefore different intrinsic distributive criteria, then their distributions should be confined within different spheres (Ibid.: 10). Whereas ability to pay will be appropriate for the distribution of sports cars in the marketplace, piety is more likely to be appropriate to the distribution of religious office. In consequence, the distribution of religious office should belong to a wholly distinct distributive sphere from that of the market (Ibid.: 10). Walzer builds on this a vision of a range of separate 'spheres of justice' within which the most important social goods are distributed according to their internal criteria (he mentions membership, security and welfare, money and market commodities, office, hard work, free time, education, kinship and love, divine grace, recognition and political power as examples of goods that require different spheres). What is important is that these distributive spheres are kept distinct and it is the role of the state to police their boundaries (Ibid.: 28). Now, within these distinct spheres there may be all sorts of unequal distributions, there may even be spheres within which a good is monopolised in the hands of a few, but as each good is confined to its proper place there is no dominant good. No good is generally convertible across all the spheres and so just because one has done well in the sphere of wealth this will not guarantee a more than just share of any other good. Indeed Walzer characterises his claim in an open-ended distributive principle. 'No social good *x* should be distributed to men and women who possess some other good *y* merely because they possess *y* and without regard to the meaning of *x*' (Ibid.: 20). Wealth shouldn't bring with it access to political power and so unequal wealth shouldn't result in unequal power, for example. This illustrates the more general point: although there are inequalities within each sphere, as the distributive principles within each sphere are different so across spheres inequalities should even out. In any case, any inequalities become less significant since without a dominant good they are less important. When we have reached a position where distributions are appropriate to their goods and spheres are kept distinct then we will have a just society. What is more, that society will exhibit a complex equality.

> Complex equality means that no citizen's standing in one sphere or with regard to one social good can be undercut by his standing in some other sphere, with regard to some other good. Thus citizen X may be chosen over citizen Y for political office, and then the two of them will be unequal in the sphere of politics. But they will not be unequal generally so long as X's superior office gives him no advantages over Y in any other sphere – superior medical care, access to better schools for his children. (Ibid.: 19)

There is no single measure against which we will be able to ensure that all match up equally, but the inequalities across the spheres will not lead to tyranny; no citizen will dominate another in all spheres. As such everyone can be regarded as of equal status, all are equal citizens of a complexly equal society where no one is dominated and no one dominates. Obviously, because political philosophy is interpretative and social meanings are relative to context, the shape of particular societies will differ greatly. However, so long as within these societies the distributive spheres remain distinct and distributive criteria accurately reflect social meanings the general point stands. There will be a diversity of different societies, each exhibiting their own form of complex equality.

Conclusions

We started this discussion of distributive justice by recognising that seeking answers to distributive questions also involved seeking answers to questions about what kind of state we want. Nozick has provided us with a vision of a minimal state, a state that is the fierce guardian of our equal rights but avoids interfering with free and voluntary distributive outcomes no matter how radical their inequality. Most of the functions of the more extensive states we are familiar with such as education, health care, road maintenance etc. are regarded as the job of the market. In contrast Rawls, Walzer and Cohen appear to favour a much more extensive social democratic state that intervenes in the market in order to ensure equality. Each of these thinkers believes that the market needs to be constrained in some way if equality is to be a real possibility. Nozick has laid out clear arguments to support his claim that any constraints on the market (except the minimal ones necessary to prevent theft and fraud) are constraints on liberty, itself an exceptionally important value. Alarmingly, constraining markets to further equality may involve using the state to coerce us into forced labour for the benefit of others. Constraining markets also means stopping people doing what they want with their own resources, stopping them from spending their money as they wish, exchanging services or giving gifts whilst at the same time taxing those resources and redistributing the proceeds to others. Nozick is particularly alarmed by this level of paternalism, where the state treats us as children who need to be sheltered from the full implications of our choices. Instead he argues that respecting people equally as adults involves letting them take responsibility for the way their lives work out, even if this means that some citizens do much better than others. Freeing us from constraint and taxation enables our achievements to, at least potentially, match our ambitions.

Against Nozick's concerns Cohen retaliates that poverty is itself a restriction on liberty. In a market economy, where you have to purchase everything you need, from food and clothes to tickets for travel, a lack of money is directly translated into a lack of freely available courses of action. If you cannot afford the ticket then you are not free to travel. The richer you are the more things you are free to do; the poorer you are the less you are free to do (Cohen 1994: 14–16). Poverty, perhaps more than taxation, interferes with liberty. Poverty also makes a mockery of the importance Nozick places on rights. It is laudable to defend equal rights to life, liberty and property but there seems to be little point in these rights if you are begging in the streets, wondering where your next meal is coming from. In unconstrained markets there are winners and losers. Without at least some redistributive measures, the losers in Nozick's minimal state are utterly reliant on what they can beg off family and friends. It may be that some people make the choice to be poor, perhaps they are lazy or they decide that they prefer the lifestyle of a surfer on Malibu Beach, but many of the worst off are poor not simply because of their choices. However, it is one of Rawls's key points that redistributive measures are not **paternalist** in Nozick's pejorative sense. Whilst Rawls broadly agrees that people should take responsibility for the choices they make, he is very clear about the unfairness involved in regarding them as responsible for matters of luck, whether brute, social or natural. Nozick's vision of a minimal state corresponds to what Rawls describes as a system of formal equality of opportunity and, like this system, it suffers from the defect of allowing these arbitrary factors to influence distributive outcomes. Rawls is clear that principles of justice should not reflect matters that are arbitrary from a moral point of view, and the class that you were born into, the talents and capacities that you were born with and the contingencies of fortune that affect you are arbitrary in this way. A more-than-minimal state might then be justified, constraining markets so as to achieve a level playing field and fair equality of opportunity for all.

You may by this point have been swayed to agree with first one then another of these positions. It is worth pausing for a moment and reflecting on whether you find the arguments for or against market constraints and redistribution more convincing. Are you more drawn towards Rawls's arguments about fairness or towards Nozick's about freedom? What do you think might be a reasonable balance between distributive equality and liberty or do you, like Cohen, think that distributive equality is necessary in order to achieve equal liberty?

If we accept, for the sake of further discussion, that constraints on markets are necessary for equality what might this mean, what sort of constraints might we be talking about? We have identified two broad approaches. Firstly, as socialism argues, we may constrain markets to the point of their destruction by eliminating market motivation. Instead of asking what sort of state we want Cohen is asking us what sort of people we want to be. On this approach the key is to foster a communal ethos of sharing, equality and respect in opposition to the individualist and instrumentalist markets that encourage us to regard others as ways of getting what we want. Cohen and other socialists such as David Miller stress the need to build and encourage a sense of community so that the poverty and suffering of our fellows moves us to its remedy and to redistribution (see Miller 1989). This stress on building a community is in effect, however, a denial of the basic pluralism that characterises contemporary democratic states. As we shall see in the next chapter, there are problems involved in assuming that everyone in society will share a single unitary moral and political vision.

The second approach to constraining markets is structural. Rawls's clear emphasis on the basic structure of society as the subject of justice rather than individual actions marks justice as fairness as an explicitly structural approach. The two principles of justice, especially the difference principle, place a range of constraints on the way that market distributions can reflect individual choices. Rawls wants to structure the basic institutions of society so that, whatever people do with their resources, any inequalities in the distribution that results benefit the worst off. Rawls is not so concerned to identify exactly what form those constraints should take; a just society may have a capitalist or a socialist economic system, or perhaps be a property-owning democracy (Rawls 1999: 242). He does not want to tie justice to arguments in economic theory about the workings of the welfare state, the proper level of income tax, the efficiency of a planned economy or whether in minimally restrained markets wealth 'trickles down' effectively to every economic class. Each of these economic arguments may be settled one way or another but the key point for Rawls is that, however they go, the economic system and constraints on the market should function so as to make the worst off as well off as they can be. Only by ensuring that this is the case can we reassure ourselves that, as fellow citizens, we are treating each other with the equal respect to which we are entitled.

Walzer's contention that justice should reflect social understandings and so that different goods are distributed in distinct spheres in accordance with distributive criteria appropriate to that sphere places more obvious and direct structural constraints on the market. He is effectively structurally limiting the range of goods that fall within the market sphere with an account of what he calls 'blocked exchanges' (Walzer 1983: 100–3). Literally he argues that our social understandings are such that there are things that money cannot buy, or at least should not buy, and so need to be beyond the reach of the market sphere. Amongst the goods he lists that money shouldn't buy are human beings, political power or office, criminal justice, public honours, love and friendship, as well as a long list of criminal sales such as drugs and certain firearms. Setting up alternative distributive spheres for these goods, or denying that some should be distributed at all, in accordance with our social understandings of them as goods, constrains markets in order to undercut the dominant status of money as a medium of exchange. Only then can tyranny be undermined and equality ensured.

Regarding justice as relative to social meanings highlights an important dispute concerning the scope of justice. In Walzer's communitarian account of justice different communities, with different social understandings of goods, will look very different. The distribution of political power according to the social meaning of power, or of wealth according to the social understanding of economic justice, could result in radically different outcomes in different societies. Justice would be a different and particular thing in different countries, reflecting different cultures and particular contexts. Rawls, Nozick and Cohen cannot agree with the basic relativism that this position seems to imply. For them, at least the fundamentals of justice must be invariant; justice is justice everywhere. On this universal account of the scope of justice an injustice is still unjust no matter who suffers it and where they live, it makes no difference which side of a border or ocean they were born on, or which religion happened to take root locally in the distant past. This is an argument about how sensitive we should be towards the diversity of our societies and the wider world. Should we, like Walzer, accept that justice should reflect that diversity in sensitive ways, or should we, like Rawls, Nozick and Cohen, argue that justice sets limits to acceptable diversity? These are difficult questions and the dispute between universalists and particularists is picked up in the next chapter.

Finally, it should be clear that distributive justice is not important simply because it is important that Andrew gets x and Brenda gets y. Principles of distributive justice are not designed simply to ensure that goods get distributed in a certain way. These principles, whichever turn out to be justified, are important because they express how we regard each other as citizens. Distributive principles distribute goods in a certain way *because* that is what appears to be necessary if we are properly to respect our fellow citizens. Differences in distributive principles reflect different conceptions of what such respect involves. Nozick thinks respecting people is about enabling them to take responsibility for their choices. Rawls agrees but argues that this involves removing arbitrary constraints from the lives of citizens. Cohen and Walzer both argue that market motivation can undermine equal respect and so they severely limit markets in order to make equal and reciprocal respect between citizens possible. What we think we owe to each other in regard to distributive justice seems to reflect and express what we think we owe to each other more generally. When thinking about distributive justice and injustice you should consider these more general questions. Ask yourself what living under different distributive principles would be like. Ask yourself whether you feel that the benefits and burdens of living together would be distributed justly in that regime, whether any citizen of that society must necessarily feel hard done by and what sort of life you could expect as such a citizen. Thinking about these questions, equipped with a broad understanding of the distinct positions outlined in this chapter, should enable you to feel more confident in your judgements of justice and injustice. You should also be more open to the idea that freedom, poverty and just distributions are matters about which individual and collective choices are important. Things are not the way they are currently just because 'that's the way things are'. Rather, the way things are is something that is worth thinking hard about, and this makes it worth posing to ourselves the critical question, 'is this how things ought to be?'.

Topics for discussion

1. Should we simply accept the claim that markets necessarily entail winners and losers? If so, should we reject markets on that basis?
2. To what extent should luck or contingency determine people's life chances?
3. How do you react to Nozick's claims that taxation is equivalent to forced labour? Is Wilt Chamberlain entitled to his earnings?
4. Do you think a convincing account of universal primary goods could be given? If not, does this mean that justice is relative to context?

5. Do you think that abstract and hypothetical arguments, as we find with Rawls's use of the original position, are the right approach to take towards identifying principles of justice?
6. How egalitarian should justice be?

Critical glossary

Distributive justice Questions of distributive justice are questions about how we should distribute the benefits and burdens of social co-operation to individuals across society.

Equality Equality is one of those values that has to be qualified in terms of (for example) equality of 'wealth', 'political power', 'opportunity' etc. This chapter explores several competing accounts of this value.

Libertarianism An extreme liberal view that stresses the importance of absolute property rights and claims that this justifies no more than a minimal state.

Communitarianism The basic communitarian idea is that human beings can only make sense of themselves as citizens, persons and moral agents through the concepts and standards inherent in the practices and traditions of their particular communities. In this way communitarians characterise human beings in social rather than individual terms.

Minimal state A conception of the state in which its functions are restricted merely to the protection of its citizens against force, fraud and theft. Also refered to as the nightwatchman state.

Paternalism The state of affairs where governments regulate the lives of citizens just as parents do for their children.

List of references/Further reading

References

Cohen, G. (1994), 'Back to Socialist Basics', *New Left Review*, 207, 3–16.

Cohen, G. (2000), *If You're an Egalitarian, How Come You're So Rich?*, Cambridge, MA: Harvard University Press.

Miller, D. (1989), *Market, State and Community: Theoretical Foundations of Market Socialism*, Oxford: Clarendon Press.

Nozick, R. (1974), *Anarchy, State, and Utopia*, Oxford: Blackwell.

Rawls, J. [1971] (1999), *A Theory of Justice*, Oxford: Oxford University Press.

Walzer, M. (1983), *Spheres of Justice: A Defence of Pluralism and Equality*, Oxford: Blackwell.

Secondary literature

Campbell, T. (2001), *Justice*, 2nd edn, Basingstoke: Macmillian.

Dworkin, R. (2000), *Sovereign Virtue: The Theory and Practice of Equality*, Cambridge, MA: Harvard University Press.

Freeman, S. (2003), *The Cambridge Companion to Rawls*, Cambridge: Cambridge University Press.

Kymlicka, W. (2002), *Contemporary Political Philosophy: An Introduction*, 2nd edn), Oxford: Oxford University Press.

Wolff, J. (1991), *Robert Nozick: Property, Justice and the Minimal State*, Cambridge: Polity Press.

CHAPTER EIGHT

HISTORICAL

Rawls II, Kymlicka and Parekh

CONCEPTUAL

Liberalism and the Challenge of Multiculturalism

Multiculturalism is probably a term with which we are all familiar. It is inescapably the case that most modern societies are made up of different religious, ethnic and cultural groups (what we can term 'the fact' of multiculturalism). Our task in this chapter is to think about what, if anything, we should do about this fact. Modern western political thought has been dominated by liberal responses to the core features of politics. In seeking to eradicate arbitrary inequality among citizens and to establish the political conditions for freedom liberalism has argued, in many forms, for the recognition of universal, individual rights. Every citizen must be treated equally and this is more easily done if we ignore differences between people or discount them as morally irrelevant. On this most basic reading of liberal principles it does not matter if you are black or white, male or female, of any particular religious faith or none, just as long as you are treated equally before a legitimate political and legal authority. On the face of it this has much to recommend it. No one should be discriminated against because of his or her race, or ethnicity, his or her gender or his or her faith. However, a series of challenges to the basic principles at the heart of liberalism has recently come to the fore. The fact of multiculturalism has brought us to question the viability and desirability of liberal solutions to the fundamental questions of political life.

Some of the most fascinating discussions surrounding multiculturalism stem from a real concern that the familiar liberal democratic political structures that we developed to cope with conflicts between different groups of human beings have themselves created new problems. Liberalism was not developed in a cultural or historical vacuum. Rather it can be viewed as a series of responses to political problems encountered in the seventeenth and eighteenth centuries. In seeking to limit the devastating effect of religious intolerance and the tendency, throughout history, to proselytise by force the principle of sovereignty was developed to divide our geopolitical space into independent, juridically equal and self-determining states. The sovereign state was considered to be the prime unit of world politics. A sovereign state had exclusive, indivisible authority within its borders and acknowledged no higher authority outside itself. The emergence of these large, territorially bounded states precipitated a massive change in modern politics. Politically these large, originally heterogeneous, units became forged into nations. The emergence of the nation-state brought with it the creation of national **identity**, over and above the distinctive cultural, religious and parochial identities of earlier times. At roughly the same time as this process took hold in early modern Europe (and as a part of this process) the Enlightenment attempt to rescue us from the injustices of the old world order began to push for 'the rights of man'. Slowly the idea that each individual could be guaranteed freedom and justice only by virtue of equal membership, or citizenship, in a nation-state gained currency and credibility. If each individual was subject (on equal terms with his or her fellow citizens) to the same set of shared institutions, which were neither subject to the arbitrary whims of some group within the state or anyone outside it, then they were free. In this way differences of wealth, class, ethnicity and religion were to be subsumed under a universal conception of justice embodied in **a unitary conception of citizenship**. The core idea here is that both the Enlightenment conception of an undifferentiated or unitary citizenship and the principle of sovereignty were developed as solutions to the problems we faced in the seventeenth and eighteenth centuries. These ideas and their institutional and legal manifestations are still massive features of the political landscape today. As political innovations they have had the most profound influence on modern and contemporary politics. Your lives are structured by your membership of a state (or perhaps the lack of one). Your lives are governed by laws designed to reflect the idea that every citizen is equal before the law.

One feature of modern and contemporary political thought is that these ideas (nationhood, citizenship, equality) are often treated as a necessary feature of politics and ethics. However, if we do begin to think more historically and view the establishment and development of the principles of sovereignty and universal citizenship as products of a time and place, it is hardly surprising that these proposed solutions to the problems of early modern Europe have, over time, thrown up new and unfamiliar problems of their own. Politics has come a long way since the Thirty Years War, the English Civil War and the French Revolution. Europe at this time was the birthplace of modern politics but the political architects of that era had no experience of ours. The nation-state is under pressure from within and from without. From within a myriad of different voices demand political recognition. Women, gays and lesbians, religious non-conformists, indigenous peoples and many others all have reason to believe that they have been denied a political voice. From the outside migrants and refugees, those whom choice or fortune have made members of alien societies, bring with them new moral and political experiences and needs. It may well be the case that unitary conceptions of citizenship that stress universal homogeneity (sameness) as a basic principle went a long way to prevent the injustices of absolute monarchy, of aristocratic privilege, and later of gender and class discrimination. But this 'one size fits all' approach may have blinded us to the different needs of different people.

Indeed a variety of multiculturalist challenges to liberalism argue that to ignore difference is by definition to ignore something that is morally valuable and that liberal institutions that do so are necessarily discriminating against those who do not share the individualism that is at the heart of liberal political culture. This last sentence has touched on two key features of the contemporary multiculturalist argument. First there is the claim that some differences between human beings are morally valuable. This claim is elaborated differently by different thinkers but a common feature of these arguments is that the liberal focus on the individual as the core unit of political and moral concern is too abstract. We are who we are, so the claim goes, because of the social context from which we inherit our values and within which we construct our aspirations. Our social context, our ethno-cultural background, serves as a filter between us and the wider world. We are not individuals in any real sense. Rather we are husbands, wives, sons, daughters, brothers and sisters, community members, students, workers etc. Still more importantly, we enact these roles within certain broader social and cultural contexts. To be a husband or wife, son or daughter within a religious community (Christian, Jewish, Muslim or any other you care to mention), or a secular western community influenced by many of these traditions, differentiates us not only as individuals but also in our social roles. The rights, duties, expectations and aspirations of people within this complex web of social roles are likely to be quite different. The core idea is that we are constituted as human beings with distinct identities by virtue of the fact that we are part of a specific social group. My perception of the world, of right and wrong, of the different value to be assigned to various social and material goods is given, in large part, by my specific identity. I would not claim the rights and freedom that I do, I would not have the same social and economic aspirations that I do were it not for the fact that I was born in a particular time and place. The claim that follows from this is that I do not need rights and freedoms as an individual because I am not an individual in this abstract sense. Rather I need rights and freedoms that mean something to me. I may need the freedom to observe certain religious holidays and practices, to make judgements about certain medical procedures, to organise my marital or family affairs in accordance with custom. Protecting these moral requirements, it is often argued, requires the legal and political recognition of group rights that are not reducible to the rights of the individuals within those groups.

This sounds fine. But how are we to decide which claims are justified and which spurious? On what grounds would we make the (intuitively sensible) claim that the desire of some Muslims to exclude their daughters from co-educational sports lessons is legitimate whereas the claim of thousands of (very bored) people to have Jedi Knight recognised as their religion in the 2001 UK census does not afford that group any special rights? More controversially, what is the difference between the above claim to have Muslim girls excused co-ed PE lessons and the claims (made by various groups) to have the right to arrange marriages or to restrict access to education or medical treatment or to practise female circumcision? Even if we do decide that bare individualism is not enough we still have some very difficult moral and political judgements to make. Is every distinct social group worthy of equal value and treatment? How can we develop a politics that is responsive to the existence of a plurality of value systems and beliefs? Is it the case that we should treat different cases differently, paying attention to the detail of meaning in each constitutive context, or is it possible to elaborate on a universal set of principles that form the common core of justice?

The second claim builds upon the first and supplements it with the charge that liberalism is not just wrong (as a political theory) but that it champions the interest of the dominant group against the real interests of other groups. The fact that I am a British or European, white, Christian, heterosexual, male liberal is important. My value system has a context, a history and I am the product, at least in part, of social conditioning. But it also means that the value system in which I was brought up and in which I developed my sense of right and wrong etc. is the historically dominant value system of my society. Change any one or more of those features that go to make up my identity and that changes rapidly. A brief glance through history and at contemporary society and we can see that those thought of as foreign because of country of origin or colour, non-Christians (or simply the wrong type of Christian), gay and lesbian people, women and even non-liberals (communists in McCarthy's America for example) have not just been ignored but actively discriminated against. They have been variously enslaved, colonised, imprisoned, burned at the stake, denied all sorts of life opportunities including education and equal work opportunities, forced into accepting certain social roles, barred from or hounded out of public office and systematically denied a political voice. It is not just that the history of liberal societies is scarred by colonialism, slavery, religious intolerance, and sex and gender discrimination, although this is true. It is also the case that in attempting to end discrimination by ignoring difference liberal societies have in fact institutionalised the value systems of white middle-class men. This charge is distinct from the first in that it is not merely claiming that liberalism is theoretically mistaken to argue that individualism is either morally necessary or a useful way to get around pluralism; rather it is arguing that liberalism itself is the product of a specific culture. What right do liberals have to insist that non-liberals observe a liberal way of life?

Within this complicated web of challenges to the dominant liberal traditions of politics are a number of distinct, but related voices. The insistence of feminists that the political norms and institutions of contemporary politics are exclusively male, and so systematically deny women freedom, will be examined in Chapter 10. Here we will focus exclusively on the issues surrounding multiculturalism and ethnocultural justice. How should we deal with a political world where the problems appear to be caused by massive ethnic, cultural, religious and moral diversity and the traditional solution has been to impose and encourage homogeneity?

The questions are very difficult and very pressing. They represent a challenge to mainstream liberalism and here we shall turn to an introductory account of four attempts to engage with the sorts of problems raised in the preceding section. This is an initial engagement with a very complex problem. Here we need to get a basic understanding of the range of claims made on behalf of **pluralism** and **multiculturalism** and an introductory understanding of some key responses to those demands. To begin with we need to acknowledge the fact of multiculturalism. This, in itself, does not commit us to any course of action or compel us to draw any moral or political conclusions. Instead imagine a continuum of responses to the fact of ethno-cultural pluralism.

liberal monism → liberal pluralism → liberal multiculturalism → multiculturalism → relativism

On the one extreme we have **liberal monism**. Liberal monism models the universalist and individualist liberal political theory that you encountered in the work of John Locke and John Rawls. Monism is often defined in opposition to pluralism, where monism recognises one way of life as just and pluralism recognises many ways of life as just. In this case I am using the term to refer to the insistence that a unitary conception of citizenship, like those developed in the Enlightenment, is the only just way to order a liberal polity. Monism is, in the context of the present debate, often used as a term of abuse. The claim, made for example in Bhikhu Parekh's critique of liberal monism (which we will examine below), is that monists champion a singular conception of right in the face of obvious pluralism, arguing that 'only one way of life is fully human, true or the best, and that all others are defective to the extent that they fall short of it' (Parekh 2000: 16). The explicit charge is that monism in defending a singular conception of equality among citizens treats individuals identically rather than equitably. However, liberal egalitarians such as Brian Barry, in *Culture and Equality*, and the earlier Rawls, in *A Theory of Justice*, argue that liberal universalism is defensible and necessary. For a robust account of this defence that appeared in response to the claims we examine below it is instructive to read Barry's severe criticism of those who would 'privatise' the disputes of a multicultural society and his defence of the claim that 'on liberal egalitarian premises, equal treatment of a difference-blind nature is what is called for by fairness' (Barry 2001: 91). Given that you have already had the opportunity to explore liberal accounts of freedom and justice in Chapters 3, 4, 6, and 7 we will not go into further detail here.

The next steps in from the left take us to two liberal attempts to accommodate diversity. First we will come to the later work of John Rawls, whose work you encountered in Chapter 6. In his later work (Rawls 1993) Rawls argues that it is possible to develop a '**political liberalism**' rather than a 'comprehensive liberalism' that can both accommodate 'reasonable pluralism' and be the object of an '**overlapping consensus**' on the moral value of the liberal principles of justice contained within it. The difference between the political philosophy of Rawls's *A Theory of Justice* and that in *Political Liberalism* is often taken to be so distinct that you will often come across references to the 'old Rawls' and the 'new Rawls'. The key claim is that in recognising the 'fact of reasonable pluralism' (Ibid.: xix) Rawls found that he had to alter his liberal theory to accommodate a variety of moral and religious viewpoints. Here Rawls specifies what 'reasonable pluralism' is, thus enabling us to see which claims we are obliged to accept as valid and which we can discount as unjust. This is still a liberal theory and argues that all reasonable people regardless of their ethno-cultural background are able to accept the same core principles of justice for the sake of stable political interaction. Beyond the requirements of politics we are urged, and required by justice, to tolerate and value the pluralism that is a fact of modern life. Then we will examine the stronger multicultural liberalism laid out by Will Kymlicka. Kymlicka's work in *Multicultural Citizenship: A Liberal Theory of Minority Rights* offers a liberal theory that argues that 'liberals can, and should, accept a wide-range of group differentiated rights for national minorities and ethnic groups, without sacrificing their core commitments to individual freedom and social equality' (Kymlicka 1995: 126). In working out his theory Kymlicka provides a basis upon which we can decide which groups should be assigned differentiated rights and attempts to make ethno-cultural pluralism, particularly as exhibited in countries containing national minorities, consistent with liberal values such as individual autonomy and self-identity. Kymlicka's core claim is that culture provides the context in which individuals make choices and that a proper recognition of this context is essential to the promotion of liberal values.

The next step in from the left, away from liberalism, brings us to multiculturalism. Here I am referring not to the empirical fact of diversity but to a political theory that attempts to take seriously the importance and role of a plurality of cultural voices in constructing principles of politics. Here we will examine the political theory of Parekh. Parekh in his influential book *Rethinking Multiculturalism: Cultural Diversity and Political Theory* argues that a political theory suited to a multicultural society must go beyond liberalism and must stress 'the centrality of a dialogue between cultures and ethical norms, principles and institutional structures presupposed and generated by it' (Parekh 2000: 14). This theory does not attempt to impose a liberal solution to the question of value pluralism. Rather it takes liberal and non-liberal points of view as equal partners in political dialogue and works from there. This claim, the multiculturalist challenge to western, liberal orthodoxy, will form the main focus of this section.

Finally, and at the other extreme of our continuum, we encounter **relativism**. Relativism argues that there are no criteria through which we can judge between the contending claims of different groups. Ethical meaning is given solely within the context of a social group and attempting to make cross-cultural judgements is at best arrogant and at worst a kind of ethical imperialism. Relativism is the very opposite of universalism and monism. Here we are not going to explore relativism. Rather we shall let it stand as a challenge. If we cannot find convincing ways to show that mediation between groups is possible and desirable then this is where we remain.

Our present task is not to become thoroughly familiar with every detail of these powerful arguments but to fill out this continuum to see what distinguishes each position from the others and to find out what principles drive each of them to their different conclusions. This gives us a context within which we can begin to explore these very difficult, sensitive and urgent questions. We should note, before we move on, that this continuum is not exhaustive. There is a huge variety of other positions and variations on each theme. Rather it is intended to be representative and to familiarise you with the conceptual tools you will need as you go on to explore this topic further. We should also reemphasise that the continuum laid out above is not intended to suggest an inevitable or necessary move away from liberal universalism to multiculturalism. They are landmarks in a contemporary argument and should be judged accordingly.

Liberal responses to multiculturalism I: Rawls and political liberalism

If Rawls's *A Theory of Justice* is a classic work of twentieth-century political theory (a status it is rightly accorded) then his later work, *Political Liberalism*, represents another distinctive and exceptionally important contribution to the canon. In this book Rawls revisits his liberal political theory in order to deal with what he viewed as 'a serious problem' in his earlier work. This serious problem 'concerns the unrealistic idea of a well-ordered society as it appears in *Theory*' (Rawls 1993: xviii). For Rawls, the unrealistic aspect of his earlier work stems from its failure to recognise both the fact and the value of pluralism. It is this, rather stunning, admission that requires that we revisit Rawls's political theory in this chapter. Our goal here is not to grasp the totality of Rawls's argument. Rather we need to get a sense of the core aspects of his claim that political liberalism can offer principles of justice for a society marked by a real pluralism of moral, social and religious ways of life.

The essence of Rawls's 'serious problem' is that his earlier liberalism required all citizens to endorse his theory of justice on the basis of what he calls a 'comprehensive doctrine'. This means that *A Theory of Justice* expected everyone to share the same moral and political values that led them to affirm the two principles of justice (see the discussion of Rawls in Chapter 7). His acknowledgement of this as a problem recognises that not only is the prospect of a genuinely shared moral societal culture empirically inconceivable but that it is morally undesirable. Pluralism is itself the outcome of human reason under conditions of freedom. Monism could only ever be maintained by the oppressive use of state power (Rawls 1993: 37). However, despite this recognition, Rawls does not want to abandon liberalism. In fact the entire object of his argument is to politicise it. The key distinction that Rawls makes is between his new 'political liberalism' and his earlier 'comprehensive liberalism'. The essence of political liberalism is the attempt to maintain impartiality between moral doctrines by refusing to address the moral topics on which those doctrines divide (Ibid.: 13). Rawls's claim is that political liberalism is a 'freestanding' conception of liberalism. That is, it develops principles of justice that apply to the interaction between citizens but beyond such interaction it does not interfere with moral, cultural or religious life. The fundamental claim is that a monistic, liberal moral culture is unnecessary for the establishment of liberal democratic justice and political stability.

The question Rawls wants to answer is profound but simply put: 'How is it possible for there to exist over time a just and stable society of free and equal citizens, who remain profoundly divided by reasonable religious, philosophical, and moral doctrines?' (Ibid.: 4). Rawls's new theory is modelled on the social-contract model developed in *A Theory of Justice*. It is developed in a similar context (a closed, democratic society) and aims to demonstrate, via the original position/social contract image, that all reasonable people would or should choose the two principles of justice as fairness that you met in Chapter 7. The fact that Rawls is working out principles that are to be applied to a democratic society is important here. It means that the political culture of the society assumes that society should be a fair system of co-operation over time, that citizens are free and equal and that this is maintained via a system of public justification (Ibid.: 14). These are the prevailing norms of society. The insight that Rawls brings to his second version of justice as fairness is that, within the broad parameters of a democratic public political culture, a wide variety of people with different moral and religious views are capable of affirming the same principles of justice.

In the context of our present discussion this is key. If Rawls is right then the liberal democratic nation-state need not be a homogenising and monistic power. The core idea is that the public political culture of a democratic society, from which we draw our principles of justice, is distinct from the social cultures of that society. Any way of life capable of proposing and abiding by fair terms of political cooperation is capable of forming part of an overlapping consensus on the two principles of justice. The ability to form such a consensus is the mark of reasonable rather than simple pluralism. There is an awful lot of information here and it is characterised by a distinctively Rawlsian phraseology that can be intimidating. The basic idea is that people can be bound by their cultural commitments in private (and so they can be parochial, different or pluralistic) yet liberal in public political life (and so part of a universal citizenship). The measure by which social groups and individual life choices are judged reasonable and unreasonable is precisely their ability to engage, on fair terms, in this public political culture. This does not require them to reach agreement on the nature of morality or to share the same God. It works, Rawls argues, because the principles of justice are to be neutral, or impartial between the different accounts of the nature and requirements of morality. This is the crux of the matter. Can *political* liberalism really be neutral between differing conceptions of the good? On what grounds may we require people to leave their religion or culture at home?

Rawls's claim is that there is nothing about the two principles of justice that any reasonable person could object to. On the other hand there is much in the various comprehensive doctrines that make up the social cultures of a society that those who do not share those views could object to. The insistence of a Protestant Christian that those of other faiths worship the Christian God and follow the doctrine of the Protestant Church is a clear example of the latter. Similarly, the insistence of a comprehensive liberal that everyone share the same view of individual autonomy can be seen to be objectionable. Rawls's argument turns on the view that people in democratic societies are both rational and reasonable. Rationality consists in the ability to form, hold and revise a conception of the good life. Being reasonable means 'desiring a social world in which they, as free and equal, can cooperate with others on terms all can accept' (Ibid.: 50). In political liberalism reasonableness is given priority. This means that the ability to engage, on fair and equal terms, in political society is the benchmark of reasonable pluralism. This, Rawls argues, does not harm those distinct ways of life or draw its principles from any one of them. Ways of life that cannot or do not meet this requirement are outlawed.

With these ideas in mind Rawls argues that it is possible for people with very different moral, cultural and religious conceptions of the good to come to what he calls an 'overlapping consensus' on his two principles of justice. This is a strong consensus in which people agree on the value of the two principles of justice to society, each regarding the principles as justified within their comprehensive conceptions, and so do not regard agreement as compromising their principles. By virtue of this fact such a consensus is more than mere ***modus vivendi***. This means that it is more than just a contingent form of accommodation between fundamentally disputing parties who may agree to disagree and settle for an agreement suited to the power relations of the day (compare this with Kymlicka's view of the possibility of consensus below). This overlapping consensus, Rawls argues, breeds 'stability for the right reasons' and binds a plurality of peoples together in a firm and lasting way.

> The fact of reasonable pluralism is not an unfortunate condition of human life, as we might say of pluralism as such, allowing for doctrines that are not only irrational but mad and aggressive. In framing a political conception of justice so it can gain an overlapping consensus, we are not bending it to existing unreason, but to the fact of reasonable pluralism, itself the outcome of the free exercise of human reason under conditions of liberty. (Rawls 1993: 144)

This then is the core of political rather than metaphysical liberalism. The burden of the rest of Rawls's argument is to show that such people could meet in the original position, under the veil of ignorance, and choose shared principles of justice that are liberal in character but do not require a unified moral foundation. Such principles are thus able to be the object of an overlapping consensus and ensure stability. It is a masterful argument and will repay closer inspection. Has it, however, really addressed the fact of pluralism?

Without prejudging the answer to our question we need to look at two claims that Rawls has not done enough to save liberalism from charges of partiality or to accommodate pluralism. The first is that political liberalism does not in fact confine itself to the political but has a far-reaching impact on the ways in which various social and cultural groups might live. The second is that the basic justification for political liberalism still privileges liberal democratic values over and above pluralism. The first charge forms, in part, the basis for Kymlicka's claim that liberalism must take cultural difference more seriously by allowing group-differentiated rights. The second informs Parekh's claim that any political theory that is suited to a multicultural society has to go further still and allow serious intercultural dialogue. In particular Parekh insists that liberal principles should not be accorded priority either as an accident of history (which he takes to be the case in Rawls's work) or as a matter of justice (Parekh 2000: 90).

Liberal responses to multiculturalism II: Kymlicka and multicultural citizenship

Kymlicka's main concern with Rawls's liberal attempt to accommodate diversity is twofold. First, he believes that Rawls's account of pluralism does not take the nature and function of culture seriously enough. Second, and as a consequence of this, Kymlicka believes that the idea of autonomy at work in political liberalism has far-reaching and damaging implications for the internal workings of various cultural groups (Kymlicka 1995: 164).

The core claim here is that cultural and social groups are not reducible to the individuals within them. Culture must be viewed as constitutive of identity and so treated as valuable in itself. This is an important idea and we touched on it earlier. Individuality seems to make perfect sense. Is it not obvious that the prime unit in the human species is a single individual? The answer to this is no. Individualism is itself the product of a time and place. Across history and across culture agents have been characterised in a large number of communal and group ways; by citizenship, by slavery, by caste, by class, by family and by gender. For those of us within the dominant moral and political traditions in the west it is important to note that even something as basic as individualism is a product of *our* cultural heritage. In prioritising (albeit for political rather than philosophical reasons) a conception of the importance of autonomy Rawls is simply not doing this. Kymlicka's point is that some cultural groups have, as an integral part of their identity and way of life, internal restrictions on individual autonomy. These may vary widely. Some groups impose restrictions on apostasy (giving up one's faith or doctrine) or blasphemy (offending against a faith or doctrine). Others enforce or encourage adherence to their way of life by disengaging their children from public education. Some groups, who see the family rather than the individual as the core social unit, may take the decision about marriage away from the potential newlyweds. Some groups clearly foster forms of what liberals would view as gender or class discrimination. The point is not that these peoples are trying to act against the liberal principle of autonomy. The fact that some groups consider the rejection of the teaching of their faith as a serious crime or sin, or perhaps merely as an act that excludes such people from various positions within that community, makes sense within the context of that group. The fact that other groups may consider one's social status a consequence of deeds in a past life and hence not subject to the liberal view that all are equal by birth is similarly important to their identity. To overrule these issues in the name of autonomy may well be to do damage to these ways of life. On the other hand to grant a group the freedom to ignore some of the basic civil liberties of some of its members may be (from a liberal perspective) to harm those individuals.

Kymlicka does not deny that sometimes we have to restrict the internal workings of various groups. A liberal society would hardly tolerate a social group that insisted on proselytising its religious beliefs in the manner of the infamous Inquisition. Similarly, a liberal people would want to deny that Salman Rushdie, author of *The Satanic Verses*, should be subject to the *fatwa* that demanded his execution (even if we acknowledge the power of the insult that many Muslims felt). However, if we are to grant cultural groups a real place in the political debate we cannot automatically deny that these differences are relevant or automatically assume that we can impose a liberal code of conduct upon them.

Kymlicka does not want to abandon liberalism. In fact he wants to argue that 'the most defensible liberal theory is based on the value of autonomy' (Ibid.: 165). However, he does think that he can go further than Rawls to accommodate multiculturalism by advocating differentiated group rights for some (but not all) minorities. Here we do not need to rehearse the liberal argument for autonomy. Rather, we need to explore Kymlicka's claim that a proper understanding of culture and of minority rights actually promotes individual freedom (Ibid.: 75).

One of Kymlicka's most important claims is that there is an irreducible link between freedom and culture. This is because Kymlicka takes seriously the view that 'societal cultures' are 'a context of choice'. Put simply, freedom involves making choices amongst various options, and our societal culture not only provides us with those options, but also makes them meaningful to us.

> People make choices about the social practices around them, based on their beliefs about the value of these practices . . . and to have a belief about the value of a practice is, in the first instance, a matter of understanding the meanings attached to it by our culture. (Ibid.: 83)

The main idea here is that meaningful individual choice takes place within a cultural context and so any political theory wishing to foster individual freedom has to take account of these contexts. This is not a hugely novel claim. Many liberals, Rawls included, so Kymlicka argues, have accepted this fact. However, in associating societal culture with the culture of the national state they misunderstand the context of choice and lay their theories open to charges of monism and homogenisation (Ibid.: 93).

Because Kymlicka wishes to retain and promote core liberal values it is inevitably the case that the sorts of choices some people will wish to make from within their societal context will clash with those liberal principles. However, he continues, forcing illiberal cultures to assimilate into the dominant liberal culture would be to ignore the importance of culture to choice. So how do we decide, in a principled way, which cultures we should accommodate and which we should encourage to assimilate? For Kymlicka the answer to this turns on how the minority culture in question developed its place within a given state.

Kymlicka does not believe that the requirement to assimilate is unjust provided that the minority in question had the option to either stay in their homeland or emigrate.

> Given the connection between choice and culture . . . people

> should be able to live and work in their own culture. But like any other right, this right can be waived, and immigration is one way of waiving one's right. In deciding to uproot themselves, immigrants voluntarily relinquish some of the rights that go along with their original national membership. (Ibid.: 97)

Kymlicka reluctantly extends this principle to refugees for practical rather than moral reasons (Ibid.: 98–9) but a basic principle has been established. In fact, most of Kymlicka's work is premised on this idea. Most states, he argues, are either multi-national or polyethnic or both. Multinationality is typical of states made up of several nations, such as those containing a number of indigenous peoples, or where historical development has included a federation of distinct national groups (such as the relations between the English and French in Canada). Polyethnic states are those characterised by immigrant populations. These, Kymlicka maintains, are the relevant sources of cultural pluralism. Drawing on this insight Kymlicka suggests three categories of group-differentiated rights that offer, in varying degrees, ways to accommodate cultural pluralism. These are (1) self-government rights, (2) polyethnic rights and (3) special representation rights (Ibid.: 27).

Self-government rights are, or should be, accorded to national minorities. Here national minorities include groups such as the Québécois (French-Canadian) and the Chicanos and aboriginal peoples such as the Inuit, native American Indian tribes and native Hawaiians. These groups, by virtue of their being a people or nation, are entitled to claim devolved political powers to be substantially controlled by members of that minority. This, argues Kymlicka, would (and in some cases does) allow them to make real choices about health, education, law, family and resource development. Here Kymlicka points to the federal system in Canada (which allows the Québécois a real voice in Canadian national politics and in their own cultural development) and the establishment of tribal reservations in the USA and of band reserves in Canada, which grants substantial powers to tribal/band councils (Ibid.: 29). Polyethnic rights are those rights properly claimed by immigrant groups. These measures

> are intended to help ethnic groups and religious minorities express their cultural particularity and pride without it hampering their success in the economic and political institutions of the dominant society. Like self-government rights, these polyethnic rights are not seen as temporary, because the cultural differences they protect

> are not something we seek to eliminate. But . . . unlike self-government rights, polyethnic rights are usually intended to promote integration into the larger society, not self-government. (Ibid.: 31)

The rights may take the form of anti-racism laws, public funding to support cultural practices, or exemption from certain national laws that may disadvantage them, given their religious practices. Special representation rights may be sought by both groups and amount to reserved places in the political institutions of the state to ensure the visibility and protection of minority opinion.

This argument is both instructive and distinct from that of Rawls. The major difference is that Kymlicka argues that even the attempt to be neutral between competing cultural claims results in a diminution of the autonomy of people. Autonomy entails the ability to make choices and the ability to make choices relies on a social and cultural context. Therefore we must take active steps to ensure that this context is taken into account. However, we still have to broach the murkiest waters in this debate. What happens when the desires of minority cultures conflict radically with the liberal principle of autonomy? The point here is that Kymlicka's argument is fine so long as we are talking about the desire to wear a turban rather than a crash helmet but what happens when we face up to the desire to enforce cultural conformity by coercively restricting freedom of conscience and religion, or by restricting access to education, or by enforced arranged marriage? Kymlicka's response again turns, in large part, on the distinction between national culture and immigrant culture. It is more legitimate to compel respect for liberal principles in dealings with immigrant minorities than it might be in dealings with national minorities. Some national minorities may claim that particularistic laws that deal coercively with blasphemy or distribute property and wealth on the basis of cultural conformity are essential to the preservation of their way of life and thus the context of choice. It is clear, Kymlicka argues, that laws of this type are wrong from a liberal point of view. What is less clear is that liberals have a right to impose their point of view on the national minority. Kymlicka fleshes out this idea by showing that the same reasons liberals have for viewing imperialism and colonisation as unjust should apply to national minorities. Imposing a liberal point of view on some foreign group is no different to imposing such views on a national minority (Ibid.: 165–6). This shows how radical Kymlicka's conception of multicultural citizenship can be and he concludes that measures such as excluding these minorities from federal bills of rights and judicial review may be a necessary accompaniment to self-government rights.

Lurking uneasily in the background to Kymlicka's theory is an awareness that according the historical status of these groups priority over the moral status of liberal principles is a pretty shaky argument (Ibid.: 170). This is not something Kymlicka goes on to address. His project aimed to show that differentiated rights are a necessary part of liberalism. Nevertheless we need to be aware that liberalism is not defended as a historically parochial way of life. It is not merely 'what we do around here'. There are moral reasons why liberals believe individual autonomy is a core value and provided that can be defended there is no reason to accord illiberal practices any moral standing. However, rather than engage with this very difficult topic, Kymlicka points out that spelling out the implications of liberal principles of freedom and equality should form the first stage not of interference but of intercultural dialogue. If groups cannot be brought to share basic principles then Kymlicka proposes two potential solutions. The first is mere *modus vivendi*. This, you will recall, is a much weaker form of consensus than Rawls's overlapping consensus but it may be all we can manage legitimately. The second is to develop mechanisms similar to international mechanisms for dealing with human-rights violations. Here Kymlicka's insight is that we often overestimate the illiberality of minority cultures. Often such national cultures are both open to claims about individual freedom and willing (more so than sovereign states) to conform to external review. As Kymlicka wryly notes,

> most Indian tribes do not oppose all forms of external review. What they object to is being subject to the constitution of their conquerors, which they had no role in drafting, and being answerable to federal courts, composed solely of non-Indian justices (Ibid.: 169).

Nevertheless we need to be aware that disagreements between groups are not just about historical priority but also about moral principles. A recognition of this has a number of implications for a critical understanding of Kymlicka's position. First, if Kymlicka's attachment to autonomy is a moral attachment (rather than a product of his societal culture), as it seems to be, then we need to explore the question of whether there is anything about it that would allow it to function as a decisive standard. It seems a little arbitrary to suggest that it trumps the moral views of immigrants but not of national minorities. Either it is a decisive moral argument or it is not. If it is not then the implications for multicultural politics are far more wide-ranging than Kymlicka allows. If it is then we need to recognise that decisive moral arguments do not necessarily wait upon consensus and we may construct laws to ensure individual freedoms. Similarly if a specific societal culture is morally necessary to autonomy, rather than contingently necessary, it is not at all clear that immigrants can or should waive the right to this freedom. If, on the other hand, any functioning societal culture will do then why make exceptions for illiberal national minorities? In attempting to widen and deepen our understanding of multicultural politics Parekh picks up on these very issues.

Parekh and multiculturalism

Parekh's multiculturalist thesis stems firstly out of a rejection of relativism and monism and subsequently from the claim that liberal attempts to respond to the fact of multiculturalism do not take the concept of culture seriously enough. In identifying the faults of these theories he lays the ground for an argument about the nature and importance of culture to human existence and argues for a politics based on intercultural dialogue. In doing this Parekh engages with the primary, but very thorny, issue of intercultural evaluation of disputed practices such as arranged marriages, polygamy, female circumcision, ritual slaughter of animals, issues of customary dress and participation in aspects of public education, all of which have aroused different degrees of concern over the years (Parekh 2000: 264–94). Parekh also addresses the relationship between minority cultures and the 'operative public values' of society. It is a comprehensive work by a contemporary British political theorist, who is also a member of the House of Lords and a very senior figure in the UK Commission for Racial Equality and the chair of the Commission on the Future of Multi-ethnic Britain.

In setting the scene for his argument Parekh considers the many questions that our enterprise must face.

> The questions relate to the cultural rights of minorities, the nature of collective rights, why cultures differ, whether their diversity is a transitional or permanent phenomenon, whether and why it is desirable, whether all cultures deserve equal respect, whether they

> should be judged on their own terms, by ours, or by universal standards and how the last can be derived, and whether and how we can communicate across and resolve deep differences between cultures. They also include questions about the state's relation to culture, such as whether it should ignore or give public recognition to its various cultures, and if the latter whether it should privilege the dominant culture or treat them all equally. (Ibid.: 9)

For Parekh the relativist answer, which asserts that there is no possibility for intercultural dialogue or evaluation, is mistaken because it ignores cross-culturally shared human properties and because it misunderstands the nature of culture (Ibid.: 127). In advancing the view that a culture is a neat, homogeneous and impenetrably bounded entity, a fact that Parekh argues is demonstrably false, relativists deny us the basic materials of moral and political mediation. Similarly, but on the opposite end of the spectrum, monism overplays the significance of our shared human nature to the extent that it ignores difference as morally irrelevant, unaccountably asserting the moral primacy of those things we share over those things that make us different (Ibid.: 18). In doing so monism fails to recognise the ways in which culture mediates, constitutes and reconstitutes moral value (Ibid.: 127). For Parekh both culture and human nature are vital starting points for political and moral reflection but in emphasising one over the other we make a grave mistake. Parekh's detailed account of human beings stems out of this idea.

> Human beings are articulated at three different but interrelated levels: what they share as members of a common species, what they derive from and share as members of a cultural community, and what they succeed in giving themselves as reflective individuals. (Ibid.:123)

The very basis of Parekh's political theory is the attempt to give adequate expression to the interplay between these three features. Relativism and monism are clearly too extreme. We must not overemphasise difference and we must not overemphasise similarity. It is a balancing act that Parekh also believes that contemporary liberal responses to diversity have failed to pull off (Ibid.: 80–113). Parekh's critique of Rawls is similar in scope and content to that offered by Kymlicka. One chief concern is that Rawls's assumption that political liberalism does not presuppose comprehensive liberalism is unconvincing. Indeed Parekh believes that political liberalism is 'conceptually and substantively parasitic upon comprehensive liberalism' in that it presupposes a conception of human individuality that is not to be found in other traditions of thought (Ibid.: 86). As a consequence of this Parekh believes that Rawls's work is deeply inhospitable to cultural plurality. He argues that Rawls's political liberalism unduly restricts political discourse. Allowing people into society provided they leave their moral and religious baggage at the door is to bar important resources from political debate. To offer only a unitary conception of individual citizenship is to deny cultural pluralism a voice from the outset.

From Parekh's point of view Kymlicka's liberal multiculturalism does not fare much better. Parekh explicitly picks up on the point that there appear to be no general or undisputed principles that inform Kymlicka's hierarchy of national, refugee and immigrant minority rights. If culture is a primary good in that it is a necessary condition for the good life then are we right to deny immigrants access to their culture (Ibid.: 103)? Parekh also believes that Kymlicka 'absolutises liberalism'. Kymlicka's pervasive suggestion that national minorities are to be given self-government rights provided they govern themselves within certain liberal parameters fails to take culture seriously enough (Ibid.: 102, 110).

Instead of relativism, monism and the attempts of liberals such as Rawls and Kymlicka to develop a minimum universalism, Parekh's theory takes the form of '**pluralist universalism**'. Pluralist universalism entails a particular view of human nature, of culture and of morality itself. We share certain attributes as members of the same species and this has some normative force but it is very thin. We share a physical and mental structure, have the same basic needs and common conditions of growth. But our nature is formed not merely from these basic characteristics but in tandem with our active participation in nature. Humans act on nature and change it and in return nature acts on humans and changes them. This dialectical (meaning a complex interplay between nature, culture and reason) account of human existence (Ibid.: 119) means that we inevitably encounter more than just bare human nature when we look at people.

> Thanks to human creativity, geographical conditions, historical experiences, and so on, different societies develop different systems of meaning, ways of looking at the world, ideals of excellence, traits of temperament and forms of moral and social life, giving

> different orientation and structure to universally shared human capacities and desires and cultivating wholly new ones of their own. (Ibid.: 120)

This is what Parekh means when he says that humans are culturally embedded. It is important to note here that because of the important place of culture in this dialectic, and because culture is by definition a social or group concept, we need to be able to conceive of people not merely as individuals but as part of a collective group or groups. For Parekh the rights of cultures are 'primary collective rights' (Ibid.: 213). This idea is key. Typically liberals claim that we should not recognise group rights because powerful groups can (and do) threaten the freedom of the individuals within their boundaries. Here liberals judge certain aspects of culture (such as arranged marriages or female circumcision) from the perspective of individual autonomy rather than the significance of each practice within the given culture. Alternatively liberals may argue that special group rights breach the core principle of equality, so that allowing a Sikh to carry a *kirpan* (a small dagger and a mandatory symbol of their faith) and proscribing the carrying of offensive weapons more generally, or allowing a Sikh to wear a turban instead of a motorcycle helmet while making the wearing of crash helmets a matter of law for everyone else, is wrong. For Parekh primary collective rights are simply not reducible to the rights of the individuals within those groups. These liberal claims against group rights 'absolutise' or privilege liberal principles. For Parekh, there is no good reason to do this (indeed doing so is inherently discriminatory) and once we recognise this then we can begin to think about equality in a more culturally sensitive way.

Because of the dramatic and dialectical interplay between nature and culture we must avoid privileging either those things that make us similar or those things that divide us when we make judgements about the best sort of life. This is the essence of pluralist universalism. 'There are universal moral values and there is a creative interplay between them and the thick complex moral structures of different societies, the latter domesticating and pluralizing the former and being in turn reinterpreted and revised in their light' (Ibid.: 127). This understanding of the human existence leads to a very specific account of morality. Moral principles do not leap out of nature. You cannot say 'this is natural therefore this is right'. This is because nature is dialectically derived. Making a judgement, or deciding that something has value (the essence of morality) must therefore be dialogical. That means that working out the moral hierarchy, the order of values must stem from cross-cultural dialogue. For Parekh 'moral values have no foundations in the sense of an undisputable and objective basis, but they do have grounds in the form of intersubjectively discussable reasons and are not arbitrary' (Ibid.: 128).

The core idea here is that a roughly equal interplay between culture, nature and cross-cultural dialogue forms the basis for morality. Simply saying 'this is nature therefore it is right' is not enough. Simply saying 'this my culture – it is right' is not enough. Because we have to take account of both, and because cultures are widely differentiated, morality is bound to be pluralistic in form. This denies relativist and monist points of view. It also denies a starting point to 'thin' or minimalist liberalism of the sort argued for by Rawls and Kymlicka as, Parekh argues, they still give too much weight to, or absolutise, liberal principles such as autonomy (Ibid.: 110). Solving disputes between moral standards must therefore be achieved through dialogue.

This is a very interesting account of the nature of morality and a strong argument concerning the importance of culture to morality. The real crunch, for all multiculturalist arguments, comes when we examine the logic of intercultural evaluation and especially the question of disputed practices. We already know that there is no single principle that we can use to solve disputes. Nevertheless there are times when society does voice concern (rightly or wrongly) about the practices of communities within its borders. Here Parekh is thinking in terms of female circumcision, ritual slaughter of animals in the Muslim and Jewish traditions, polygamy, refusal by Gypsies and the Amish community to send their children to schools and so on. In proposing a method of evaluation premised on his moral theory Parekh starts with one major point that does not immediately spring from his earlier work. Because Parekh is about to outline the core principles of a political dialogue rather than a philosophical dialogue he begins by noting that political dialogue takes place within specific societies. Because of this empirical fact 'we start and cannot but start with what I shall call society's operative public values, which provide the context and point of orientation for all such discussions' (Ibid.: 267). Every society has a shared normative framework and this is the default position in moral and political debate. Disputed practices offend against this shared value system but that does not mean we have automatic reason to ban or condemn them. Culture, whether it is the culture of the majority or the minority, is important and so the disapproving society is obliged to give reasons for its disapproval and to listen to the reasons why the offending party believes the practice to be morally and culturally valuable. This is implied by Parekh's earlier work. The details of Parekh's account of the dialogue need not concern us here but it is important to note that while everyone has a duty to respect the moral importance of culture the burden of proof is on the minority. Unless it can be shown that the offending practice is essential to the way of life of a cultural community, or that the practice does not actually offend against the operative public values of society (but merely the aesthetic taste of society), then 'the operative public values of the wider society should prevail' (Ibid.: 272).

Here then we have the fundamental concepts at work in Parekh's multiculturalist political thought. Human nature is both universal and embedded and thus morality is discursive or dialogical and not universal or ahistorical. Appeal to nature or to culture is not enough. Even an appeal to religious principles is not enough and this is often thought of as a trump card. Religion is interpreted and culturally embellished and we stand accountable to morality for that embellishment. The fact that Parekh does emphasise the place of the operative public values of society may seem a little surprising given that he is the most multicultural thinker on our continuum. But one thing is certain: the response 'this is the way we do things around here' in the face of disputed claims fails to live up to the requirements of morality. Similarly we need to be aware that moral ideas such as autonomy are also culturally coloured. They may be central to our self-understanding (or we might think they are) but they are not non-negotiable. The key insight is that there is always an obligation to take seriously claims from minority groups that the disputed practice is valuable and if that claim is sustained then it is the operative public value system that has to amend its view and develop. Offending against the operative public morality establishes only a *prima facie* case against the practice. This is the core of pluralist universalism.

How then does this structure our thinking about politics? First it gives us reason to approach the core features of the modern state critically. The modern state, as it has developed over the last three centuries in Europe, asserts the territorial identity of its members in a way that transcends and cuts across cultural communities. It also, Parekh argues, abstracts away class, ethnicity, and religion in favour of a homogenising and unitary conception of citizenship that treats each individual identically. In short the thrust over the last 300 years has been to privilege territorial over all other forms of identity (Ibid.: 180–3). It is hardly surprising that Parekh goes on to argue that

> the task of exploring new modes of constituting the modern state and perhaps altogether new types of political formation is particularly acute in multicultural societies. They need to find ways of pluralizing the state without undermining its unity and the ability to act decisively in the collective interest (Ibid.: 195).

Despite the heavy emphasis that Parekh places on the operative public values of existing societies there is an implicit critique of their dominance. There is no principled reason to accept the moral authority of these legal structures. Rather, Parekh offers conservative and prudential reasons (stability etc.) for accepting the authority of these values, a legacy of his modified but still Oakeshottian world view (see Chapter 9). Recognising group rights and the importance of culture should have a dramatic influence on the structure of the modern state, including a possible dispersal of sovereignty and legal jurisdiction.

Critical ideas

What then, are the core issues at stake between the different points on our continuum? The real crux of the issue is whether, or how, we should respond to the empirical fact of multiculturalism. Should we develop a **unitary, difference-blind citizenship** with equal rights? Or should we develop a **differentiated citizenship** with difference-sensitive rights? Here our answer may well turn on how much weight we give to the importance of individual autonomy as against embedded or constitutive identity. If we favour individual autonomy then it is very possible that group identity will suffer. If we prevent groups from encouraging compliance with tradition (by educating their young members only in traditional ways, forcing them to marry internally to the group, etc.) that group may well become both resentful and diluted. If on the other hand we respect the needs and desires of groups then we have to recognise that occasionally individuals will suffer. We need reasons to back up our preferences here. Answering these questions requires us to reflect on the very nature of human existence and society.

If we do acknowledge the importance of social and cultural ties – either as something constitutive of identity (Parekh), or as a context within which individuals make choices (Kymlicka), or as the only outcome of human reason under conditions of liberty (Rawls) – we have further questions to answer. First, what groups are to be accorded moral and political recognition? Why Muslims and not Jedi Knights? Why Somalis and not Manchester United football supporters, who also have their own dress codes, rituals and icons? Many different groups have many different reasons for being taken seriously as a group. What distinguishes a culture from any other interest group demanding special rights from government? Some seem to claim that a religious base to a culture distinguishes it. But this would be to discriminate against secular cultural groups and poses the equally difficult question 'what makes a religion a religion?'. What is the difference between Christianity and Scientology (which is not accorded the status of religion in much of the world) or the desire to be recognised as a Jedi Knight? One of the reasons liberals attempt to be neutral between various claims is to avoid the controversies of this very argument. If all are equal before the law then the state does not discriminate between different groups. This liberal claim is met with some derision by communitarians and multiculturalists, who argue that not to make special provision for ethno-cultural goods is to discriminate against them and the people whose lives are led and make sense within those boundaries.

But people are capable of revising their conception of the good, moving within and between cultural assumptions and boundaries. Ensuring they have the freedom to do this is to ensure they respect the basis of political interaction. It is to ensure that the groups are themselves reasonable (Rawls) or able to respect autonomy and pluralism (Kymlicka). Parekh's concern with this answer is that to assume the value of autonomy is to privilege liberalism from the outset and to prejudge the question of the value of different cultural perspectives. There are two arguments here. First there is the moral argument. Which is more important, individual freedom or cultural freedom? How might we strike a principled balance between them? Second there is the political argument. If there is a dispute about this moral question how do we solve it? Can we reach an overlapping consensus on political principles of the public political culture in question? Should we simply develop a *modus vivendi*? Should we foster intercultural dialogue and embrace the changes this brings?

There is an important codicil to this political argument. Debates about how to solve these issues always take place in a particular time and place. How should we govern the relations between the claims of minority groups and the dominant viewpoint? In a variety of ways the three representatives of our continuum all argue that if there is no compelling evidence to the contrary then the dominant view must prevail. Only Kymlicka, when writing about indigenous peoples, demurs from this point. What is doing the work here? Is it a principled answer or is it a default argument stressing historical precedence? How happy are you with the playground retorts 'well, we were here first' or 'there's more of us so watch it'? In particular it seems that Parekh, and to a lesser extent Kymlicka, have moral reasons to reject this type of claim.

These questions are urgent and difficult. Engaging with them requires patience, sensitivity, the ability to make informed normative judgments and the willingness to subject those judgments to the scrutiny of others. In this chapter you have met some of the most effective attempts to do precisely this and it is here that you must pick up the baton and continue running.

Topics for discussion

1. How would you describe the fact of multiculturalism and its impact on modern society?
2. What sorts of arguments can you put forward in defence of the liberal principle of autonomy?
3. What are the key differences between the arguments of Rawls, Kymlicka and Parekh?
4. Why are cultural rights important?
5. Which is more just: a unitary conception of justice or a differentiated conception of justice? Why?

Critical glossary

Multiculturalism A term used in two distinct ways. The first is descriptive: multiculturalism describes the fact of ethno-cultural pluralism in society. The second is normative and argues for a genuinely multicultural approach to political theory (see Parekh's argument).

Identity What makes us who we are? The answer to this question is hotly contested but the debate falls into two broad camps. The first is that our identity is formed primarily by our membership of a single species – we have moral standing because we are human. The second (constitutive) idea is that our identity is formed in the specific social and cultural groups that we live in – we have particular moral standing because we gain such standing from our ethno-cultural context.

Unitary citizenship — A unitary conception of citizenship argues that all citizens should be treated the same way by virtue of their status as equal citizens. Cf. differentiated citizenship.

Pluralism — Pluralism argues that there are many, equally valuable, conceptions of what is right or wrong. Cf. liberal monism.

Liberal monism — Liberal monism models the universalist and individualist liberal political theory encountered in the work of Locke and Rawls. Monism is often defined in opposition to pluralism (q.v.), where monism recognises one way of life as just and pluralism recognises many ways of life as just.

Political liberalism — Rawls's *Political Liberalism* (1993) is defined in opposition to his 'comprehensive liberalism' as laid out in *A Theory of Justice* (1971). The latter is defined in terms of a moral attachment to the principles of liberalism and the former as a political mechanism for accommodating reasonable pluralism.

Overlapping consensus	Overlapping consensus represents a political (and in Rawls's terms moral) accommodation based on the just nature of an agreement on how to get along. For Rawls a political order based on overlapping consensus is the goal of politics as it promotes 'stability for the right reasons' and is likely to be far more stable than 'mere' *modus vivendi* (q.v.) politics.
Relativism	(See also glossary for the Introduction) The idea that values have validity only in a particular social or historical context. In this context relativism is much more radical than pluralism, which still attempts to find reasons for limiting the validity of some claims.
Modus vivendi	In Rawls's political thought *modus vivendi* represents a political accommodation, a compromise based on instrumental reasoning – a way of getting along. However, for Rawls a political order based on overlapping consensus (q.v.) is the goal of politics as it promotes 'stability for the right reasons' and is likely to be far more stable than 'mere' *modus vivendi* politics.
Pluralistic universalism	Parekh's expression of the universal tenets of multiculturalist political theory. At its core is the refusal to privilege those things that unite us over those things that make us different.
Differentiated citizenship	A differentiated conception of citizenship argues that different citizens may have different social, cultural

and religious needs and so must be treated differently in order to be valued equally. Cf. unitary citizenship.

List of references/Further reading

There is plenty of reading available for this topic. In the first instance it would be a good idea to read the primary texts discussed here.

Kymlicka, W. (1995), *Multicultural Citizenship: A Liberal Theory of Minority Rights*, Oxford: Oxford University Press.
Parekh, B. (2000), *Rethinking Multiculturalism: Cultural Diversity and Political Theory*, Basingstoke: Palgrave.
Rawls, J. (1993), *Political Liberalism*, New York: Columbia University Press.

For a forthright monist/egalitarian response to these positions see

Barry, B. (2001), *Culture and Equality*, Oxford: Polity Press.

For secondary reading on the debates see

Bellamy, R. & Hollis, M. (eds) (1999), *Pluralism and Liberal Neutrality*, London: Frank Cass.
Gutmann, A. (ed.) (1994), *Multiculturalism: Examining the Politics of Recognition*, Princeton: Princeton University Press.
Haddock, B. & Sutch, P. (eds) (2003), *Multiculturalism, Identity and Rights*, London & New York: Routledge.
Kymlicka, W. (ed.) (1995), *The Rights of Minority Cultures*, Oxford: Oxford University Press.

SECTION IV

CHALLENGES TO UNIVERSALISM AND FOUNDATIONALISM

CHAPTER NINE

HISTORICAL

Burke and Oakeshott

CONCEPTUAL

Conservatism: Reason vs Tradition

So far in this introduction we have covered a wide range of approaches to politics and to the way that political thought should proceed. It may be, however, that there are a number of common themes that should be identified and addressed. These include the claims that:

1. *it is possible to abstract from history and context in order to identify a better or best world.* We find this thought in Plato's claim that we can gain knowledge of a true reality behind the observed world and that the forms constitute 'ideal patterns laid up in heaven'. We find this also in John Rawls's conception of the original position or in theories that utilise a state of nature to abstract from the contingencies of social life in order to identify the best form of political order. Both socialism and utilitarianism claim to get behind our local understandings and to identify either the material basis of society or the real basis of human motivation and morality in pleasure and pain.
2. *we identify this ideal through the exercise of philosophical reason.* This is the point of Plato's philosopher-rulers and of the Simile of the Cave. Likewise reason underpins Aristotle's restriction of citizenship in the *polis*. It is also as hypothetical exercises of reason in the identification of the best political order or of natural law that Rawls conceives of the original position and the social contract theorists of the state of nature.

3. *we should attempt to reconstruct the world so that it accords with this reasonable ideal.* This thought is implicit in the prescriptive nature of much normative theory. Plato outlines the just *polis* because he is recommending that we establish it. In the same way Hobbes, Locke, Owen, Marx, Bentham, Rawls, Nozick and Parekh are all offering arguments about why we should reform our political institutions and practices to match particular rational ideals. Much normative political thought is concerned with 'putting the world to rights'. Implicit in this approach is the further thought that the world is the sort of place that will be receptive to our attempts to change it.

In an example from closer to home, this whole approach to politics is embodied in the way different political parties or groups claim to provide us with distinctive visions of a 'better future' and attempt to convince us that at least our bit of the world should be remade in line with the most popular vision.

We need to ask ourselves whether we should accept this conception of political philosophy at face value. We can look back over a long and violent human political history and it seems that much of that violence has been justified by a confidence in having identified the eternal ideal. The less savoury aspects of Christian history illustrate well the violence that truth is capable of bringing with it. In the same way the history of the twentieth century provides numerous and particularly stark examples of the horror that can accompany attempts to reconstruct the world along rational lines, from the terrors of Stalinism and Nazism to the well-intentioned redrawing of European borders in the post-First World War peace settlements. Conservatism invites us to look again at both the rebuilding project itself and the tools we might have at our disposal in the identification and pursuit of a suitable project. Conservative thinkers question the suitability of the tools, such as human reason, for the jobs they are asked to do. The suggestion is that the thinkers we have looked at so far are trying to do something akin to building an entire house armed only with a sledgehammer. They also ask whether the architect's plans are suitable for the context in which they are to be applied. Is it desirable, or even possible, to draw up a single set of plans for a building that will be built many times to that one set but will be put to different purposes by different people in different circumstances? Is there perhaps something about human relationships, with one another and with the world, that might lead us to be concerned about this entire way of conceiving of politics? The grounds of this conservative questioning are varied. Many proponents and commentators on conservatism tie it to a range of beliefs in natural law, a providential order reflecting a divine purpose and original sin. It is one of Michael Oakeshott's central contentions that these beliefs are not necessary underpinnings for a conservative disposition (Oakeshott 1962: 183–4) and one of the most helpful general books on conservatism, by Anthony Quinton, is written to demonstrate that the most important elements of conservatism are secular in nature. This chapter will predominantly focus on the secular and political possibilities involved in asking and answering these questions with a conservative disposition.

In asking these questions conservatives are questioning the universal in the light of the particular, the hypothetical and abstract in favour of the situated and historical. They question whether the blind faith in the power of reason to deliver us from our problems might not be misplaced. They also question whether the complexity of social and political relations might not be such in order to ensure that the outcome of rational abstraction fails to apply to the real world. Finally, conservatives want to draw our attention to way in which that failure to apply can have disastrous consequences. Given this stress on context and history it may seem strange that, to some extent, this chapter detaches conservative thought from the historical contexts to which it responds. However, it is an important claim of conservative thinkers themselves that, from the historical responses and self-understandings of conservatives, we can draw out the features of an attitude or disposition towards certain sorts of change and certain types of political action. In this chapter we shall illustrate this disposition by briefly working through the ideas of Edmund Burke and Oakeshott. Both Burke's *Reflections on the Revolution in France* and Oakeshott's *Rationalism in Politics* are works in a polemical style. They contain strong arguments mixed in with harsh invective and strident warnings about taking the wrong attitude towards politics. Together they form a good introduction to conservative thought.

Burke's *Reflections on the Revolution in France*

Burke's *Reflections* was written in 1790 as a letter to a gentleman in Paris concerning the 1789 French Revolution. This revolution, under the banners of liberty, equality and fraternity, against the monarchy and the *ancien régime* was received by many as a victory of progress and justice. The year 1789 has come to be regarded as a turning point in European and world history, a date from which we measure the growth of mass ideologies and the basis of modern ideas of human rights. Burke refers to the revolution as 'the most astonishing that has hitherto happened in the world' but then goes on to foreshadow its degeneration into a violent regime where 'you see nothing but the gallows' (Burke 1968: 92, 172). Correctly identifying the revolution as a momentous historical event, rather than celebrate the victory of liberty, Burke was concerned that 'rage and phrenzy will pull down more in half an hour, than prudence, deliberation, and foresight can build up in a hundred years' (Ibid.: 279–80). His conservatism was formulated as a response to the revolutionary fervour that followed 1789, both in France and also amongst many learned Englishmen who seemed to take France as an example to be admired. He was worried that what he saw as a fundamental threat to a free and civilised way of life others saw as a model for the development of free and just states across Europe.

Burke regarded society as a closely knit whole consisting, not of an agglomeration of individuals who just happen to coexist in the same territory, but of groups of people whose very identities are social and shaped by the history of common experience that identifies them as the people they are. Our identities and loyalties are tied up with the 'little platoon we belong to in society' and, through the natural way those platoons link together, our society more generally. Our relations with the polity are extensions of our 'family affections'; national bonds are akin to 'domestic ties' that link us together in the image of 'a relation of blood'. This is an **organic** conception of society, of a nation as a naturally organised living body, an 'immortal corporate body', in which each part (or platoon) has a well-defined role for the good of the whole and its members (Ibid.: 299, 135, 120, 247). A revolution must be seen as a traumatic upheaval in this body. Burke does not doubt that the French Revolution can be seen as a well-intentioned utopian attempt to realise a better world by tearing down the old and that some good may actually have been done. 'Those who destroy everything certainly will remove some grievance. They who make everything new, have a chance that they may establish something beneficial' (Ibid.: 374). Any benefit, however, is a matter of chance and bought at a price. For Burke, the revolutionaries are like utopians; 'considering their speculative designs of infinite value' they are committed to disregarding 'the actual arrangements of the state as of no estimation' (Ibid.: 155).

A claim that the world should be remodelled in accordance with a rational ideal involves ignoring our actual organic and social particular interests and attachments in favour of abstract and disembodied 'loose theories' that aim to reinvent those interests and attachments. In casting aside the organic and living social ties that have been nurtured over time political revolutionaries show themselves willing to 'cut up the infant for the sake of an experiment' (Ibid.: 277). By placing their faith in an ideal and in the power of human reason to identify and implement that ideal the revolutionaries are endangering the very things that underpin our social identities, the local and national ties that bind us together and make us who we are. This is exactly the approach to political order that the social-contract theorists seem to adopt. By going back to first principles in a state of nature peopled by unconnected individuals they aim to identify the sort of political regimes that can command our loyalty, independently of any consideration of our particular social and political circumstances and any preexisting ties.

Burke is adamant, in opposition to the Platonic approach and to the social contractarians, that the 'science of constructing a commonwealth' is not an activity that can be approached in the abstract, simply by an application of reason. Our politics and society are too complex for such a simple approach to succeed. The intricate web of relationships that characterise any society and the 'gross and complicated mass of human passions and concerns' are such that it is no easy task to link social causes and consequences, or even to identify which causes and consequences are of the greatest importance (Ibid.: 152). Predicting, in the abstract, the effect of any political action is too difficult a task for us to pursue with any confidence of success. It may be that we can construct a vision of society that caters perfectly for one aspect of human concern, and another vision to cater for another aspect, and so on. However, the 'abstract perfection' of these visions 'is their practical defect'. Human societies are engaged in the pursuit of a complex mass of interests and concerns and any simple vision that perfectly embodied a single concern to the exclusion of others would be 'fundamentally defective' in ignoring the impact and importance of that complexity (Ibid.: 151, 153). Indeed, in ignoring this complexity 'very plausible schemes, with very pleasing commencements, have often shameful and lamentable conclusions' (Ibid.: 152). The failure of the 'fallible and feeble contrivances of our reason' when faced with the complexity of actual circumstance highlights the 'ignorance and fallibility of mankind' when we place too great a faith in theory and speculation (Ibid.: 121, 376). Taking a sceptical stand against the philosophical drive to abstraction that characterises the social-contract theorists for example, Burke announces:

> I cannot stand forward, and give praise or blame to any thing which relates to human actions, and human concerns, on a simple view of the object, as it stands stripped of every relation, in all the nakedness and solitude of metaphysical abstraction. Circumstances (which with some gentlemen pass for nothing) give in reality to every political principle its distinguishing colour, and discriminating effect. The circumstances are what render every civil and political scheme beneficial or noxious to mankind. (Ibid.: 89–90)

It is this thought that informs Burke's concerns about the revolutionaries' attempts to portray 1789 as the establishment of English liberties in France. The project of transplanting a political system from one set of circumstances to another, just like that of developing a constitution for all circumstances, ignores the complexity of social relations that makes its impact uncertain and disregards the complex contexts that render this abstract approach inappropriate.

Many French revolutionaries greatly admired what they took to be England's constitution of liberty. Burke claims that they have misunderstood what sort of achievement this constitution is. It is not that Englishmen were once unfree and then established a constitution that gave them their freedom. Whilst the English had their own revolution in 1688, Burke is concerned to impress on his reader that this was a revolution to preserve ancient laws and liberties, not to tear them up and start afresh. The English revolutionaries wished, as Burke does a century later, to understand their liberty as a inheritance from their forefathers, built on a body of inherited institutions and with reference to a principle of reverence for antiquity. They claimed their liberties not on abstract principles as the rights of man, but instead as the historical rights of Englishmen. In understanding their claims as hereditary titles based on the long history of English institutions they implicitly understood that the practical wisdom involved in inhabiting a particular social world, or context, is a better tool than any 'theoretic science'. Rather than referring to a 'general or prior right', liberties are more securely claimed as the entailed inheritance of the people of a particular kingdom, an inheritance that is to be passed on into the future as it has been passed to us. This dependence on context to underpin claims that cannot be substantiated in the abstract and then applied is a natural way to proceed and embodies 'wisdom without reflection', a

practical wisdom based on our collective experience rather than a **theoretical** and critical reason (Ibid.: 117–19). On the other hand, the French revolutionaries 'despise experience as the wisdom of unlettered men' and so cast aside the wisdom of experience embodied in distinctive French institutions (Ibid.: 148). Burke claims that the enormity of the loss entailed by destroying that experience through the destruction of historical and longstanding institutions cannot be estimated, as 'from that moment we have no compass to govern us' (Ibid.: 172). These institutions embody our 'inbred sentiments' or what Burke calls 'prejudices'.

By **prejudice** Burke does not mean quite what we would usually mean. While we both use the term to refer to the presence of a sort of 'prejudgement', and we might regard this as indicative of a close-minded and unreasonable attitude, Burke regards prejudices more positively as a considered judgement of experience that relieves us of the burden of making (possibly mistaken) judgements of our own. Prejudices are an institutional and psychological compass that can guide us in our decision-making. So, whilst the revolutionary disregards historical experience and so has to make do without prejudices and rely instead on the unsteady and precarious philosophical reason of a few individuals, Englishmen

> cherish them because they are prejudices; and the longer they have lasted, and the more generally they have prevailed, the more we cherish them. We are afraid to put men to live and trade each on his own private stock of reason; because we suspect that this stock in each man is small, and that the individuals would do better to avail themselves of the general bank and capitol of nations, and of ages (Ibid.: 183).

Our traditions and prejudices embody the 'collected wisdom of ages' and should not be lightly set aside. To do so would be to break our connections to our history and to undermine the continuity of the political community. If there is no reverence for established tradition then the practical wisdom of experience is not passed through generations, and generations would not 'link' with one another. 'Men would become little better than the flies of a summer', each generation dying off and passing nothing but the bare fact of their existence on to the next (Ibid.: 193). Instead of placing our trust in the feeble reason of individuals to come to terms with past generations and to plan for the lives of future generations,

> where the great interests of mankind are concerned through a long succession of generations, that succession ought to be admitted into some share in the councils that are so deeply to affect them. If justice requires this, the work itself requires the aid of more minds than one age can furnish (Ibid.: 282).

Our exercises of reason must be situated in our particular contexts in order to be practical, and we can admit the council of generations in reflecting that context, listening to the voice of experience embodied in our inherited traditions and prejudices.

Let us stand back for a minute and take stock of our exploration of Burke's thoughts so far. We have identified two closely related ideas that are central to his conservatism. Firstly, he claims that, in contrast to the individualism of the social-contract thinkers and the revolutionaries, our identities are inherently social and therefore tied up in the particular contexts in which that social identity has developed. Secondly, against the abstraction of contract theories and their reliance on theoretical reason, Burke reminds us of the practical wisdom tied up in our collective institutional experience that provides a surer guide than individual reason when political decisions need to be made. He invites us to recognise that an understanding of the importance of context, tradition and the centrality of the social are vital to an understanding of the particular relationships we have with the people around us, the nation that we are a part of and the institutions that shape and transmit our identities, values and communal self-understandings.

Faced with this reading of our lives together Burke 'cannot conceive how any man can have brought himself to that pitch of presumption, to consider his country as nothing but *carte blanche*, upon which he may scribble whatever he pleases' (Ibid.: 266). This understanding of identity and tradition also makes it clear why, as far as Burke is concerned, change of any sort becomes a very serious matter indeed. When a person lives all their life under certain institutions, nurtured and protected by them, their ideas, habits, desires and expectations have become accommodated to them. They have adapted to a mode of life for which their particular upbringing within that mode of life especially suits them. By any 'sudden alteration' of those institutions and the habits of activity and judgement that go with them 'multitudes may be rendered miserable', change is a 'sudden violence to their minds and their feelings' (Ibid.: 281, 265–6). We have unavoidably developed a set of expectations about the world and change confounds those expectations. Change introduces into our social world an instability that is unsettling and disorientating; radical change may mean that we fail to recognise the world around us as the one that we grew up in, leading us to feel lost and uncomfortable. Given the way in which our identities and characters are formed within and shaped by a nation's institutions, it is hardly surprising that any change to those institutions must be regarded as some sort of loss and therefore to be regretted. We can see why Burke thought that the massive instability involved in 'a revolution will be the very last resource of the thinking and the good' (Ibid.: 117).

It is the recognition of the importance of stability in our relationships with each other and the world around us that leads Burke to place particular stress upon the institutions that do the most to reinforce that stability in the English context: the constitution, property, the monarchy, the Church and a regulated liberty. We have already touched on Burke's attitude towards the English constitution. He regarded it as an ancient constitution, the origins of which are lost in the distant past, and although it has been reinforced, explained and even improved, its fundamental principles are to be regarded as 'forever settled'. It is this ancient constitution, enshrining ancient laws and liberties, which provides the only security we have for our particular laws and liberties (Ibid.: 100, 117). Regarding the constitution in this way involves recognising it as a major historical and contemporary source of the political stability, and with it the stability of expectations, necessary for any of us to lead comfortable lives. We have inherited this constitution from our forefathers as a form of property that we hold together, just as we have inherited our ordinary property from them. The more mundane understanding of the institution of property and of property rights also serves stability in a similar way. We each have a vested interest in accumulating property, not because we are selfish but because we wish to perpetuate our property in our families and so perpetuate our families too. The possessors of family wealth, Burke claims, are the natural security for hereditary possession and the ongoing transmission of property. They possess a far-sightedness embodying their concern for future generations that the unpropertied masses cannot. As such, property must be protected from invasion and attack by granting it a predominance, out of all proportion to population numbers, in the representative government. The landed aristocracy constitute, for Burke rightly, the whole House of Lords and a significant portion of the Commons (Ibid.: 140–1). Only in this way can the security that stable property rights provide be maintained over time. The inherited nature of the constitution and of property come together in a monarchy based on a principle of hereditary succession. It is important for Burke that the English Revolution had reaffirmed the historical English constitutional tradition of an hereditary monarch as head of state, unlike the French Revolution against such a form of political authority. Continuity, stability and tradition were maintained in this conservative revolution.

Burke also emphasises the stabilising role of the Church as the basis of all civil society. Man, Burke claims, 'is a religious animal' and atheism is against our reason and instincts. We seek to explain the world in spiritual terms that are embodied in traditions and institutions that transcend individual lives. In England the Christian religion has been a great source of civilisation over a long history, lending structure, meaning and stability to significant parts of people's lives. The church has been a bulwark against the uncouth and degrading superstition that would arise if it took a lesser role in public life. Burke is concerned that the revolutionaries were revolting against traditional authority in general, political and ecclesiastical, and that such an attitude may spread to England (Ibid.: 186–8). He regards the establishment of the church, enshrining links to the state, and the consecration of the state that this entails, as necessary to instil a 'wholesome awe upon free citizens' (Ibid,: 190). It is not that Burke fears liberty, indeed he claims to 'love a manly, moral, regulated liberty as well as any gentleman', but that the association of state and church will encourage a care in its exercise (Ibid.: 89).

Burke regards the liberties of an Englishman as of great importance. However, at the same time he is clear that liberty exercised without wisdom, tuition or restraint 'is the greatest of all possible evils' (Ibid.: 373). Liberty needs to be protected and regulated by the virtue and awe inculcated by our religious traditions and also by a strong government. A feeble or precarious government, or a changeable and unstable one, is no remedy for the dangerous exercise of liberty. Unrestrained freedom is arbitrary freedom and a strong state with an established church can provide the necessary constraints that will enable us to all exercise our freedoms together without threatening the stability of our social inheritance. We should exercise our freedom in the enjoyment of the comfortable surroundings in which we find ourselves rather than in virulent criticism of the very institutions that have made us who we are. 'It has been the misfortune . . . of this age, that everything is to be discussed' (Ibid.: 188). Instead of discussion and reflection we should focus on enjoyment and stability. We should inhabit our contexts, not change them.

It is clear that, because of the way in which our identities are tied up with particular contexts, the difficulties that social complexity poses for political action and a scepticism about individual reason, Burke is suspicious of change, emphasising tradition and continuity instead. However, he does not urge an injunction against all change. Instead he recommends a healthy caution and a scepticism towards the necessity of any particular change and the adoption of a certain attitude towards any change that may be necessary. One of Burke's most quoted passages is 'a state without the means of some change is without the means of its conservation' (Ibid.: 106). He explicitly recognises the dangers of stagnation. An attempt to hold steady to practices and institutions that no longer reflect current circumstances is potentially as reckless as attempts to reform institutions that do not need to be changed. In either case we end up with a set of institutions out of step with the world we inhabit. The key, for Burke, is not to throw the baby out with the bath water but to combine a disposition to preserve with an ability to improve. He advocates the adoption of twin principles of conservation and correction, which should operate to keep the useful parts of established practice and add to them what circumspect and cautious changes become necessary (Ibid.: 106, 280). Operating in this manner political change follows 'the pattern of nature'. As in nature change is evolutionary and organic, a gradual development in which the various transitory parts of a body may undergo revision but the body as a whole retains a permanency and a consistent identity. As we inherit, enjoy and transmit evolving traditions we draw on

> a stupendous wisdom, moulding together the great mysterious incorporation of the human race, the whole, at one time . . . [being] never old, or middle-aged, or young, but in a condition of unchangeable constancy, moves on through the varied tenor of perpetual decay, fall, renovation and progression. Thus, by preserving the method of nature in the conduct of the state, in what we improve we are never wholly new; in what we retain we are never wholly obsolete (Ibid.: 120).

Armed with a vision of natural development and cautious renewal, we can see that Burke is not concerned with change as such, but only with the unnatural and revolutionary change that breaks violently with our inherited traditions in an attempt to wipe the slate clean and start again. The social-contract theorists and the French revolutionaries envisaged just such a fresh start, basing social life on a contract between individuals or between individuals and the state. Whilst everything we have read of Burke tells us that he does not think highly of this conception of politics, surprisingly he also thinks that it is possible to regard society as a contract. However, this is not a contract as Hobbes, Locke or Rousseau envisage it. Instead he regards social life as a partnership in all art and science and in virtue and perfection.

> As the ends of such a partnership cannot be obtained in many generations, it becomes a partnership not only between those who are living, but between those who are living, those who are dead, and those who are to be born. (Ibid.: 194–5)

The vision of a partnership across generations reinforces the image of our institutions and traditions as a cherished inheritance that we hold in trust for those who come before and after us. This in turn reinforces a reverence towards that inheritance and justifies a conservative disposition towards change.

Oakeshott's *Rationalism in Politics*

Burke's championing of tradition over reason and of a caution based on a recognition of complexity and uncertainty is echoed strongly in Michael Oakeshott's *Rationalism in Politics*. This collection of papers was published in 1962 and constitutes a spirited restatement of the conservative disposition we identified in Burke. Like Burke's *Reflections*, Oakeshott's essays were a response to the experience of radical political upheaval and a first-hand understanding of the damage revolutionary politics can inflict. During the previous fifty years Europe had been devastated by two world wars and there had been political revolution in Russia, Germany and elsewhere. The revolutionary **ideologies** of fascism, Nazism and communism had overthrown the old European political order. Even those countries not directly under the sway of these ideologies did not escape dramatic political change. In Britain the masses were drawn into politics by an expansion of democratic suffrage, most notably to women. The British state had also adopted a much more intrusive or active understanding of legitimate state activity with the advent of the welfare state and comprehensive education. Faced with change at this pace we should not be surprised if a powerful restatement of conservatism was regarded as necessary by some. Oakeshott self-consciously takes on this task, most notably in the essays 'Rationalism in Politics', 'Rational Conduct', 'Political Education' and 'On Being Conservative' (Oakeshott 1962: chapters 1, 4, 5 & 7).

Oakeshott contrasts conservatism with **rationalism** in a recognition of what he characterises as two distinct ways of understanding the activity of politics and the character of the person associated with each. He thought that almost all politics had become rationalist and that the rationalist stands for

> independence of mind on all occasions, for thought free from obligation to any authority save the authority of 'reason' . . . he is the *enemy* of authority, of prejudice, of the merely traditional, customary or habitual. His mental attitude is at once sceptical and optimistic: sceptical, because there is no opinion, no habit, no belief, nothing so firmly rooted or so widely held that he hesitates to question it and to judge it by what he calls his 'reason'; optimistic, because the Rationalist never doubts the power of his 'reason' . . . to determine the worth of a thing, the truth of an opinion or the propriety of an action. Moreover, he is fortified by a belief in a 'reason' common to all mankind. (Ibid.: 1–2)

Reason enables the rationalist to acquire knowledge, which for the rationalist is technical knowledge or knowledge of technique. This knowledge of technique is the sort of thing that can be precisely formulated as a set of rules or directions that could, in principle, be written down in a book. For example, the technique (or part of it) of driving in Britain can be found in the Highway Code and for baking a cake in a cookery book. Likewise the rules of scientific method formalise the technique of scientific discovery (Ibid.: 7–8, 10). The rationalist is sure that 'there is no knowledge which is not technical knowledge' and, as such, every department of intellectual activity should be guided by the appropriate technique (Ibid.: 11, 17). The technical approach is envisaged as a more general application of the rationalism associated with the scientific method. It begins first with a purging of the mind to eliminate the influence of different prejudices and false assumptions. In this way the mind, purged of any taint of the past, can be viewed 'as a neutral instrument, as a piece of apparatus' for the use of the reason which is common to all human beings (Ibid.: 86).

In their political activity rationalists subject the institutional inheritance of society to an intellectual scrutiny in which each institution has to demonstrate its worth. 'Nothing is of value merely because its exists' and if the application of the appropriate rational technique provides knowledge of possible improvements then those improvements should be pursued. For the rationalist, political activity is about solving problems in the same way as the engineer solves a problem. Indeed, rationalist politics takes on the character of social engineering where a problem is perceived, a rational solution identified and society brought into perfect accord with that solution (Ibid.: 4). In this way we can understand rationalist politics as the pursuit of perfection and with it, since the rational solution just is the rational solution, uniformity (Ibid.: 5). Oakeshott characterises rationalist political engineering as 'the pursuit of perfection as the crow flies' and contends that this rationalist understanding of politics as the pursuit of ideals dominates our political activity. From the pursuit of simple ideals of freedom, equality, racial purity or happiness to the more complex ideals of liberalism, Marxism or democracy, 'political activity is understood as the enterprise of seeing that the arrangements of a society conform to or reflect the chosen abstract idea' (Ibid.: 59, 79, 116). The rationalist is inspired by a vision of government as a 'vast reservoir of power' and dreams of the purposes to which it could be put. The rationalist will develop a vision of a project that, if implemented, would be for the general benefit of mankind and understands the government of men to be all about harnessing this power in order to impose their favourite project on the rest of society. The rationalist is a 'private enterprise politician' who thinks that 'to govern is to turn a private dream into a public and compulsory manner of living' (Ibid.: 191–2, 186). Oakeshott claims that European history is littered with these rationalist projects. He identifies these with many of the views that we have encountered in this book. These include Robert Owen's project, which Oakeshott regards as the most sublime rationalism, the French revolutionaries' attempt to found a society on the ideals of the 'Declaration of the Rights of Man', Jeremy Bentham's utilitarian political and legal philosophies and the rationalist communism of Karl Marx and Friedrich Engels (Ibid.: 6, 25–6). We might just as well include Plato, Jean-Jacques Rousseau and John Rawls in this list as well.

In the face of this corrosive rationalism, tradition or habit is dismissed as primitive and obsolete. The past is an encumbrance to be shaken off. The rationalist mind must not be 'clouded by the fumes of tradition' and so traditions are destroyed (Ibid.: 4). They are replaced by 'ideology', the political vision of the rational project to be pursued in politics. Ideologies claim to consist of a set of abstract principles that correspond to the ideal. This ideal is an independently premeditated scheme of ends to be pursued, identified in advance of political activity, which political activity is to be engineered to match. It is difficult to create ideologies *de novo* (as if wholly new) and so they will probably start life as abridgements of already existing political traditions and the ideas they contain. However, once the ideology is identified the tradition is set aside or superseded and the ideological abridgement takes on a life of its own, regarded as independently justified and as the 'sole guide' (Ibid.: 116, 122). Rationalist politics is 'ideological politics', the competition of these ideologies for control of the massive power of the state and the attempt, once that control is achieved, to use that power to engineer society so that it conforms to the ideology. It is this vision of remaking society in line with a rational ideal that unites under the rationalist banner revolutionary France, communist Russia, Nazi Germany and the post-war British creation of a welfare state. Although very different, these political enterprises are united by their rationalist character.

Oakeshott's rationalist is a very similar character to Burke's revolutionary or man of ability. It is no surprise therefore that the rationalist and the revolutionary are supposed to face similar problems. In their pursuit by political means of a premeditated ideal both seek certainty. Technical or theoretical knowledge is regarded as certain and treated as if there is certainty about the consequences of its political application. The rationalist really seeks to use political power to escape the messy world of politics with its emphasis on bargaining and compromise. The very complexity of the social and political world makes the rationalist project of bringing about perfection on earth difficult. This is why, Oakeshott claims, faced with the 'intricacy of the world of time and contingency so unmanageable', the rationalist 'is bewitched by the offer of a quick escape into the bogus eternity of an ideology' (Ibid.: 29). A successful rationalist politics would require certainty about the influence of our political actions upon the world. If we are to wipe the slate clean and build again, the claim is that we have control over what we build and the impact that our building will have. Complexity, however, so impairs our ability to accurately forecast future events 'that our activity of amendment is often found to lead us where we would not go' (Ibid.: 124). Innovation and change is always an uncertain undertaking, an equivocal enterprise based on a faith in forecasting consequences that complexity renders imprudent. Like Burke, Oakeshott does not envisage an improvement that is not also a loss.

This is not simply the loss of the things with which we are already intimate and familiar, where any change is akin to losing an irreplaceable friend. More generally,

> innovation is an activity which generates not only the 'improvement' sought, but a new and complex situation of which this is only one of the components. The total change is always more extensive than the change designed; and the whole of what is entailed can neither be foreseen nor circumscribed. Thus, whenever there is innovation there is the certainty that the change will be greater than was intended, that there will be loss as well as gain. (Ibid.: 171–2)

Rationalist politics, and its attempt to remake the world in line with an ideal, will always fail and history shows us that that failure will have possibly terrible consequences. Real politics is wrapped up with the transitory and the circumstantial, bringing with it the complexity and uncertainty that undermines rationalism as an approach to politics. What is it in the rationalist picture of the world that leads its adherents up this dangerous blind alley?

Oakeshott is certain that the rationalist has misunderstood important aspects of knowledge. To put this point in the language of earlier chapters, he has an inadequate understanding of epistemology. There is something about a plumber or an electrician that sets them apart from somebody who has read books about plumbing and wiring. They have experience, a practical and hands-on knowledge of their subject, in a way that someone who knows all the theory but has not been through a long apprenticeship has not. The rationalist politician, with his theoretical ideal for implementation, is like the person who tries to rewire his house or fit a new boiler armed only with a careful reading of a good book on the subject. The amateur plumber or electrician is likely 'to be pulled up short by an explosion; but all that happens in politics [when the rationalist gets his hands dirty] is war and chaos' (Ibid.: 94). Political activity, like any sort of activity, involves relying on 'practical knowledge'. This second sort of knowledge, alongside technical knowledge, is called practical as it 'exists only in use' and 'cannot be formulated in rules'. Instead of knowledge that can be adequately codified and written down, practical knowledge finds its expression in 'customary or traditional ways of doing things . . . in practice'. As a result it will lack the appearance of precision and certainty that technical knowledge exhibits but instead matches the imprecision of the world (Ibid.: 8, 10). It is this customary and traditional knowledge that is not taught and learned but imparted by a master and acquired through long practice by an apprentice. It is this sort of knowledge, the knowledge gained from the experience of working alongside a practising master, that the plumber or electrician has that cannot be learned from rules and books. Despite having a good recipe it is not possible to bake a good cake unless one has some experience of cooking. The rationalist, asserting that knowledge is certainty and that therefore only technical knowledge is real knowledge, denies that this practical understanding is knowledge at all (Ibid.: 11). Oakeshott, on the other hand, claims that technical and practical knowledge can never be wholly separated. The rationalist thinks first of the mind and reason, then of reason as providing ideas of right and wrong and true and false and only then in terms of its application in activity. Oakeshott regards this as a fundamental error of understanding. The mind is not an 'apparatus for thinking'. Instead, the mind is constituted by, or made up of, a complex interaction of ideas and activity. Whilst we may be able to think about notions such as right and wrong conduct in the abstract this is only something we can do because of our experience of conducting ourselves. Abstract thought about conduct is not something we do and then apply to conduct; it is itself a reflection on our conduct and cannot exist in advance of it. We cannot simply think it then do it, according to rules laid down in advance of activity. '*Doing* anything both depends upon and exhibits knowing how to do it' and so any activity at all depends upon practical knowledge of the way things are done. The notion of activity, of doing things, would make no sense at all without this notion of practical knowledge (Ibid.: 89–90). This notion of the practical knowledge involved in any activity involves understanding that any activity places limits on the sorts of things that can be done in that context, and how they can be done. The activity of building a house so that the roof stays on, water stays out and the inhabitants can live comfortably has built into it certain limits that are intrinsic to the pursuit of this activity. Rationalism, constructing abstract ideals as if there was no such thing as practical knowledge, disregards the possibility of a proper understanding of the appropriate limits to an activity. As such, it always risks failure by overstepping the bounds of the practically possible.

Practical 'rationality' is not, as technical rationality is, mere 'intelligence' but is instead 'faithfulness to the knowledge of how to conduct the specific activity we are engaged in', and rational conduct is 'acting in such a way that the coherence of the idiom of activity to which the conduct belongs is preserved' (Ibid.: 101–2). Maintaining the coherence of the 'idiom' is simply a way of saying that our actions should be appropriate to the activity in which we are engaged. Instead of trying to bring the method of geometry (Thomas Hobbes) or of engineering (Marx) to bear in politics, we have to recognise that geometry and engineering are distinct activities and that each is distinct from politics, an activity with its own appropriate way of doing things. Instead of imposing patterns from outside, there are patterns of acting inherent in activity. Some elements of this pattern are more obvious than others and we call these elements 'customs, traditions, institutions, laws, etc.'. These do not express our knowledge; practical knowledge just is these things. 'We do not decide that certain behaviour is right or desirable and then express our approval of it in an institution; our knowledge of how to behave well is, at this point, the institution' (Ibid.: 105). Traditions or habits of behaviour are not chosen or conceived but acquired just as we acquire a fluency in our native language. In this way, political education is 'learning how to participate in a conversation'. Politics in any community is just like language and conversation in involving more than individual activity; they are all necessarily social activities that we learn over time to participate in. Just as learning a language is not a matter of reading a dictionary but of learning words in use, a political education involves an immersion in tradition from an early age. Long before we might read about politics we are acquiring, through that immersion, the intimate and intricate knowledge of our political tradition that will later enable us to make any sense of a book on politics. Knowledge of our political tradition is therefore not of an abstract idea, but always of the intricate detail of a concrete and coherent manner of living (Ibid.: 129). A properly practical education enables us to function appropriately within this tradition, it gives us the power to do the right thing without hesitation even if we cannot explain what we are doing and why in abstract terms. Practical knowledge takes the form of habits of behaviour and an intuitive understanding of our institutions and, as such, relies on and is itself a force for stability (Ibid.: 63).

Just as it did for Burke, the idea of tradition has a complicated relationship with the concepts of stability and change but with Oakeshott we get a clearer picture of this relationship, unattached to any obscuring organic metaphor. A tradition of behaviour is

> neither fixed nor finished; it has no changeless centre to which understanding can anchor itself [nor a rationalist give a clear

> account of]; there is no sovereign purpose to be perceived or invariable direction to be detected; there is no model to be copied, idea to be realised, or rule to be followed. Some parts of it may change more slowly than others, but none is immune from change. Everything is temporary. Nevertheless, though a tradition of behaviour is flimsy and elusive, it is not without identity, and what makes it a possible object of knowledge is the fact that all its parts do not change at the same time and that the changes it undergoes are potential within it. Its principle is a principle of *continuity*: authority is diffused between past, present, and future; between the old, the new, and what is to come. It is steady because, though it moves, it is never wholly in motion; and though it is tranquil it is never wholly at rest. . . . Everything is temporary, but nothing is arbitrary. (Ibid.: 128)

This quote captures the flexibility inherent in Oakeshott's view of traditions. Traditions respond elastically to novel situations that may appear to disrupt our largely settled institutions. The disruption of outside influence or internal incoherence may present our tradition with what looks like a crisis. Oakeshott's claim is that these crises necessarily appear within a tradition of political activity and, since we have no access to alternative resources, they must always be met by utilising the resources that are left within our traditions. There is no guide outside our familiar traditions that we can turn to. If we are disorientated by crisis we need to return to our traditions and to the resources and tools with which we are most familiar and attempt to meet the challenge as best we can. In this way, political activity is like sailing a ship on a 'boundless and bottomless sea; there is neither harbour for shelter nor floor for anchorage, neither starting-place nor appointed destination. The enterprise is to keep afloat on an even keel' with access only to the resources on board (Ibid.: 126–7).

This measured response to political crisis contrasts sharply with the rationalist response. When the pursuit of one ideal fails, all the rationalist can do is find another project to replace it and start again in the pursuit of a different ideal. Oakeshott recommends that a conservative approach to politics become not the pursuit of any ideal, but instead the 'pursuit of intimations'. 'Politics is not the science of setting up a permanently impregnable society, it is the art of knowing where to go next in the exploration of an already existing traditional kind of society' (Ibid.: 58). Knowing where to go next when institutions don't dictate an answer will involve amending existing arrangements 'by exploring and pursuing what is intimated in them'. Accepting the complexity of the world and the uncertainty that is therefore invested in our actions makes the pursuit of competing dreams and ideals dangerous. Oakeshott gives voice to the key conservative vision of managing disaster through tradition rather than reason. 'Our mistakes of understanding will be less frequent and less disastrous if we escape the illusion that politics is ever anything more than the pursuit of intimations' in traditions. Even rationalists, in pursuing their ideologies, are pursing a single, exaggerated intimation (Ibid.: 124–5).

By now the outline of Oakeshott's conservatism should be plain. Conservatism cannot be summed up in a set of principles for politics, nor is it an idea that men follow or a doctrine we can look to for guidance. Rather conservatism is a disposition. Oakeshott's clearest account of this conservative disposition is in 'On Being Conservative' in *Rationalism in Politics*.

> The general characteristics of this disposition are . . . a propensity to use and to enjoy what is available rather than to wish for or to look for something else; to delight in what is present rather than what was or what may be. . . . There is no mere idolising of what is past and gone. What is esteemed is the present . . . not on account of its connections with a remote antiquity . . . but on account of its familiarity. . . . To be conservative, then, is to prefer the familiar to the unknown, the tried to the untried, fact to mystery, the actual to the possible, the limited to the unbounded, the near to the distant, the sufficient to the superabundant, the convenient to the perfect, present laughter to utopian bliss. Familiar relationships and loyalties will be preferred to the allure of more profitable attachments; to acquire and enlarge will be less important than to keep, to cultivate and to enjoy; the grief of loss will be more acute than the excitement of novelty or promise. (Ibid.: 168–9)

Keywords include stability, certainty and familiarity at the expense of improvement, speculation and perfection. We find nothing strange in the idea that a craftsman works much better with, and is happiest with, the familiar tools he has had for years than he ever could with a new set, however good they may be. It is only a small extension to think about our political institutions and traditions as the tools of our political activity. Our politics will go better if we work with what we have, perhaps changing tools one at a time when they wear out, rather than trying to replace an entire toolbox at once. Oakeshott wants to claim that man, as a tool-using animal, is predisposed to this conservative disposition (Ibid.: 179). As circumstances change the conservative will recognise that accommodations must be made but will find it difficult to celebrate. It is not that there is any guarantee that things are better without change, or that improvements could not be made. Rather, things in the present are familiar because we are attached to them and we are therefore capable of relaxing and enjoying them. Something of that possibility of enjoyment is lost whenever continuity is disrupted. Faced with changes we turn to the familiar in the intuitive attempt to throw our weight 'upon the foot which for the time being is most firmly placed' since 'change is a threat to identity, and every change is an emblem of extinction' (Ibid.: 170–1).

In politics this conservative disposition encourages us to regard the role of government as specific and limited. Governing should not be about formulating a plan or embarking on an enterprise; it is not about imposing beliefs or making people better; it is not about directing people or galvanising them into action, nor is it about leading or co-ordinating; this is the rationalist misunderstanding of politics. Instead we must recognise that projects and enterprises are things that are undertaken by individuals. 'Each of us is pursuing a course of his own', alone or with like minded others, and politics should be concerned with enabling us to pursue our chosen activities. Governing is not about riding roughshod over people's projects but rather it is about providing and maintaining general rules of conduct for people to observe in their individual pursuits (Ibid.: 187, 184). Governing is 'not the management of an enterprise, but the rule of those engaged in a diversity of self-chosen enterprises' (Ibid.: 189). The ruler is like an umpire, policing the activities of participants in the name of general rules of conduct. If we regard ourselves as individually pursuing different projects we must acknowledge that the activities we undertake are likely to clash with those of other individuals. The conservative thinks that faced with the possibility of conflict it is better to have some sort of rules rather than none at all and that government should be about enforcing traditional rules of procedure for resolving that conflict. These general rules of conduct are necessary if any of our projects are to have a chance of success; without them a society descends into 'a chaos of conflicting ideals' and our common life is severely disrupted. In sum, conservatives 'know the value of a rule which imposes orderliness without directing enterprise' (Ibid.: 178, 188, 59, 194). Elsewhere Oakeshott makes more explicit this contrast between a society that is ruled in the pursuit of a single project or ideal and one that is ruled by general and minimal rules of conduct that enable individuals to pursue their own projects. He characterises them as a contrast between an 'enterprise association' and a 'civil association' (Oakeshott 1975: 112–22). Conservative politics is concerned with achieving and maintaining a civil association and avoiding the dangerous excesses of enterprise politics.

Conclusions

It may be helpful to think about conservatism and its contrast to a more activist style of politics by way of two common proverbs. The rationalist or revolutionary would be keen on the proverb 'you can't make an omelette without breaking eggs'. When your goal is perfection then sacrifices that may be necessary along the way will appear justifiable. What is a little suffering for a few compared with building the ideal for us all? The conservative is quick to point out that this attitude has a habit of getting out of hand and 'a little suffering' descends all too easily into chaos and horror. The optimism of the early days of the French Revolution were soon forgotten as the Terror and the guillotine took hold and was a distant memory when Napoleon's armies tore up Europe. Likewise, the liberating plans of early communism were used to justify Stalinism and the gulags. Conservatives, on the other hand, would feel happier with the proverb 'better the devil you know than the devil you don't'.

What do we gain from a conservative understanding of politics? Above all we gain a wariness about pursuing ideals in politics. Conservatism always counsels caution and, if its counsel is followed, we are less likely to be taken in by the next guy along with a big idea. The conservative encourages us to regard revolutionaries and visionaries in the same way as we might regard those salesmen who travelled the American West and with whom westerns have made us so familiar. Just as the salesman claimed to have formulated and bottled a universal tonic capable of curing any ill, the visionary (Oakeshott's rationalist) claims to have formulated a cure-all for our social and political ills. Just as the 'medicine' may taste bad at first but cure everything we are assured that some suffering will be necessary in implementing the vision but everything will be so much better afterwards. Conservatism points out that more often than not the cure-all made people worse, not better, but that this was not apparent until the salesman had left town with your money. Likewise, it is less often the ideologue than the ordinary person swayed by visionary rhetoric that suffers when the rationalist project backfires.

In writing about the French Revolution Burke was responding to a set of specific historical events whilst Oakeshott appears more self-consciously general in his account of a conservative disposition. However, the basic thrust of their conservatism is remarkably similar. They have similar reasons for championing stability over change. Both recognise the deep, and very real, sense of loss that any change involves. Whilst both Burke and Oakeshott accept the necessity of change, they wish to keep change bounded; change should be gradual and not revolutionary. When we accept changes it is with reluctance and out of a desire to maintain continuity with the institutions that have structured our lives up to now. Change is not about remaking the world to fit an ideal. The world, both natural and social, is a complex place that it is beyond the power of human reason to understand. Our individual reason is **imperfect**; it is not capable of formulating plans and understanding the full consequences of acting upon them, nor can it help us to predict the untold consequences of our actions. It is this intellectual imperfection that means that we have to place our trust in our traditions and institutions as they embody the 'historically accumulated political wisdom of the community' (Quinton 1978: 11). Tradition opposes reason and practical knowledge opposes theoretical or technical knowledge. Although we find it also in Burke, Oakeshott best draws out this epistemological basis for conservatism, making plain what is at stake between practical and theoretical conceptions of knowledge. Conservatives have doubts about the straightforward application of theoretical knowledge to the real world and so place their faith in the practical knowledge of tradition. The stress must be on context and detail over abstraction, on the particular rather than the universal. Familiar context puts us at our ease and makes us feel at home, abstraction from this can disorient us and leave us stranded. Recognition of this might make politics and politicians less prone to well-meaning disaster.

Finally, this conservative understanding of politics appears to relegate political philosophy to an explanatory role. As Oakeshott explains,

> Political philosophy cannot be expected to increase our ability to be successful in political activity. It will not help us to distinguish between good and bad political projects; it has no power to guide

> or direct us in the enterprise of pursuing the intimations of our tradition . . . it must be understood as an explanatory not a practical activity. (Oakeshott 1962: 132–3)

However, if we think about what is going on when we pursue the intimations of our traditions, or actually try to work through Burke's principles of conservation and improvement, we must be struck by the role of judgement. We do not mindlessly pursue this intimation rather than that one, as the whim takes us. Nor do we conserve some aspects of tradition and improve others without thought. We are faced in any situation with a variety of options, each of which we might think of as the pursuit of a different intimation. What we cannot avoid is the necessity of making a judgement about which intimation we *should* pursue, a judgement about how our traditions *ought* to apply in this situation. It is implicit in everything we have read about conservatism that there are better and worse ways of proceeding when we are faced with difficult circumstances. We cannot avoid making normative judgements about what we ought to do and how we ought to act. In recognising the necessity of normative judgements we are opening the door once more for a normative and practical role for political philosophy (Haddock 2004). This conclusion suggests that the picture painted of the rationalist and the revolutionary may be overdrawn. Instead of contrasting conservatism with the caricature of the rationalist who develops an abstract idea and attempts to impose it on the world we might envisage a less forceful rationalist. It may be possible to abstractly outline an ideal but, instead of attempting to realise it impractically, treat it as a regulative ideal. In this way we can hold an ideal in mind when faced with difficult normative decisions. A regulative ideal can guide our judgements in a way that tradition, since tradition will not often speak loud enough or in a single voice, cannot. Whilst the political caution urged on us by conservatism is a useful antidote to the overzealous political pursuit of projects, the normative character of political philosophy cannot be dismissed so easily.

Topics for discussion

1. How recognisable is the rationalist in both the thinkers we have looked at in this book and in contemporary politics?
2. Are conservative worries about 'reason' a healthy antidote to the 'unrealistic' philosophy of earlier chapters?

3. Do you accept the conservative argument about the importance of unreflective prejudice?
4. Might there be any problems with the conservative reliance on tradition?
5. Should we think of political community as an enterprise or a civil association?

Critical glossary

Organicism	An organic view of social institutions regards them as similar to living creatures and therefore subject to similar laws of development.
Theoretical/practical wisdom	A distinction between the knowledge or wisdom we can gain through the abstract use of reason and that which is contained in the social practices of society and our intimate understandings of those practices.
Prejudice	Literally prejudgement. For conservatives it refers to the normative judgements already inherent in the traditions and institutions of a society.
Ideology	Generally any systematic political doctrine. For Oakeshott ideologies are rationalist abridgements of tradition used to justify an enterprise politics.
Rationalism	Generally the claim that the world is knowable only through reason and that reason therefore has a critical role to play in assessing claims to justification.
Imperfection	The conservative understanding that man's faculty for reason, or his capacity to act morally, is flawed and cannot therefore be relied on in political justification.

List of references/Further reading

References

Burke, E. [1790] (1968), *Reflections on the Revolution in France*, ed. with an introduction by C. Cruise O'Brien, London: Penguin.

Haddock, B. (2004), 'Contingency and Judgement in Oakeshott's Political Thought', *European Journal of Political Theory* (forthcoming).

Oakeshott, M. (1962), *Rationalism in Politics and Other Essays*, London: Methuen (there is an expanded edition published by Liberty Fund under the title *Rationalism in Politics and Other Essays* (1995) but the pagination differs significantly from the 1962 edition).

Oakeshott, M. (1975), *On Human Conduct*, Oxford: Oxford University Press.

Quinton, A. (1978), *The Politics of Imperfection*, London: Faber and Faber.

Secondary literature

O'Sullivan, N. (1976), *Conservatism*, New York: St. Martin's Press.

Scruton, R. (2002), *The Meaning of Conservatism*, 3rd edn, South Bend, IN: St Augustine's Press.

There are also good chapters on Burke and Oakeshott in:

Boucher, D. & Kelly, P. (eds) (2003), *Political Thinkers*, Oxford: Oxford University Press.

Forsyth, M. & Keens-Soper M. (eds) (1993, 1996), *The Political Classics*, Oxford: Oxford University Press, 3 vols, vols 2 & 3.

CHAPTER TEN

HISTORICAL

Feminism and Antifoundationalism

CONCEPTUAL

What's Wrong with Universal Justice?

There has, up until now, been something fundamentally wrong with this book. This is the stark claim made by some of the positions we shall examine in this chapter. What this book has apparently done wrong is to think of political philosophy as a tool for helping us to solve, or at least think more clearly about, moral or political dilemmas. The varied positions in this chapter, and the feminists and postmodernists we examine are a varied bunch, are united by a claim that, in one way or another, political philosophy has been far more a part of the problems that need to be addressed than it has been a part of the solution. The very aspects of political philosophy that have seemed virtues, its universalism and abstraction for example, are conceived of as central to the problems it causes us. This is a fundamental challenge to the role of normative political theory and, if successful, will mean that the whole enterprise will need to be rethought.

In this chapter we will encounter the liberal feminism of Susan Moller Okin, the difference feminist 'ethic of care' position of Carol Gilligan and Joan Tronto and the anti-foundationalist postmodernism of Richard Rorty. The challenge they collectively pose to normative theory as it has traditionally been conceived is extensive, and united by several complaints. The first concern is that normative political philosophy functions so as to set up and reinforce clear distinctions and dichotomies. These consist of abstractly conceived pairs of terms that appear innocuous but actually function in such a way as to privilege one side of the distinction and relegate the other. In this chapter we shall encounter criticisms of dichotomies set up in terms of distinctions between men and women, public and private, man and animal and even true human and pseudo-human. In each case what appear to be sensible and unobjectionable distinctions function so as to reinforce and justify a set of unequal power relations and often to downgrade the moral status of people who find themselves on the wrong side of a distinction. It is a central theme of this chapter that we need to look again at the way philosophy does this.

A second worry is that political philosophy, as understood by many of the people addressed in this chapter, sets up such high standards for objectivity in moral judgement, conceived of in terms of moral absolutism and universalism, that it causes as many problems as it can possibly hope to solve. This is made clear when our attention is drawn, by Rorty, to the ways in which a conviction that moral right is on your side, an absolute right, can seem to justify all sorts of terrible things. Secondly, an understanding of morality in such universalist and absolute terms encourages a vision of the world that is painted in black and white. Actions are either right or wrong, people are either good or bad and states are either just or unjust. One point of an ethic of care is to draw attention to the way that approaching moral dilemmas in this abstract manner actually obscures the heart of such dilemmas, that there is often no clear-cut right and wrong. Moral decisions come instead in various shades of grey where whatever we do is wrong and morality is about attending to the local and particular information that will help us to make the difficult moral judgements concerning what is necessary in particular situations. A propensity to view the world in absolute and universal black and white is conducive to the blind pursuit of just principles or rules, whatever their cost or impact on the real lives of real people. Finally, many of the views we encounter in this chapter will want to draw our attention to the way in which a belief that morality must be objective and universal is a handicap when it becomes clear that such an objective and universal account of justice cannot be justified. If what is referred to by Rorty as foundationalism fails then, if we are handicapped by a belief that this is the only possible ground for morality, we will be blinded by this belief and prevented from recognising the alternative moral resources we may have to hand such as moral sentiment, sympathy and care. It is only the moral foundationalist and universalist who is inclined to think, with Friedrich Nietzsche, that 'if God is dead then anything goes'. Those who have not been seduced by this dominant conception of political philosophy will have been aware all along that these alternative resources are to hand, and will be in a position to draw on them when the problematic nature of political philosophy is made clear to us.

Feminism

Normative political philosophy, usually regarded as one of the weapons we can use against inequality, has reinforced **patriarchy**, the systematic political, social and cultural subordination of women to men, for thousands of years. Feminism is a body of thought that analyses the patriarchal nature of society, criticises the continued existence of patriarchy but, as a first step, draws our attention to it. In twenty-first-century western democracies we often pat ourselves on the back that we are equal societies, where women are liberated and one sex no longer dominates the other. However, brief reflection ought to lead us to reconsider this self-congratulation. Whilst positions of authority are no longer the sole province of men, men still hold an overwhelming majority of powerful posts. Likewise they seem to have the best jobs, with many women working in the most poorly paid and part-time jobs. Women often get paid less than men in similar jobs and usually get promoted more slowly. Finally, there is still all sorts of social pressure, exerted through families, the media and the state, on people to slot into a well-defined set of **gender** roles. Women usually stay at home and look after children whilst men usually 'bring home the bacon'. Childless women and jobless men are not social outcasts, but are still often regarded as failures to be pitied. Women also still do the bulk of domestic work. Try to think critically about whether this analysis matches your experiences.

Inequality is a concern that political philosophy has sought to address but, argue feminists, this gender-based inequality seems to have passed political philosophers by. 'The great tradition of political philosophy consists . . . of writings by men, for men, and about men' (Okin 1980: 5). As such, it seems to have missed women out altogether, or treated them as something peripheral. This cannot continue, feminism argues, since we have a commitment to the democratic values of freedom and equality, whereby it is argued that people should not be constrained by social or innate differences from achieving success or well-being (recall John Rawls in Chapter 7). Political theory, which up until now has masked these inequalities, must now address them by adequately incorporating both sexes theoretically. But

> it is by no means a simple matter to integrate the female half of the human race into a tradition of political theory which has been based, almost without exception, upon the belief that women must be defined exclusively by their role within the family, and which has defined them . . . as outside the political (Ibid.: 286).

In this chapter we will outline two very different approaches to this task. Both approaches challenge the claims of political theory to have dealt with women adequately and both challenge political theory's claim to be universal. How can it be universal if it can't properly account for half the human race? Both approaches judge political theory a failure, not because it actively discriminates, but at least partly as a result of its gender-blindness. This may be surprising, as gender- or colour-blindness have often been taken to be virtues, but gender-blind thought has tended to take the traditional, patriarchal understandings of worker and citizen and simply treat them as if they now cover women as well as men. Instead, feminism argues that we need to rethink the way that our theories take gender into account. The two approaches we shall outline fall each side of what is called the 'equality–difference debate'. The 'equality' approach accepts that the universalist claims of political theory are appropriate but currently misguided. Men and women are fundamentally the same but current gender roles mask this equality. What is needed is a rethink of the role of the family in political theory coupled with a recognition of the fact of interdependence, and then proper equality of opportunity and treatment can be realised. Rather than stress equality, the '**difference**' approach focuses on important differences between men and women. Difference feminists argue that political theory's universalist claims fail because they pay insufficient attention to these important differences. Moreover, once these differences are recognised it will become apparent that our theory should be less universal anyway.

Equality: Okin and liberal feminism

Okin's liberal feminism in *Justice, Gender, and the Family* is a clear exemplar of this equality approach. She diagnoses the problem political theory has accommodating women as the result of most theories' assumption of a traditional gender-structured family and the sexual division of labour that it entails (Okin 1989: 8, 6). That political theory does assume the gendered family becomes obvious with a little thought. Firstly, political theories almost invariably take mature, independent adult humans as the subjects of their theorising without ever considering how they got to be that way. Human beings do not spring into being as independent adults; someone brought them into the world and raised them, whatever political theorists might think. Secondly, the attitude of political theory to 'work' demonstrates this assumption of the gendered family. When work is mentioned (pretty often by someone like Rawls or Robert Nozick) it is work in the marketplace that is referred to and not the domestic work of child-rearing and house-keeping. There also seems to be the assumption that workers do not have duties as primary carers for pre-school infants. No mention is made of ways for workers to fit child-rearing into their working day. The assumption is also widespread that women are primarily responsible for rearing children. These basic assumptions can be summed up in the claim that political theorists, and society more widely, generally assume that 'workers have wives at home' (Ibid.: 5, 13). This assumption seems built into the structure of the workplace and other important social institutions. For example, the school day does not match the working day and the school year is punctuated by extended vacations that are not a part of the work calendar. The assumption of the school timetable would seem to be that in any family one partner stays at home and takes care of the children. Both our theory and practice seem to make these assumptions and the impact on gender inequality is marked. Women earn less than men and are promoted more slowly since they usually have to take a career break in order to have a family, while their partner does not. This means that women are often reduced to following their husbands around the country as they move from job to job. If they do work women are more likely to work part time in order to fit around the school day. Women also, whether they work or not, continue to do the bulk of the domestic and child care work.

Equality feminism is clear that this way of organising the division of labour between the sexes is not a natural necessity but a social construct. Indeed whilst sexual differences are obviously down to nature, since only women have wombs and so can bear children, Okin approvingly quotes Simone de Beauvoir's claim that 'one is not born, but rather becomes, a woman' (Ibid.: 106). Whilst male and female are natural categories, man and woman are socially constructed. We are brought up and socialised into certain gender-based roles based on gendered expectations. Furthermore, different societies have conceptualised gender roles differently and this encourages us to recognise that while sex is natural, it is up to us how we react to it. Since gender is socially constructed it is a legitimate and necessary subject for political philosophers, even though they largely ignore it. This lack of attention to gender cannot be justified. Political theories are centrally concerned with questions of how and why persons can be treated unequally or differently and with the consideration of what legitimates unequal social institutions (Ibid.: 8). Rawls's arguments for moving away from equality to the difference principle are examples of this. The assumed naturalness of gender works alongside liberal assumptions of a sharp distinction between the 'public' life of work and politics and the 'private' domestic life to guarantee that the family is opaque to the light of justice.

There are three broad reasons advanced by equality feminism to explain why political theory cannot continue along its current path. Firstly, women must be included for the sake of completeness. A theory of justice that applies to only half the population is not going to be acceptable (Ibid.: 14–15). Secondly, equality of opportunity for women and children is undermined by gender injustice. In the same way as poverty or education are important for justice and equality because of the influence they have over people's lives (Rawls considers them as a part of the subject matter of accounts of the basic structure of society and of social primary goods) so is the family. 'The family is a crucial determinant of our opportunities in life' (Ibid.: 16). As such it must be taken into account by any liberal theory at least. Finally, 'a just family is . . . [the] essential foundation' of a just society (Ibid.: 17). The family is the first school of justice and moral development for citizens. The first and most important example of an adult relationship that children experience is usually within the family. Okin contends that it makes a lasting difference whether that relationship is one of 'justice and reciprocity . . . [or] one of domination and manipulation' (Ibid.: 17). Any political theory that regards either universality or equality as at all important will not be able to avoid taking this feminist challenge seriously.

When equality feminists such as Okin turn their attention to possible ways of taking gender on board they often take liberal methods very seriously. Okin, for example, thinks that a modified version of Rawls's 'original position' (see Chapter 7) in which the parties are made fully aware of the gendered nature of current society and where the veil of ignorance screens sex is a strong basis for a successful approach (Okin 1989: 101, 174). This enables a focus, alongside the usual focus on poverty for example, on the difference between sex and gender. When we ask what the parties in this reformulated original position would agree to Okin believes we would reach an acknowledgement that 'the disappearance of gender is a prerequisite for the *complete* development of a nonsexist, fully human theory of justice' (Ibid.: 105).

What practical steps might be taken to achieve this aim? The first step is simply to recognise that the family is a political concern (Ibid.: 111). We have already mentioned the way in which this is so because of the family as the point of production of gendered relationships and as the first school of future citizens. To this we need to add the recognition that the sexual division of labour within the family introduces power relationships based on dominant and subordinate economic and reproductive positions. If one partner controls the family income it is very likely that they will control the family in broader ways. We must also recognise that the family is the way it is because of past and present political decisions. The state regulates and sanctions marriages and divorces: in many countries you can't be married to more than one person at the same time, for example, or you may be imprisoned. The state also makes judgements about how to treat sexual and domestic violence within families and about illegitimate ways of raising and educating children. It should be clear that the family is already political; 'the issue is not whether, but *how* the state intervenes' (Ibid.: 131). Recognising this, a second step would be to conceptually separate child-bearing from child-rearing. Whilst child-bearing is a function of sex, current distributions of responsibility for child-rearing are a function of socially constructed gender. Since the gender-structured family is one central vehicle by which social expectations of gender roles are expressed it would be a good strategy to concentrate here.

In the final section of *Justice, Gender, and the Family*, called 'Towards a Humanist Justice', Okin addresses this issue head on. Here she argues that we must rethink the sexual division of labour altogether. Any fair and just solution

> must encourage and facilitate the equal sharing by men and women of paid and unpaid work, of productive and reproductive labour. . . . A just future would be one without gender. In its social structures and practices, one's sex would have no more relevance that one's eye color or the length of one's toes. No assumptions would be made about 'male' and 'female' roles; childbearing would be so conceptually separated from child rearing and other family responsibilities that it would be a cause for surprise, and

> no little concern, if men and women were not equally responsible for domestic life or if children were to spend much more time with one parent than the other. It would be a future in which men and women participated in more or less equal numbers in every sphere of life, from infant care to different kinds of paid work to high level politics. Thus it would no longer be the case that having no experience of raising children would be a practical prerequisite for attaining positions of the greatest social influence. . . . If we are to be at all true to our democratic ideals, moving away from gender is essential (Ibid.: 171–2).

This vision of a genderless society is not simply a statement of a utopian and therefore unrealistic ideal; Okin has practical and concrete suggestions about what measures we can take in order to make progress towards this more equal society. Firstly, legislation and public policy should generally make no assumptions of gender-based social differentiation. They should assume that shared parental responsibility is the norm and that it should be facilitated as far as possible. This might involve such practical measures as state subsidy for high-quality child care (in Britain progress is being made in this direction). It is necessary, however, to go much further than this. Policy makers should start with the 'reasonable assumption that women and men are equally parents of their children' and that they share all the paid and unpaid work that goes with this role (Ibid.: 175). This will necessitate a rethink of the way in which our current work and education practices are structured since we cannot cling to the 'assumption that every worker has "someone else" at home to raise "his" children' (Ibid.: 176).

Changes in the workplace might involve restructuring to suit a workforce that are also parents, with a parental role to play. Pregnancy should be conceptually disconnected from policies about care provision and treated instead in the same way as any other temporary disability. Parental leave from work around the time of a birth should be available to both parents on the same terms. Currently in Britain the mother is entitled to far more paid maternity leave than the father is paternity leave; what assumption do you think this is making about the parenting role of each sex? Okin also recommends that, as far as possible, employers should adopt flexible work hours and practices for parents with young children. Finally, employers could be encouraged to provide high quality on-site day care (Ibid.: 176–7). School provision also needs to be rethought so that education combats rather than reinforces gender stereotyping. Positive discrimination in employment might be used to ensure that equal numbers of teachers and head teachers are drawn from each sex. Children should be educated in the politics of gender and inequality just as they are currently taught about racial or religious discrimination. Old-fashioned home economics classes that taught girls how to cook and sew should be replaced with new classes that teach all children to be responsible parents and to manage a family life. Finally, schools should provide high quality pre- and post-school programmes in order to synchronise the school with the working day (Ibid.: 177). The ramifications of these changes over a short period of time would be far-reaching. Most notably of all they would remove incentives and disincentives for men and women to unthinkingly adopt certain roles simply because that is the way they've been done in the past. Active parents would now be found in every influential position in society, more less equally distributed by sex (Ibid.: 179).

Okin recognises that not all people would feel happy rejecting the traditional conception of the sexual division of labour and adopting this new model of family life. Instead they may agree with their partners and together choose to organise their affairs so that they match traditional understandings of the family. Okin does not want to forbid this arrangement according to the traditional model. She does, however, think that both women and children need to be protected from the potentially vulnerable and dependent position that this places them in. Okin's suggestion is that in such a relationship we recognise both the paid work done outside the home and the unpaid work done inside it as work that contributes equally to the well-being of the family. Recognising the equal contribution made by each we can assign equal legal entitlement of each to all family earnings. For simplicity's sake employers should divide all wage cheques in half and pay each half to a different partner. This would remove a significant degree of the inequality, dependence and possible subordination that have been widely experienced by the non-wage earner in such relationships (Ibid.: 181).

Okin has these two models of family life, both designed to be more just and more equal than our current arrangements. Both are designed to remove gender from the field of consideration as an issue of inequality. This focus on equality and equal opportunity reaffirms the liberal commitment to equality and to a universalist approach to political theory. Okin's concern with liberalism's universalist claims is not that they are misguided, simply that as things stand liberals fail to live up to these claims. The current approach to political theory serves to mask that failure. The role of the equality feminist is to place this failure before our noses so that we can remedy it. As such, this type of feminist approach is not a challenge to universalist normative theory at all, but just a challenge to our claims to have lived up to our ideals. This approach is firmly placed within the confines of political theory as traditionally conceived.

Difference: Gilligan, Tronto and an 'ethic of care'

That feminism should aim for a genderless society is disputed by difference feminism. Rather than accept their sameness, difference feminists stress the idea that there are essential differences between the moral and psychological outlooks of men and women and that our theories should reflect these differences. Political theory is identified as part of a problem to be overcome, as it has usually ignored, or actively attacked, these differences in the name of justice. In this section we will examine the views of some difference feminists who oppose this '**ethic of justice**' with an '**ethic of care**'. We are familiar with the sort of ideas that are associated with an ethic of justice. Justice theorists treat normative questions as questions of conflicts of rights between autonomous individuals and attempt to deal with these conflicts by the identification and application of abstract principles. This understanding of the normative enterprise is challenged in Carol Gilligan's *In a Different Voice* and Joan Tronto's *Moral Boundaries*.

Gilligan's background in psychology underpins her ideas. She worked for some time with the important psychologist of moral development Lawrence Kohlberg. Kohlberg's research led him to outline a six-stage process of moral development, charting this development from a child's to a mature moral perspective. Key steps in this development were at stage one, where people behave morally simply to avoid punishment; stage three, or the 'good boy' stage, where one's moral judgements are focused on gaining the approval of those closest to you; and stage six, which is a mature perspective consisting of universalisable and prescriptive abstract moral judgements based on a commitment to fairness (Tronto 1993: 65). Rawls's theory of justice might be regarded as the sort of perspective appropriate to someone at stage six of moral development. What studies tended to show was that women are most often diagnosed as arresting at stage three and so are judged morally immature on this scale. Unlike men, who often progress to stage six, women appear incapable of rational moral reasoning. Reacting to this work with Kohlberg, Gilligan questioned what seemed to be a gender-differentiated pattern in levels of moral maturity. Did this differentiation reflect a real moral underdevelopment of women, perhaps justifying patriarchal society on the basis of women being morally more like children than mature moral reasoners? Or was there something altogether different going on?

Gilligan revisited the studies of moral judgement conducted by Kohlberg to check for bias in the conduct or analysis of the tests and found none. The only alternative was that there is something about the conceptual framework of the social scientists engaged in formulating criteria for moral development that consistently leads to the diagnosis of female underdevelopment. Perhaps what the researchers had failed to appreciate was the possibility that women view themselves and morality in a way that is different from men. Perhaps this different experience of morality is missed or discounted in male-developed tests of moral development and, importantly for us, is not taken into account by normative theorists either. To explore this thought Gilligan conducted her own studies of moral judgement in which she did claim to identify a 'different voice' and that this voice seemed to find expression predominantly in women. Gilligan characterises this different voice as an 'ethic of care'.

> The moral judgements of women differ from those of men in the greater extent to which women's judgements are tied to feelings of empathy and compassion and are concerned with the resolution of real as opposed to hypothetical dilemmas. . . . In order to go beyond the question, 'How much like men do women think, how capable are they of engaging in the abstract and hypothetical construction of reality?' it is necessary to identify and define developmental criteria that encompass the categories of women's thought. . . . [We must] derive such criteria from the resolution of the 'more frequently occurring, real-life moral dilemmas of interpersonal, empathetic, fellow-feeling concerns' . . . which have long been the centre of women's moral concern. . . . Women's construction of the moral domain relies on a language different from that of men and one that deserves equal credence in the definition of development. (Gilligan 1982: 69–70)

Women, it is suggested, think of moral dilemmas in different ways, using different moral concepts, and so any understanding of morality and moral development that has no space for a recognition of this is radically incomplete. The development of an understanding of an ethic of care is a step towards a fuller understanding of morality.

Tronto explores this different voice, characterised as an ethic of care, and draws out three key characteristics of the ethic in contrast to the mainstream ethic of justice (Tronto 1994: 79). Firstly, an ethic of care treats as central a range of moral concepts that is significantly different from those stressed by an ethic of justice. Women seem to conceptualise moral dilemmas in a distinctive way, not as a clash between rights or principles but as situations which necessarily entail hurt. Morality is concerned with finding ways to minimise the general experience of that hurt. Rather than think of the moral person as one who observes abstract principles of right conduct, the 'moral person is one who helps others; goodness is service, meeting one's obligations and responsibilities to others' (Gilligan 1982: 66). The central conceptual distinction is not between right and wrong but instead between selfishness and responsibility. The ethic of care reflects not a formal logic of fairness, but an underlying logic of relationships where morality is a matter of *taking care of* the responsibilities that go with being enmeshed in the web of relationships we find ourselves in. Sometimes we are faced with conflicting responsibilities and there may be no principled way of identifying what the right or wrong thing to do is; whatever we do may involve hurt to someone. There is an acceptance here of a moral greyness, a refusal to see the world in the stark black and white terms of an ethic of rules and principles. Secondly, an ethic of care is tied to concrete circumstance rather than expressed in abstract and hypothetical rules or principles. Moral dilemmas cannot be assessed in abstract terms but need to be attentive to the actual consequences of particular actions on the lives of the people affected. In a passage that could almost be directed at Rawls's method of coming to principles of justice through a hypothetical original position Gilligan notes that

> an injunction to care . . . [is] a responsibility to discern and alleviate the 'real and recognisable trouble' of this world. . . . Hypothetical dilemmas, in the abstraction of their presentation, divest moral actors from the history and psychology of their individual lives and separate the moral problem from the social contingencies of its possible occurrence. . . . However, the reconstruction of the dilemma in its contextual particularity allows the understanding of cause and consequence which engages the compassion and tolerance. . . . Only when substance is given to

> the skeletal lives of hypothetical people is it possible to consider the social injustice that their moral problems may reflect and to imagine the individual suffering their occurrence may signify (Ibid.: 100).

An ethic of care is a form of *particularism* rather than universalism. Instead of abstracting from the particulars of a dilemma, women's moral understanding is characterised by an 'insistence on the particular' (Ibid.: 101). This centres on our actual responsibilities and the possible hurt in real relationships that reflects a clear understanding of basic human interdependence. An ethic of care stresses the fact of interconnection between the self and the other. Selfishness and violence, through the interconnected web of relationships we are a part of, hurt and destroy everyone to some degree whilst the activity of care enhances the self and others. This is the third aspect of an ethic of care that Tronto identifies, its expression in the actual activity of care. This activity accepts the thought that individual lives are fundamentally connected to each other and therefore embedded in the social context of particular relationships. This vision of connection as a fundamental fact of moral existence contrasts sharply with political theory's usual vision of autonomy as all-important.

Having identified care and the responsibilities that go with caring as important aspects of human life, a conception of care must be a central category in our attempts to understand and explain the social world. Tronto attempts to make significant steps in this direction, exploring the way in which care interrelates with our other moral and political concepts. We have already seen that from this perspective a morally good person must, among other things, strive to meet the particular demands for care they encounter. Moral societies must likewise provide an adequate level of care for their members. Tronto is very clear that in making these claims she is not making the further claim that only care is important for morality. An acknowledgement of the importance of care is not supposed to oust our recognition of the importance of other concepts such as honesty and fairness. An ethic of care is, in Tronto's reading, not a total account of morality to replace and ethic of justice but is instead a necessary supplement to justice (Tronto 1994: 126).

If care is to be treated as a central moral category we need to gain a better understanding of what it is and what it entails. Tronto offers the following definition of care. At a general level she suggests that

> caring be viewed as a *species activity that includes everything that we do to maintain, continue, and repair our 'world' so that we can live in it as well as possible*. That world includes our bodies, our selves, and our environment, all of which we seek to interweave in a complex, life-sustaining web (Ibid.: 103).

We do not have space to fully examine the ramifications of this definition but we can draw out some important implications. It is immediately clear that the concerns of care are very different from those of justice. The moral scope of care is not restricted to human interaction as justice usually is. Instead care is something that can be directed at our environment and other objects. Nor is care an individualist notion in the way that justice seems to be. Any relationship of care assumes at least two connected people and possibly many more. From this perspective human beings are necessarily social. This social nature is also expressed in the way that the activity of caring is culturally constrained. What will count as adequate and appropriate care will depend on the culture within which that caring takes place. Finally, caring is a ongoing process that is a constant aspect of the lives of every one of us (Ibid.: 103).

In contrast to an ethic of justice, which may be based in one's own needs, care involves adopting 'a perspective of taking the other's needs as the starting point for what must be done' (Ibid.: 105). It is worth thinking about how different this is from the approach of the social-contract theorists we have looked at, which justifies leaving the state of nature on grounds of self-interest. There is also a contrast with theories of distributive justice such as Nozick's, where I try to establish what I have a right to, and also with Rawls's, where the parties in the original position reason with an eye on getting as large a share as possible in the distribution of social primary goods. This is also notably different from an ethic of justice more generally in the stress that is laid on the particular. There is the thought that we must concentrate on the real hurt of real people in the actual relationships that we are in. There is also the recognition that notions of adequate care will vary from context to context and culture to culture, as will the understanding of whose responsibility it is to meet needs for care. A clear example of this is in the different ways that different cultures treat the care of the elderly: some regard it as a family matter, others as an issue that the state must get involved in. In spite of this particularism, 'care is nonetheless a universal aspect of human life. All humans need to be cared for' in ways that do not depend on culture; we are all helpless infants at the outset of our lives, and may be helpless at various points throughout it also (Ibid.: 110). It is true, however, that context dictates how these needs are to be met.

There is also some question about whether the different voice that is identified and explained in an ethic of care is as particular as many feminists seem to treat it. While Gilligan never quite committed herself wholly on the question of whether this different voice is necessarily tied to gender other people have been less careful. In fact, Tronto argues that the different voice may not be a distinctively female voice but may instead be a much more general or universal phenomenon associated with the experience of subordination. She draws attention to psychological studies that show that the supposed difference between men and women expressed in the different voice also describes the differences between working and middle classes and between the white majority and ethnic minorities. The ethic of care may not be female but be instead a function of marginalisation and exclusion. An ethic of interconnectedness, care and responsibility that stresses the importance of local relationships may be a natural response of the powerless to their subordination (Ibid.: 82–91).

If an ethic of care is not gendered but linked instead to subordination and inequality more generally then there is no way we can ignore it as a political concern. Even though caring activities are currently undervalued by society (much of it is unpaid and that which is paid is treated as low-status work) we cannot sidestep the conclusion that care is a central concern of human life. We must also recognise that care is a already a central concern of politics. The traditional public/private distinction that served to keep women out of public life is no longer as sharp. Many women are now in the workplace and in public office, taking the ethic of care with them, and this is an achievement of liberal feminism that needs to be acknowledged. Also importantly, many care functions are now the province of either the market or the state. Increasingly through the twentieth century the care for children, the sick and elderly and the preparation of meals for example have found their way further and further into the public sphere. Care is now unavoidably political and we have to attempt to understand its importance as a political value. Central to this importance is the recognition of interdependence and of the fact that we all require care at some time. Further, the relationship of mutual concern and responsibility that is central to an ethic of care may help us to understand 'the qualities necessary for democratic citizens to live together well in a pluralistic society, and that only in a just, pluralistic, democratic society can care flourish' (Ibid.: 161–2). Awareness of the centrality of care in our lives should encourage us to rethink the notion of democratic citizenship not in terms of the abstract fiction of equality that we find in discussions of justice and citizenship, but instead in terms of a frank recognition of current inequality. What is needed is an admission that beneath the veneer of supposed equal citizenship is a range of very real inequalities masked by the abstract approach of an ethic of justice working alone. Supplementing justice with care, we will be more attentive to the real inequalities and regard equality not as an abstract ideal, but instead as a real political goal to strive for (Ibid.: 164). Care should therefore take its place alongside the other liberal and democratic values of rights, fairness, due process and legal and political obligation but as it does so we must recognise that we must rethink the way in which we theorise democracy. It would, however, make 'citizens more thoughtful, more attentive to others, and therefore better democratic citizens' (Ibid.: 169). Tronto explicitly regards this as an attempt to reconcile an ethic of care to an ethic of justice.

Both difference feminists and equality feminists challenge the role of political philosophy. Both regard it as contributing to the historically subordinate position of women and therefore as part of a problem that needs to be overcome. Central to both challenges is an injunction to take seriously the facts of human interdependence in a comprehensive way. They do differ about the depth of this challenge to political theory, with equality feminists wanting a traditional universalist approach recast to take account of the gendered nature of current society and difference feminists challenging the universalising approach generally in favour of a more particularist account. Difference feminists may therefore accuse equality feminists of not taking interdependence seriously enough and therefore of failing to adequately shake off the shackles of male philosophy. As a result they are confined by patriarchy while at the same time reinforcing it with their acceptance of a liberal, justice-based approach. Equality feminists on the other hand can express concern at the potential relativism and conservatism of an ethic of care. It may be relativist because in its attention to the particular rather than the universal it may be so shaped by cultural difference as to simply reflect local practice. In doing so it may be conservative since attention to context and detail makes a critical distance difficult to achieve and also conservative in the stress on the maintenance and repair of current relationships. More worryingly for the equality feminists, stressing the essential differences between men and women, highlighting the nurturing and caring qualities of women over men, seems not so much to challenge traditional patriarchal gender roles as to reinforce them; if women are so much more suited to care than men then it may seem natural that they should raise children and take on low-status care roles, reinforcing their subordinate social positions. Essentialising difference in this way (arguing that there are essential elements to womanliness that are different to the essential elements of maleness) may be a dangerous strategy to adopt for a feminist committed to ending female subordination.

Rorty: antifoundationalism and the shift from epistemology to politics

The claim that political thought has sytematically neglected more than half of the human species is clearly a very serious charge. However, the second challenge to political thought that we examine in this chapter claims to be even more serious. The antifoundationalist challenge to normative political thought is, perhaps, the most comprehensive of all such challenges. Over the course of a formidable career Richard Rorty, whom we have chosen to represent this tradition because of his clarity, has sought to debunk the pretensions of philosophy. His argument strongly reinforces the suggestion that not only is traditional philosophy not part of the solution, it is in fact part of the problem. Throughout this book we have encouraged you to think about the foundations of politics. Over the millennia we have seen that philosophers have sought to base their prescriptions on true foundations. Yet for Rorty it is this very enterprise (the search for and objectification of foundational claims in political thought) that is the focus of criticism. For this reason Rorty is often described as an **antifoundationalist**. The fact that the search for foundations characterises modernist and Enlightenment philosophy is what leads to the description of Rorty as a **postmodernist**. **Antifoundationalism** is the more technical term here. It indicates a critical approach to the idea that it is possible to find universal foundations that can support normative arguments. **Postmodernism** is a more general term referring to a series of movements in literature, art, architecture etc. that seek to abandon the formalities and aspirations (pretensions) of modernism. Rorty's ambition is to encourage us to move beyond epistemology and to find a new way to engage with politics (Rorty 1989: 68). This simply means that Rorty wants to see debates about the political move away from debates about what we can *know* about the moral and social world and to help us envisage ways of thinking about politics that are distinctively postmodern.

Rorty's critical gaze has fallen on many aspects of contemporary life. However, in order to keep this introductory engagement focused we will draw on only a limited range of Rorty's writings. The principal writings that we will refer to here are *Contingency, Irony and Solidarity* (1989), which is perhaps the most powerful statement of Rorty's antifoundationalism in its relation to social theory, and an Oxford Amnesty lecture entitled 'Human Rights, Rationality and Sentimentality' (1993), which offers a clear expression of how Rorty sees the immediate future of political thought. The opportunity to consider the antifoundationalist approach to normative political thought is, we believe, an essential part of any contemporary introduction to political thought. Armed with a basic understanding of the nature of political theory your challenge is to engage with Rorty's position and to reflect on the future, if indeed there is a future, of normative political thought. This requires a sophisticated and honest approach to your subject and to a reading of Rorty. Whether you agree or disagree with Rorty's position one thing is certain: no one can engage fully with contemporary political thought without having confronted the antifoundationalist challenge to its very basis.

Let us begin with an examination of Rorty's critique of philosophy. It might seem a little strange to think of a philosopher as being critical of philosophy. However, Rorty is only concerned to criticise systematic or foundational philosophy, that type of modernist or Enlightenment philosophy that searches for what is 'out there', the 'truth', 'knowledge' or moral certainty. The sort of theory that we have examined in this book falls into this category. Plato's view of a moralised universe and Aristotle's conception of human teleology rest on the 'truth'. Hobbes sought the 'truth' in his scientific method, Locke sought it in revelation and natural law; the list could go on and on. Rorty, on the other hand, allies his type of philosophy to the arts, to romantic poetry, to novelists such as Charles Dickens and Vladimir Nabokov and to the argument that philosophy (like literature) is a creative enterprise rather than a search for existing universal foundations. Philosophy, he insists, should not be tied to the 'truth'. Rorty's bold programme is laid out in the introduction to *Contingency, Irony and Solidarity*, where he argues that

> a postmetaphysical culture seems to me to be no more impossible than a postreligious one, and equally desirable. . . . More important, it would regard the realization of utopias, and the envisaging

> of still further utopias, as an endless process – and endless proliferation of Freedom, rather than a convergence toward an already existing Truth. (Rorty 1989: xvi)

Even in this short passage there is much to get us thinking. The first thing to note is Rorty's claim about the desirability of a post-metaphysical and post-religious culture. We need to know why this is desirable and what it might entail. Second there is a sense here, and throughout his work, of genuine optimism about the prospect of a post-modern world emancipated from the shackles of foundationalism. We need to imagine, with Rorty, what this would be like. How would social and political life change if we were not to rely on the distinctions and judgements that we draw from moral and political thought?

For the sake of ease we can divide Rorty's critique of foundational philosophy into two distinct parts. The first set of arguments claims that foundational philosophy is wrong because it is aiming at an impossible goal. The second set of arguments claims that foundational philosophy should be abandoned because it has such disastrous consequences for humanity. Taking the first set as our launching point we immediately gain a flurry of insights into the nature of antifoundationalism. In most of its incarnations antifoundationalism is made up of a series of sophisticated and critical arguments about the nature of truth. At least in part this is Rorty's initial point. Philosophy is aiming at the impossible because there is no truth 'out there' to find. On this reading the search for truth is very much like the search for the nature of God or the nature of man (Ibid.: 5, 8). On the basis of discoveries about such truths philosophers claim authority for their political prescriptions. Denying that there is a truth obviously makes this philosophical enterprise problematic. This is precisely what Rorty has in mind. Truth is not a property of the world. Rather it is a property of language.

> We need to make a distinction between the claim that the world is out there and the claim that the truth is out there. To say that the world is out there, that it is not our creation, is to say, with common sense, that most things in space and time are effects of causes which do not include human mental states. To say that the truth is not out there is simply to say that where there are no sentences there is no truth, that sentences are elements of human languages, and that human languages are human creations. (Ibid.: 4–5)

The idea that philosophy is a voyage of discovery rather than creation is the very thing that Rorty wishes to debunk. There is no doubt that Rorty wants to rid us of the tendency to search for the truth. However, rather than embark on an extended critique of the idea of truth itself Rorty is happy to take another tack.

Rorty's favoured self-description is 'pragmatist'. There is a history of pragmatist thought and it is a technical description but for our purposes we can rely on the common-sense understanding of the term. Rorty's principal reason for rejecting the claims of foundational philosophers is practical.

> The best, and probably the only, argument for putting foundationalism behind us is . . . it would be more efficient to do so, because it would let us concentrate our energies on manipulating sentiments, on sentimental education. That sort of education sufficiently acquaints people of different kinds with one another so that they are less tempted to think of those different from themselves as only quasi-human. (Rorty 1993: 122–3)

This quotation contains several important points. First we have a bold statement of Rorty's pragmatic rejection of foundational philosophy. This rejection is based on doubts about causal efficacy rather than concerns with the epistemic status of claims to moral knowledge (Ibid.: 119). The fact is that we seem to have been looking for 'the truth of the matter' for 2,000 years without success. Rorty wants to suggest that it is about time that we started doing something else. In fact, Rorty argues, the greatest benefit of dropping the search for elusive foundations is the potential for far greater creativity in social and political thinking. His goal is to release this creativity and he intends to do so by showing the possibilities that this move would provide. Second we are introduced to the vehicle for this creative development. Rorty's emphasis on sentimental education, or manipulation, is key here. The idea is that morality and justice wait on our ability to sympathise with others, to view them as people like 'us' and so understand and deplore their suffering. This redescription of what it is to make a moral judgement has a rich history. Rorty refers to David Hume, who famously argued that 'corrected (sometimes rule-corrected) sympathy, not law-discerning reason, is the fundamental moral capacity' (Ibid.: 129). If this is a more adequate assessment of ethics then Rorty's final point gains even more force. Rorty's claim that once we have got on with the moral and political job of sentimental education we will be less tempted to view others as only quasi-human carries with it a stinging criticism of the history of moral philosophy. Rorty, as we noted in the opening paragraph of this section, believes that not only is philosophy not part of the solution to our social and political ills, it is in fact part of the problem. Philosophy, in its foundational form, has lead to the dehumanisation of human beings. This is some charge. In the opening sections of his Amnesty lecture Rorty recounts the story of Serbian guards torturing and degrading their Muslim prisoners during the last war in Bosnia. He goes on to to remind us of a rich and varied history of 'man's inhumanity to man' recalling the actions of the Crusaders in the Middle East, slavers and slave owners in the USA, and the Nazi perpetrators of the Holocaust. With piercing insight Rorty likens the Serb camp guards to Thomas Jefferson, President of the USA, telling us that

> like the Serbs, Mr. Jefferson did not think of himself as violating *human* rights. The Serbs take themselves to be acting in the interests of true humanity by purifying the world of pseudohumanity. In this respect their self-image resembles that of moral philosophers who hope to cleanse the world of prejudice and superstition. This cleansing will permit us to rise above our animality by becoming, for the first time, wholly rational and thus wholly human. (Ibid.: 112–13)

The comparison between moral philosophy and ethnic cleansing comes as something of a shock, especially for moral philosophers. Rorty's point is that the search for moral knowledge has led us to make distinctions between those who count as full humans and those who don't make the grade. Over history the infidel, the Jew, the black person, the woman, the child, the homosexual (the list could go on) have been treated as less than fully human because they do not meet the standards of the 'true' human of the moment. It may seem a little harsh to lay the blame for this at the doorstep of the philosopher. After all philosophers tend to be ordinary decent people trying to do a little good. But then, Rorty claims, so are the other perpetrators of these terrible acts. The point is that they all had reason to think they were doing good. They are all ordinary. Our tendency to view these people as barbarous is itself a product of the history of philosophy. Even concentration camp guards act towards those they see as fully human in what we would consider an appropriate way. They may breakfast with their family, kiss their children goodbye and then go to work to help cleanse the world of pseudo-humanity. The philosophically generated tendency to divide the world into true and pseudo is, Rorty claims, at the root of this. Little wonder then that he thinks we have pragmatic reasons for dropping it.

In its place Rorty wants to describe a more appropriate attitude to morality, one that avoids the problems listed above and releases the creativity we so desperately need in ethics. Rorty's ideal postmodern moral hero is described as an **'ironist'**.

> I shall define an 'ironist' as someone who fulfils three conditions: (1) She has radical and continuing doubts about the final vocabulary she currently uses, because she has been impressed by other vocabularies, vocabularies taken as final by people or books she has encountered; (2) she realizes that argument phrased in her current vocabulary can neither underwrite or dissolve these doubts; (3) insofar as she philosophizes about her situation she does not think that her vocabulary is closer to reality than others, that it is in touch with a power not herself. Ironists who are inclined to philosophize see the choice between vocabularies as made neither within a neutral and universal metavocabulary nor by an attempt to fight one's way past appearances to the real, but simply by playing the new off against the old. (Rorty 1989: 73)

A final vocabulary is simply a set of words we carry around and employ to justify our actions, beliefs and lives. All humans do it. The difference between the modern and postmodern moral agents is that the former believe theirs to be true and the latter view theirs ironically in the sense laid out above. This does not mean that we have to ignore our moral and cultural history. Rather 'intellectual and moral progress becomes a history of increasingly useful metaphors rather than of increasing understanding of how things really are' (Ibid.: 9). We can still draw on Plato and Immanuel Kant but only for the cosmopolitan utopias they imagined and inspired us to reach for (Rorty 1993: 119). The alternative to this ironism is described disparagingly by Rorty as a common-sense approach. The common-sense approach is to believe that our final vocabulary is the appropriate language to use when judging the lives and beliefs of those who have alternative vocabularies. Put this way it does seem absurdly self-righteous.

The question we need to ask ourselves is how this proposed change to our attitude towards ethics would effect politics. The answer is that irony in ethics has little or no direct effect on politics. Moral principles approached this way cannot underwrite anything. There is, however, an important indirect effect. An ironic approach to ethics frees us from the desire to search for the truth of the matter and in doing so it leaves us with the space to get on, as Rorty puts it, with the business of sentimental education. Before we go on to examine the idea of politics as sentimental education or manipulation we need to think about the consequences of irony a little further. Irony seems very close to relativism in that it does not give us the critical vocabulary necessary to make discriminating judgements between good and bad forms of society. Without these foundations is it not the case that Rorty's favoured liberal society, based as it is on a specific series of moral and social norms, will collapse? Rorty offers us two basic reasons why this is not likely. Firstly, he writes, 'the idea that liberal societies are bound together by philosophical beliefs seems to me ludicrous. What binds societies together are common vocabularies and common hopes. The vocabularies are, characteristically, parasitic on hopes' (Rorty 1989: 86). Philosophy, like religion, never did the job it claimed in the first place and just as we have carried on regardless of the progressive secularisation of society (what Nietzsche called the 'Death of God') it is likely that we will survive the death of metaphysics. In fact it is more likely as metaphysics has always been less of a public activity than religion. Secondly, irony forms a sympathetic backdrop to liberal politics. Rorty describes a liberal (following Judith Shklar) as someone who thinks that cruelty is the worst thing we can do. Irony militates against the urge to discriminate between different people, lifestyles and vocabularies. In doing so it implicitly encourages us to expand the range of people we should avoid being cruel to. Irony does not underwrite liberalism as the moral theory of the foundational liberals we have examined through the course of this book claimed to have done. But in resisting the urge to discriminate between 'us', the bearers of truth, and 'them', living without truth, we remove an important barrier to the sympathetic identification of 'us' with 'them'. Of course Rorty realises that we have no answer to the question 'why not be cruel?' but the very need to have that question answered is the product of our metaphysical upbringing rather than a necessary requirement of morality itself (Ibid.: 94). Ultimately, Rorty argues, irony is a private affair of little or no social (public) use. This itself is the product of Rorty's rejection of the foundational role that philosophers have assigned themselves and in our recognition of this we learn to face our political challenges in a different way. Rorty's postmodern approach to politics is framed by this prior argument. In turning to examine Rorty's liberalism and his support for the development of a human-rights culture we are presented with a challenge and with the hope for human solidarity.

Our liberalism, our belief that cruelty is the worst thing we can do, is a cultural artefact, a product of our time and place. This means that liberalism is a contingent matter but given that Rorty finds this contingent fact agreeable enough there is nothing more we need to say about it. Following the work of the Argentinian jurist and philosopher Eduardo Rabossi, Rorty argues that we are living in a human-rights culture, itself 'a new, welcome fact of the post-Holocaust world' (Rorty 1993: 115). It is our approach to this contingent but welcome fact that Rorty wants to change. First of all we have to stop trying to get behind or beneath this fact in a search for its philosophical presuppositions (Ibid.: 115–16). It will not do any good anyway. Indeed, as we have seen, it may do serious harm. In any case the development of a human-rights culture 'seems to owe nothing to increased moral knowledge, and everything to hearing sad and sentimental stories' (Ibid.: 119). The sheer horror of the Holocaust has had a tremendous impact on our lives.. We wonder, with Nabokov's *Pnin*, how there can be any justice in a world where people were so brutally murdered. We look upon genocide and intolerance with fresh rather than with jaded eyes, determined to prevent such an atrocity occurring again. We commit troops to regions where our self-interest is not concerned and we take a far closer interest in the freedoms of men and women who we will never meet. We do not need philosophical certainty to help us here because this human-rights culture rests on 'an unjustifiable and ungroundable but vital sense of human solidarity' that has been developing since the Second World War. But is this not a little weak? What tools do we have to confront the concentration camp guard? Surely telling him sad and sentimental stories such as '"this is what it is to be like to be in her situation" . . . or "Because her mother would grieve for her"' (Ibid.: 133) is not the answer. Indeed it is not, but sustaining and developing a human-rights culture has got more to do with how we bring up our children and educate our students than how we confront those who fall short of the standards of human solidarity that we desire. In Chapter 1 you came across Plato's attempt to convince Thracymachus that his egoistic account of justice was wrong. Rorty picks up on this, arguing that in order to see the end of the egoistic world view of Thracymachus we do not have to convince him that he is irrational; all we have to do is make sure our children don't grow up to be like him. In giving up the pretensions of philosophy we have to alter our entire approach to politics and this is a move that requires courage. It requires courage because it requires that we acknowledge that we are never going to have a trumping argument when faced with the cruel and the powerful. It requires courage because we are enjoined to 'recognise the relative validity of [our] convictions' yet required 'to stand for them unflinchingly' (Rorty 1982: 155). Rorty recognises (and even shares) the frustrations and burdens that this can bring. How difficult is it to stand up for principles we know to be contingent? How hard is it to acknowledge that we have 'to wait for the strong to turn their piggy little eyes to the suffering of the weak'(Rorty 1993: 130)? But this is the nature of social life free from the dangers of philosophy. Here we can teach our children that people who do not appear to be like us are humans too and that they suffer and feel pain and humiliation like anyone else. We can encourage them to read Dickens and Nabokov to come to terms with cruelty on an enormous scale and to help them learn that cruelty is the worst thing we can do. We can learn to speak about morality in a new register that enables us to tell sad and sentimental stories that help us to expand our understanding of cruelty and how 'people like us' are affected by it. This is politics after epistemology.

Conclusions

This chapter has explored three bold challenges to the very enterprise of political thought. In summary, we can identify three distinct ways in which these positions challenge the universalism and foundationalism of normative theory. Each challenge regards normative theory (in its traditional modes) as part of the problem, but each characterises this fact in a distinctive way. The equality feminists challenge not so much the claim that universalism and foundationalism are necessary features of a proper political theory as the claim that political thought has reached these basic standards. The difference feminists make a more strident claim. The claim here is that the universal and foundational aspirations of political theory prevent it from adequately characterising the moral and political experience of more than half the world's population. The universalist project should, they argue, either be replaced wholesale or be supplemented by a particularist care-based approach. Rorty, on behalf of the antifoundationalists, mounts the most far-reaching challenge. His claim is simply that political theory has dramatically misunderstood the nature of social and moral life to the point where the mere attempt to theorise our way out of political difficulty aggravates the problems we face. These challenges are the among the most serious that contemporary political theory has to face and they cannot be sidestepped.

Topics for discussion

1. Is an ethic of care a necessary supplement to an ethic of justice?
2. Should feminists recognise essential differences between men and women?
3. Is liberal feminism feminist enough?
4. What are the principal reasons that Rorty gives for rejecting philosophy? Of these which do you find the most convincing?
5. How would you describe the postmodern approach to our ethical vocabularies?
6. How comprehensively has Rorty made the case for a postmodern approach to politics. Should we consider modernity 'over'?
7. If the view that cruelty is the worst thing we can do is simply *our* parochial view and if the ability to tell and listen to sad and sentimental stories is the prerogative of the wealthy and leisured, what can we do to foster and extend our human-rights culture?

Critical glossary

Patriarchy	The state of affairs in which political, social and cultural institutions are dominated by men, who thereby occupy the dominant role in a sexual division of power.
Gender	The social roles occupied by men and women. Feminism is concerned to separate gender, which it regards as socially constructed, from sex, which is natural.
Difference	A theoretical recognition that the things that divide us, such as culture or gender, are as important as those that identify us as equal members of the human race. Difference is conceptually tied to a pluralist conception of value.

Ethic of justice	A universalist conception of morality which is expressed in abstract rules and principles. It is primarily concerned with justice and right and wrong.
Ethic of care	A particularist conception of morality which is expressed in terms of relationships and responsibilities. Its prime concern is with the minimisation of hurt.
Particularism	In contrast to universalism, the view that moral principles must be identified in reference to particular contexts and social institutions.
Antifoundationalism	Literally an opposition to foundationalism in philosophy, where foundationalism is the objectification or reification of the moral, social and cultural values that are then taken to justify politics.
Postmodernism	In political theory the range of attempts to think critically about politics without relying on foundational truths and objectivity. As a term of art it has meanings beyond political theory and is itself contested.
Ironist	Rorty's description of someone with the appropriate postmodern attitude to our value systems (what he calls our final vocabularies).

List of references/Further reading

Feminism

References

Gilligan, C. (1982), *In a Different Voice: Psychological Theory and Women's Development*, Cambridge, MA & London: Harvard University Press.
Okin, S. M. [1979] (1980), *Women in Western Political Thought*, London: Virago.

Okin, S. M. (1989), *Justice, Gender, and the Family*, New York: Basic Books.
Tronto, J. (1993), *Moral Boundaries: A Political Argument for an Ethic of Care*, New York & London: Routledge.

Secondary literature

Bryson, V. (1992), *Feminist Political Theory: An Introduction*, Basingstoke, Macmillan.
Jaggar, A. & Young, I. (1998), *A Companion to Feminist Philosophy*, Oxford: Blackwell.
Pateman, C. (1988), *The Sexual Contract*, Cambridge: Polity Press.
Wollstonecraft, M. [1792] (1992), *A Vindication of the Rights of Woman*, London: Penguin.
Young, I. (1990), *Justice and the Politics of Difference*, Princeton: Princeton University Press.

Rorty

The best place to begin an engagement with Rorty is with his own work. The Amnesty Lecture is commendably brief and packed with insight but in general his work is eminently readable and enjoyable.

Rorty, R. (1982), *The Consequences of Pragmatism*, New York & London: Harvester Press.
Rorty, R. (1989), *Contingency, Irony and Solidarity*, Cambridge: Cambridge University Press.
Rorty, R. (1993), 'Human Rights, Rationality and Sentimentality' in S. Shute & S. Hurley (eds), *On Human Rights: The Oxford Amnesty Lectures*, New York: Basic Books.

For secondary reading there are many good sources and new journal articles come out regularly, such is the fascination with Rorty's position. Of the many available books the following all make distinctive contributions to our grasp of Rorty's work.

Festenstein, M. & Thompson, S. (eds) (2001), *Richard Rorty: Critical Dialogues*, Cambridge & Malden, MA: Polity Press.
Geras, N. (1995), *Solidarity in the Conversation of Humankind: the Ungroundable Liberalism of Richard Rorty*, London & New York: Verso.
Guignon, C. & Hiley, D. (2003), *Richard Rorty*, Cambridge & New York: Cambridge University Press.
Malachowski, A. (ed.) (1990), *Reading Rorty: Critical Responses to 'Philosophy and the Mirror of Nature' (and Beyond)*, Oxford & Cambridge, MA: Blackwell.

HISTORICAL

Afterword

CONCEPTUAL

Current Engagements in Political Thought

Richard Rorty's work is rich and complex. His critique of foundationalism in philosophy is powerful and his redescription of politics is both moving and challenging. If we agree with Rorty then the assumed role of the philosopher should be passed to the poet, the novelist and the literary critic, who can generate within us a hope for a future free from cruelty and marked by a rise in human solidarity. However, it is important that we do not give you the impression that the antifoundationalist and postmodern turn heralds the end of political theory. Rorty is only one voice (albeit a powerful one) in the ongoing conversation in contemporary political thought. In very general terms political theory has accepted the force of the antifoundationalist position, acknowledging that the ways in which we have constructed 'knowledge' have been problematic. This recognition does not, however, necessarily feed in to the postmodern redescription of politics that Rorty imagines. This is not the place to embark on a full-scale exploration of alternatives but a few brief examples of the attempt by political theorists to adapt will help us gain some perspective.

Among the responses to the antifoundationalist turn have been both a resurgence of interest in historicist and communitarian thought and an expansion of what is often termed constructivism in political thought. We will take historicism and communitarianism together here and examine them first, as Rorty has much in common with these traditions although they come to different conclusions. Historicists and communitarians recognise to a greater or lesser degree the historical, geographical and moral contingency of one's commitments. Nevertheless they recognise, as Rorty does, the important role that these commitments play in forming our identity and our social and political aspirations. Interestingly Rorty draws heavily on the historicist and communitarian sources when he constructs his picture of social criticism and this is not just a coincidence. Historicists such as G. W. F. Hegel and communitarians such as Michael Walzer share a similar view to Rorty on the practice of social criticism. Walzer, for example, also attempts to redescribe liberal politics in a manner that distances it from the foundationalist universalism that pervades classic liberalism (Walzer 1990). In doing this he does not follow Rorty to the conclusion that in acknowledging the fragility of philosophical knowledge we give up on the public role of the theorist. Instead Walzer seeks to argue for interpretation rather than discovery or invention as the appropriate mode of social criticism, arguing that if the social critic recognises the appropriate limits of his or her activity we gain new insights, new *political* knowledge rather than *philosophical* knowledge (Walzer 1981: 3). In making this fascinating argument Walzer also comes to redescribe human rights and universalism, explaining how the core principles at the heart of human rights (the universal rights to life and liberty) are reiterated over time in such a way that they become vital tools for the social critic even if they are deployed in very different ways to those imagined by mainstream liberals.

Walzer's redescriptions tell a more powerful and critical story about the nature of universal ethics than that which Rorty is prepared to proffer. Crucially it does not rely upon a foundationalist conception of universal rights and it recognises the reality of political and moral heterogeneity (Walzer 1994). The debate between Rorty and Walzer would focus on the epistemic standing of what Walzer calls political knowledge but interestingly Walzer only claims the standing appropriate to any participant in a democratic debate. In acknowledging that the social critic has no special theoretical status Walzer is implicitly claiming that the engaged social critic (the post-foundational political theorist) is still a powerful voice in the contemporary debate. This character may well work side by side with the novelist and the literary critic but their stories are just as compelling. Key to Walzer's contribution to the contemporary debate is his claim to have described the reiterative emergence of what he calls 'a thin universalism'. Here universalism is understood in contrast to what he calls 'covering-law universalism' (what we have come to know as foundational universalism) but Walzer does argue that it can give moral authority to universal conceptions of individual rights to life and liberty.

There are other attempts to salvage the critical project of political theory. One of the most interesting of these is often termed **constructivism**. In this vein philosophers such as John Rawls and Onora O'Neill redescribe (in this case) the Kantian liberal project in the light of the criticisms levelled against Kantian foundationalism (O'Neill 1989, 1996; Rawls 1993, 1999). Here the central concern is to retain the objective status of normative judgement without basing it on partial or unjustifiable foundations. You have already come across the later work of Rawls (Chapter 8). To a large degree *Political Liberalism* was an explicit attempt to get his argument about the two principles of justice off the ground without resorting to what he termed comprehensive liberalism. Here comprehensive liberalism is foundational liberalism and a useful point of comparison with Rorty and Walzer is Rawls's *Law of Peoples*, in which he also revisits the case for universal human rights. As was the case with both Rorty and Walzer, Rawls's recognition of the force of the antifoundationalist position forces him to pose the question in a different way. No longer does he ask 'what are universal human rights?'; rather he asks what a liberal society should be committed to in international politics and thereafter whether it would be appropriate for liberals to expect non-liberals to adopt the same principles (Rawls 1999). In approaching the issue this way Rawls also redescribes the idea of universal human rights in terms of the minimum conditions that must hold if there is to be a stable relationship between liberal and what he calls decent non-liberal peoples. At the base of Rawls's constructivism is a theory, also described as a thin universalism, concerning the minimal conditions of decency and well-orderedness that are conducive to social and political co-operation. In doing this modern social-contract theory Rawls believes he has moved away from those aspects of liberal political theory that the antifoundationalists find objectionable but has retained a justifiable and critical moral and political project capable of attaining a level of objectivity.

Whether the constructivist or historicist turn meets or transcends the objections of the antifoundationalists and postmodernists is still up for debate. But that is the point; the debates go on and thinking about our moral and political world is every bit as important now as it has ever been. The insights that we take from Plato and Aristotle, from the modern and contemporary theorists and from the critical theorists become *our* tools, used in different ways and with different purposes in different times and places. Implicit in the way that we have conceived this is the claim that the resources are available, historically and conceptually, to enable political thought to meet this challenge.

List of references/Further reading

The ongoing debates surveyed at the end of the chapter form the basis of a mass of literature in the field. The primary sources cited here are:

O'Neill, O. (1989), *Constructions of Reason: Explorations of Kant's Practical Philosophy*, Cambridge: Cambridge University Press.

O'Neill, O. (1996), *Towards Justice and Virtue: A Constructive Account of Practical Reasoning*, Cambridge: Cambridge University Press.

Rawls, J. (1993), *Political Liberalism*, New York: Columbia University Press.

Rawls, J. (1999), *The Law of Peoples*, Cambridge, MA & London: Harvard University Press.

Walzer, M. (1987), *Interpretation and Social Criticism*, Cambridge, MA: Harvard University Press.

Walzer, M. (1990), 'The Communitarian Critique of Liberalism', *Political Theory*, 18, 1, February, 6–23.

Walzer, M. (1994), *Thick and Thin: Moral Argument at Home and Abroad*, Notre Dame, IN & London: Notre Dame University Press.

Index

Major references are in **bold** type